► The IELTS Test: overview

Introduction

IELTS stands for *International English Language Testing System*. The test consists of four modules – Listening, Speaking, Reading and Writing – and takes two hours and 45 minutes to complete.

This book provides preparation for the Listening and Speaking modules, which all candidates take, and also for the Academic Reading and Writing modules, which are normally taken by candidates intending to use English for study purposes. General Training versions of these modules are also available and, while much of the material in the book would provide useful practice, there is no specific exam preparation for these modules in this book.

The test result is published in the form of a report, which places candidates on a scale of one to nine according to language ability. There is a score for each of the four modules and also an overall score.

IELTS can be taken at test centres in over 100 countries. Test dates are fixed, and tests are normally available throughout the year in most areas. Further information and a list of local centres is available on the IELTS website – www.ielts.org .

IELTS modules: details

Listening   Time: 30 minutes

There are four sections. The first two sections are concerned with social needs. In **Section 1**, you will hear a conversation in a social situation, for example, two friends discussing holiday plans or an interview at an accommodation agency. In **Section 2**, you will hear a monologue on a general subject, for example, a short talk on healthy eating or tourist information.

The last two sections are concerned with educational or training contexts. In **Section 3**, you will hear a conversation between up to four people, such as a tutorial discussion between tutor and student, or several students discussing an assignment. In **Section 4**, you will hear a monologue, such as a lecture or talk of general academic interest.

The recordings may include a range of accents including British, US or Australian English. For this reason, different accents are used on the recordings accompanying this course. You can also help yourself further by listening to as wide a variety of English as possible, on the radio or television, for example.

QUESTIONS
There are 40 questions in total, including multiple choice, short-answer questions, completion and matching tasks, and diagram labelling. Each one requires a specific approach and specific skills, and these are outlined in the **Task Approach** sections in the book.

The recording is played **only once**, but you are allowed time to read the questions beforehand. You are allowed an **extra ten minutes** at the end of the test to transfer your answers onto the answer sheet. Take care when transferring your answers – you will lose marks if you make spelling or grammar mistakes.

MARKING
One mark is awarded for each of the 40 questions, and the result is translated into a score on the IELTS nine-band scale.

Academic Reading   Time: 60 minutes

The three reading passages contain up to 2,700 words, which means that you will need to read efficiently, using appropriate reading skills for each task, in order to complete the paper in the time allowed. The course includes a varied selection of reading texts, and you can help yourself further by reading from as wide a range of sources as possible, such as newspapers, magazines and journals.

QUESTIONS
There are 40 questions in total, including multiple choice, short-answer questions, completion and matching tasks, and True/False/Not Given. Each one requires a specific approach and specific skills, and these are outlined in the **Task Approach** sections in this book. Passages come from magazines, journals, books and newspapers, and the topics are of general interest.

You must write your answers on an answer sheet, but there is no extra time for this. Take care when transferring your answers – you will lose marks if you make spelling or grammar mistakes.

MARKING

One mark is awarded for each of the 40 questions, and the result is translated into a score on the IELTS nine-band scale.

Academic Writing   Time: 60 minutes

There are two tasks. The instructions specify the minimum number of words for each task and also recommend the amount of time you should spend on each one. It is important to follow these guidelines, because Task 2 carries more weight in marking than Task 1 and you will need to give the appropriate time to each part in order to get good marks. Answers must be written on the answer sheet. They must be written in full, not in note form.

Task 1: You are given a diagram or table of some kind and you have to present the information in your own words. For example, you may have to consider a set of statistics and then write a description outlining the key features. You have to write at least **150 words** for **Task 1** and you are recommended to spend 20 minutes on it.

Task 2: You have to discuss a current issue, present and justify and opinion or analyse and assess a development or problem. You have to write at least **250 words** for **Task 2** and you are recommended to spend 40 minutes on it. You will lose marks if you write less than the required number of words.

MARKING

Scripts are assessed according to the following criteria:

- **Task Achievement** (Task 1): Have you satisfied all the requirements of the task? Have you presented a clear overview of all the key features?
- **Task Response** (Task 2): Have you discussed all parts of the task? Have you developed and supported relevant ideas and arguments, and made your position clear?
- **Coherence and Cohesion** (Tasks 1 & 2): Is your writing well organised? Is there a clear progression of information and ideas? Are sentences and paragraphs logically linked?
- **Lexical Resource** (Tasks 1 & 2): Have you used a good variety of appropriate vocabulary? Is your spelling and word formation reasonably accurate?
- **Grammatical Range and Accuracy** (Tasks 1 & 2): Have you used a good variety of structures? Is your grammar and pronunciation reasonably accurate?

The overall result is translated into a score on the IELTS nine-band scale.

Speaking   Time: 11–14 minutes

The interview between the candidate and an examiner is in three parts.

Part 1 Introduction and interview (4–5 minutes)
In the first part, the examiner will ask a number of general questions. Be prepared to introduce yourself, to say where you come from and to talk about such topics as your family or home, your country or city, your job or studies, your interests or hobbies.

Part 2 Individual long turn (3–4 minutes)
In this part, you are given a card outlining a particular topic and asked to talk about the topic for one to two minutes. You have one minute to prepare and make notes if you wish. Be prepared to describe people, places or events and to explain their significance to you.

Part 3 Two-way discussion (4–5 minutes)
In the last part, the examiner asks questions linked to the topic in Part 2 and develops a discussion of more abstract issues. Be prepared to listen carefully and respond appropriately, to express opinions and preferences and give reasons.

MARKING

Performance is assessed on the following criteria:

- **Fluency and Coherence:** Do you express ideas and opinions clearly and coherently, without long hesitations?
- **Lexical Resource:** Do you use a wide range of vocabulary?
- **Grammatical Range and Accuracy:** Do you use a wide range of structures and make only a few minor mistakes?
- **Pronunciation:** Are you easy to understand? Do you use English pronunciation features naturally?

The overall result is translated into a score on the IELTS nine-band scale.

1 ▶ Read all about it!

Lead-in

1 Work with another student. Study the pictures and say what each person is reading and why.

A

B

C

D

E

F

LANGUAGE CHECK
spend (time) + … -ing
e.g. I **spend** about 15 minutes *walking* to work.
- How much time do you spend on these things every day? TV/computer/ newspaper/homework?

2 Take it in turns to ask and answer the questions below.

1 Which of these things have you read most recently? When?
2 Which do you most enjoy reading? Why?
3 Is there anything you don't like reading? Why not?
4 What do you spend most time reading in a typical day?

▶ **EXAM LINK** Speaking

In Part 1 of the IELTS Speaking module, the examiner will ask general questions about your life and habits. Questions 1–4 above are typical Part 1 questions, but note that photographs are <u>not</u> used in this part of the Speaking module.

Focus on grammar *Present simple*

> ▶ **EXAM LINK**
>
> The **present** and **past simple** make up 80% of all verb phrases in English. They are also the foundation of successful speaking and writing in the exam, so it's important that you use each tense appropriately and accurately.

KEY LANGUAGE
Present simple
▶ p. 153
Present simple -s or -es
▶ p. 154
e.g. *sees, watches*
• There is a list of verbs normally only used in the present simple (stative verbs) on page 153.

---

1 Study the following sentences and complete the notes below.

a) Trains to London leave every hour.
b) We often play football together.
c) Acid turns blue litmus paper red.
d) I don't understand the question.
e) She's revising at the moment.
f) I work as a legal secretary.
g) She picks up new languages quickly.
h) We like Chinese food very much.

1 The only sentence which is not in the present simple tense is ..... . It describes something which ....
2 The present simple is used to describe:
  a) actions or events that happen .... , e.g. sentences a), b) and ..... .
  b) a scientific fact or a general truth, e.g. ..... or g).
  c) a mental or emotional state, e.g. ..... or ....
3 .... such as *often* or *quickly* cannot go between the verb and object NOT *She picks up ~~quickly new languages~~*.

2 Four of the following sentences are not correct. Underline them and make the necessary corrections.

1 He teaches at King's College.
2 She speaks well Arabic.
3 What means this word?
4 I don't remember the way.
5 The rains often begins in July.
6 I always take the bus to work.
7 He watchs too much TV.
8 It doesn't take long to prepare.

3 Write true sentences about yourself, using some of the following phrases.

for breakfast   *get up*   *friends*   *weekend*   *(not) enough time*

4 Work in pairs to ask and answer questions. Give true answers starting with expressions from the Essential language box below.

1 Will English be important in your future career?
2 Do you think you'll ever live abroad permanently?
3 What's the best way of learning vocabulary?
4 Is correct grammar important in the IELTS exam?
5 Do you know which areas of your English you need to work on?
6 Do you do enough English practice outside the class?

> ▶ **ESSENTIAL LANGUAGE**
>
> I hope so/hope not   I think so/don't think so because …
> I don't know/I'm not (really) sure. Maybe …

Focus on reading 1 *Introducing reading skills*

SKILLS PRACTICE

► Skimming

Skimming is looking quickly through a text to get a general idea of the subject. For example, you skim a newspaper to see which articles interest you, without reading everything in detail. In an exam, you skim a text to find the parts you need to study carefully. This saves reading the whole text several times.

1 Skim the newspaper extracts and find at least TWO which deal with each of the following topics.

Topic	Extracts		
1 Education	....	....	
2 Space exploration	....	....	
3 Family matters	....	....	
4 Business and work	....	....	....
5 Medical matters	....	....	
6 Technology	....	....	
7 Crime and punishment	....	....	

► Scanning

Scanning is looking quickly through a text to find specific names, facts or figures. For example, you might scan a list of television programmes to find the name and time of a programme. In an exam, you scan a text for information to answer a question.

2 Scan the extracts for information to answer the following questions.

1 In which Brazilian state did prisoners riot?
2 How long do grandparents spend looking after their grandchildren?
3 What is the name of America's most recent spacecraft?
4 In which month is Yuri Malenchenko due to return to Earth?
5 What is the maximum time junior doctors in Europe will be able to work in future?
6 How long was the world's longest marriage?
7 According to research, what food can help protect you from cancer?
8 What was Volkswagen's annual profit?

A

SEOUL: South Korea's largest mobile phone operator is to offer users a new service that it says will repel mosquitoes. Subscribers can download a sound wave that is inaudible to human ears but annoys mosquitoes within a range of about a metre.

B

Hospitals must urgently change the way they work or some could be forced to shut at night when new European rules come in, the leader of Britain's doctors warned. From August next year, under the European Working Time Directive, junior doctors must spend no more than 58 hours a week working.

C

The use of **digital photography** and emailing of digital images are popular among PC users – both young and old. A third of the over-55s use their PCs for storing/sending and receiving digital photographs – almost the same as 15- 24-year olds.

D

Researchers in Milan say that **pizza-eaters** are less prone to certain cancers. A study of 8,000 Italians found that those who ate at least one pizza a week were 59% less likely to contract cancer of the oesophagus. They credit tomato sauce.

E

The death of Liu Yang-Wan at the age of 103 brought an end to the world's longest marriage. Mrs Liu had been married to her husband Liu Tung-Yang for 86 years and four months. They had 110 children, grandchildren and great-grandchildren.

G A fortnight late, the US's latest **Mars** rover, named *Opportunity*, was launched from Cape Canaveral. It should arrive at its destination early next year.

F

Two days of riots by 28,000 prisoners in 29 jails across **Brazil's** São Paolo state left 20 people dead. The riots had been co-ordinated by prison gang leaders using mobile phones.

H

Unemployment in Germany hit 9.4% in June, leaving some 4.4 m people out of work. American unemployment rose to 6.4%, its highest level for nine years.

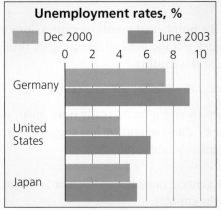

I NEARLY 20% more women than men are now applying for a place at university in Britain, new figures have revealed. A record 437,615 people have applied to begin degree courses in October, the Universities and Colleges Admissions said.

J **Grandparents** are being used as unpaid babysitters by their overworked children. On average, grandparents spend six and a half hours a week looking after their grandchildren.

K

Net profits at **Gucci** tumbled by 97% in the last quarter compared with a year ago. The luxury-goods group made just €1.2 m ($1.4 m) and ran up an operating loss.

L

Volkswagen, Europe's biggest car maker, announced that annual profits had doubled to €1.6 billion ($1.9 billion). Sales in the United States were particularly buoyant as a result of the strong dollar.

M

Police had no difficulty apprehending a gang of thieves who stole money from a football club. The robbers made their escape on a pitch-marking machine, but forgot to switch off the line painting mechanism. Officers simply followed the white line to find them.

N **Staff** at a primary school in the UK have given up a day's wages to buy books for their pupils. Twenty workers from the cleaners to the headmistress, as well as the local MP, made the sacrifice, raising almost £900. Without the donation teachers would have been unable to stock the library with new books.

O

A **cosmonaut** orbiting the Earth in the International Space Station, Yuri Malenchenko, 41, is to marry Yekaterina Dmitriev, 26, next month. As he is not due back until October, the wedding will be conducted by telephone.

▶ Reading for detail

When you **read for detail**, you study part of a text very carefully, to make sure you understand exactly what the writer means. You do this when you are following instructions and don't want to make a mistake, for example. Exam questions like True/False/Not Given or multiple choice usually require detailed reading.

3 **Read the extracts more carefully and say whether the following statements are True or False.**

1 Thieves who robbed a football club used an unusual vehicle to get away in.
2 Young people use their computers for digital photography much more than older people.
3 The launch of the most recent American spacecraft went exactly as planned.
4 The unemployment rate in Germany is higher than in the United States.
5 The number of people applying for a university place in Britain has never been higher.
6 Children at a UK primary school had to save up to buy new books for their school library.

▶ Guessing unknown vocabulary

The extracts contain a number of words or expressions you may not know, but you can probably work out the general meaning by thinking about the part of speech and looking at the context.

e.g. *Net profits at Gucci **tumbled** by 97% …* (extract K)

tumbled is clearly a verb and it could really only mean *went down* or *went up*. But the phrases *just €1.2* and *operating loss* suggest *went down*. *Tumble* actually means *to fall down quickly and suddenly*.

4 **Try to work out the general meaning of the words in italics. Think about the part of speech and the context.**

1 … a sound that is *inaudible* to human ears … (extract A)
2 … pizza-eaters are less *prone to* certain cancers. (D)
3 The riots had been *co-ordinated* by prison gang leaders using mobile phones. (F)
4 Sales in the United States were particularly *buoyant* as a result of the strong dollar. (L)
5 Police had no difficulty *apprehending* a gang of thieves … (M)

KEY LANGUAGE
Parts of speech
▶ p. 147

> ▶ **EXAM LINK** Reading
>
> In the IELTS Reading module you have just one hour to read three long texts and answer 40 questions on them. To do this successfully in the time it's important to choose which reading skills to use for which tasks.

DIY Learning strategy *Introduction*

Look at these comments from students. Do you share any of their concerns?

I tend to read slowly, word by word. How can I increase my reading speed?

Long texts frighten me. What can I do to read more confidently?

How can I build up my vocabulary?

What's the best way of improving my writing?

How can I stop making the same mistakes every time?

I find natural English really hard to understand. How should I practise?

No two language students have exactly the same strengths and weaknesses, and no course, however long, can meet each individual's needs completely. That's why it's so important to look for ways of helping yourself to learn successfully.

The DIY (Do It Yourself) sections in this book are designed to help you get the most from your course. Each section suggests useful learning strategies to help you develop effective study skills and also continue learning outside class. Following the advice can make a big difference to your rate of progress.

DIY Learning strategy *Find time for reading*

The best way to improve your reading skills is by reading as much English as possible. Reading outside class will also increase your vocabulary and your grammar range. It doesn't matter what you read. The more variety the better! Just remember these rules:

- Choose subjects which interest you. If that means academic articles, fine, but sports, fashion, crime or even celebrity gossip can be just as good!
- Avoid anything complex or boring. Reading should be pleasure not pain!
- Ignore difficult words if they aren't important to the general meaning. Remember you won't have a dictionary in the exam.
- Keep a record of any interesting words or expressions you find.

DIY LEARNING PROJECT

1 Select an English newspaper, magazine or book. Borrow it, buy it, or locate it on the Internet.
2 Choose one section to read in detail – it needn't be very long.
3 Read it quickly first, to get the general idea. Then read more carefully. Only use a dictionary to check words you really need to know. Ignore the rest.
4 Be prepared to tell a partner about what you read and how you felt about it.
5 Make a note of any interesting expressions.

Focus on reading 2 *Reading academic texts*

SKILLS PRACTICE
▶ Identifying topic

Extracts A–D below contain advice for university students about reading academic texts. Study question 1 below before you begin reading.

1 The main topic of a paragraph is often introduced in the first sentence. The topic of extract A has been underlined. Underline the word or phrase which introduces the main topic in the first sentence of extracts B–D. Do this as quickly as possible.

A

Skimming is a well-tried way to see if a book is relevant or not. Of course, it has limitations. You can skim to find out whether or not you are dealing with such material as information, argument or description, but not to extract deeper meaning. For that there is no substitute for
5 careful reading that allows you time to think and question.

B

Experimenting a little with reading speed can help you to read more efficiently. For example, you are more likely to remember the first half of a sentence if you read quickly enough to reach the second half. If you read too slowly, your short-term memory does not retain
10 information and meaning. Short-term memory can, in any case, retain only about six items at any one time. The least efficient way to read is to try to understand every single word before you reach the end of the sentence (Buzan 1974: 3). If you are a slow reader, reading slightly faster may encourage you to remember more, but you can only try this
15 for yourself to see how effective it is.

C

One useful technique is to search the first lines of paragraphs for signalling words such as *In summary*, *First of all*, *Finally* or *By contrast*. These often show the structure of a passage of text and you can use them to grasp the general meaning and organisation of what you are
20 about to read. Signalling words are pauses in the text which point out to the reader what has just been said, what is about to come, and what is about to be explained in more detail.

D

Every degree subject develops its own specialist vocabulary which some readers perceive as jargon. For example, academic fields like
25 computer sciences have developed a jargon which includes such expressions as *dynamic random access memory* and *core dump*. When jargon is used by members of the same profession, it can be efficient and effective language. For those who understand it, jargon is a kind of verbal shorthand which makes long explanations unnecessary.
30 For the non-specialist, however, too much jargon per page is irritating. Your strategy should be to ignore it and continue reading. That is exactly what children do when they do not understand a word.

Adapted from *Successful Study for Degrees* by Rob Barnes

Locating information

2 Which extract A–D:

1 provides information about the short-term memory?
2 gives examples of phrases which can help you understand a text?
3 gives examples of phrases which may be difficult to understand?
4 mentions when careful reading is important?

Reference links

3 The word *it* in extract A, line 2 refers to the word *skimming* in the sentence before. Pronouns like *this, that, these, those* are often used to avoid repetition in this way. Which word or phrase do the words in bold below refer to?

1 **Extract A**
For *that* … (line 4)

2 **Extract B**
try *this* for yourself (14–15)

3 **Extract C**
These often show … (18)

4 **Extract D**
That is exactly what … (31–32)

> **► EXAM LINK** Reading
>
> Identifying the main topic of a paragraph, locating specific information and recognising reference links are all key reading skills which will help you to tackle exam reading tasks successfully.

EXAM PRACTICE
Summary completion

4 Complete the following advice by writing one or two words taken from extracts A–D in the spaces.

Summary of Reading Advice

- Use **1** .... to find out if the information in a book is likely to be useful or not. (A)

- To discover the deeper meaning of a text you need to think and **2** .... as you read. (A)

- Don't try to understand **3** .... as you read. (B)

- You may remember more if you try to read a bit **4** .... (B)

- It's a good idea to study the first **5** .... of each paragraph. (C)

- Look out for signalling words like *First of all* or **6** .... , which can help you understand the general meaning and **7** .... of the text. (C)

- The best way to deal with jargon and other vocabulary that you don't understand is to **8** .... it. (D)

Focus on speaking *Discussing a topic*

SKILLS PRACTICE

1   Work in pairs to discuss what you read for the DIY Learning Project (page 11).

Say: which newspaper, magazine or book you chose, and why
which part you read in detail and what it was about
whether you enjoyed reading it or not, and why

> **Useful language**
>
> The newspaper/book **I chose** was … because …
> The part **I read** in detail was …
> The reason **I chose** it was …
> The thing **I liked/enjoyed** about it was …

2   Tell your partner ONE interesting word or expression you found while reading. Make sure you know what it means and how to use it. Check in a dictionary or with your teacher if necessary.

Desert island dilemma

3   Work in groups of three or four.

Imagine that you are going to spend two weeks on a desert island together. You want to improve your English during that time but you can take only TWO of the following, which must be shared among you. Work together to discuss the different options and agree which ones you would you choose. Be prepared to explain the reasons for your choices.

* An English grammar book
* An English/English dictionary
* The complete works of Shakespeare (in one volume)
* A supply of newspapers (dropped daily by plane)
* A set of popular novels, e.g. detective, sci-fi, romance
* A set of DVDs of classic films*, e.g. James Bond, Sherlock Holmes
* A set of DVDs of famous TV comedies*
* A set of CDs of well-known pop songs* with lyrics
* A 12-hour pronunciation course with CDs*

*You will have the necessary electrical equipment (powered by solar energy!)

> **▶ ESSENTIAL LANGUAGE**
>
> **Expressing a personal opinion**
> **I think/feel** is the most common way of giving your opinion when speaking.
> **In my opinion/view** is more formal in speech and more suitable in academic writing.
> *I think* (that) the important thing is …   NOT ~~I am thinking …~~
> *In my opinion*, it's a serious problem.   NOT ~~According to my opinion …~~
>   NOT ~~In my opinion, I think …~~

IELTS VOCABULARY BUILDER

Word families

1 Form nouns from the following verbs. Use a dictionary to check your answers.

1	admit	*admission*	7	develop	....
2	announce	....	8	employ	....
3	appear	....	9	encourage	....
4	apply	....	10	predict	....
5	assist	....	11	resist	....
6	cancel	....	12	solve	....

2 Complete the following sentences using words from the exercise above.

1 The experts' .... about an upturn in the economy have not come true.
2 I heard a station .... about the delayed Glasgow train.
3 We are currently looking at a number of possible .... to the problem.
4 The price of .... to the museum includes a helpful guidebook.
5 The proposed new .... laws have met .... from trade unions.

Prepositions

3 Add suitable prepositions to complete the following sentences.

1 I don't spend much time ...... housework ...... a rule.
2 He worked ...... a waiter last summer.
3 It can be difficult to get a taxi late ...... night.
4 He's applied ...... a place on a Law course.
5 Some students were interviewed ...... telephone.
6 Our education system is different ...... the British one.
7 People carry umbrellas to protect them ...... the sun.
8 Most people eat rice ...... breakfast.
9 I don't usually go ...... bed until midnight.
10 I hope to build a successful business ...... the future.

Pronunciation: Syllables

4 Words consist of one or more syllables, each containing a vowel sound. Study the examples and put the words below into the correct group. There should be five words in each group.

1-syllable words e.g. *have, find*	**2-syllable words** e.g. *study, careful*	**3-syllable words** e.g. *remember, decision*

breakfast	detail	encourage	law	telephone
cheap	develop	future	solve	time
country	difficult	interview	taxi	train

2 ▶ Take note

In this unit you will practise:

- **Listening skills:** Letters and sounds; listening for gist; listening for specific facts
- **Writing skills:** Reading and describing data; paragraphing; linking expressions; reference links
- **Speaking skills:** Discussing likes and dislikes
- **Grammar:** Frequency adverbs and expressions
- **Vocabulary:** TV programmes; word partners
- **DIY Learning strategy:** Good learning habits

Exam Focus
Writing: Tasks 1, 2
Speaking: Part 1

Lead-in

1 Work in pairs. Match each picture A–F with one of the listening situations 1–6 listed below. The first one has been done as an example.

1 Directions/instructions
2 News bulletin
3 Lecture
4 Conversation between friends   *A*
5 Traffic report
6 Public announcement

2 Work with a partner to choose answers from the list 1–6 above. For which kind(s) of listening:

1 do you often make notes?
2 can you ask questions if necessary?
3 are you often helped by what you can see?
4 do you choose certain parts to listen carefully to?
5 is there often a problem of background noise?

3 With your partner discuss which kind of listening you find easiest to understand, which you find hardest, and why?

Focus on listening 1 *Letters and sounds 1*

1 Here are the pronunciation symbols for two English sounds. You will find symbols like these in many dictionaries.

/iː/ is the sound in *we* or *see*	/eɪ/ is the sound in *make* or *day*

Write the following as words in the box above.

1 One number between 1 and 10 which has the sound /iː/ as a word.
2 One number between 1 and 10 which has the sound /eɪ/ as a word.
3 Eight letters from the alphabet which have the sound /iː/.
4 Four letters from the alphabet which have the sound /eɪ/.

SKILLS PRACTICE
▶ Recognising letters

2 🎧 Listen and choose the name that you hear spelt out.

1	A	Basker	B	Beckar	C	Backer
2	A	Jagger	B	Gadget	C	Geiger
3	A	Chervil	B	Schiver	C	Shrivel
4	A	Hindani	B	Henbane	C	Hempian

3 🎧 Listen and write down the name that you hear spelt out.

1 .... 2 .... 3 ....

Focus on speaking *Discussing likes and dislikes*

SKILLS PRACTICE

1 Study the Essential language below, and then say how you feel about different types of reading matter. Choose from the following.

daily newspapers	romantic novels	non-fiction
thrillers	biographies	classic novels
science fiction	historical novels	gossip magazines
fashion magazines	poetry	scientific journals

> ▶ **ESSENTIAL LANGUAGE**
>
> **Discussing likes and dislikes**
> These verbs can be followed by a noun, e.g. *books* or by an *-ing* form, e.g. *reading*.
>
> **Likes**
> (really) **like**/**enjoy**/**love** … very much
>
> **Dislikes**
> **don't like**/**don't enjoy** … (very much/at all)
> (really/absolutely) **hate**
>
> *We **enjoy** reading very much.*
> *I really **like** the Harry Potter books.*
>
> *My brother **doesn't like** studying at all.*
> *I absolutely **hate** horror stories.*
>
> All these verbs are transitive and need an object, e.g. *I like **something** very much.*
> NOT ~~I like very much.~~

EXAM PRACTICE
▶ Part 1

2 Work with a partner. Choose one set of questions each, A or B, then take it in turns to interview each other. One person should take the role of the examiner each time. Try to use a range of expressions to talk about your likes and dislikes.

A
- How often do you go to the cinema?
- What's your favourite kind of film? What do you enjoy about it? Why?
- Who's your favourite actor or actress? What do you like about him or her?
- Is there any kind of film that you don't like very much? Why?

B
- How much time do you spend watching TV a day?
- What's your favourite programme? What do you like about it? Why?
- Which kind of programme are you least likely to watch? Why?
- Which kind of programme is most popular with young people in your country?

▶ **EXAM LINK** Speaking

You can be asked to talk about things you like or dislike in all three parts of the IELTS Speaking module. To do well, you'll need to be able to express your feelings confidently and correctly, using a variety of expressions. Don't forget to give reasons too!

Focus on listening 2 *Introducing listening skills*

SKILLS PRACTICE
▶ Listening for gist

When you **listen for gist**, you want a general idea of the topic. You don't need to know the details or understand every word. This is like the reading skill of skimming.

1 Listen to five short extracts and decide which type of listening each one is. Choose a letter from the list a)–i) below for each answer.

a) directions
b) job interview
c) film or play
d) news bulletin
e) lecture
f) conversation between friends
g) instructions
h) traffic report
i) public announcement

1 ....   2 ....   3 ....   4 ....   5 ....

▶ Listening for specific facts

▶ **EXAM LINK**

In the IELTS exam it's important to know the best way to listen for each task type.

When you **listen for specific facts**, you want particular information like a person's name, a price or a telephone number. Again, other details aren't important and you don't need to understand every word. This is like the reading skill of scanning.

2 Listen to five short extracts and write down the names of the places that you hear.

1 ....   2 ....   3 ....   4 ....   5 ....

3 Listen to five short extracts and write down the numbers that you hear.

1 ....   2 ....   3 ....   4 ....   5 ....

Focus on grammar *Expressing frequency*

1   We use adverbs like *sometimes, usually* or *never* and other frequency expressions to describe how often something happens. There are three possible positions in a sentence for these frequency expressions. Study the information below and answer the questions.

Initial   [   ] he gets up early.
Middle   (before main verb except *to be*) He [   ] gets up early.
                  Or He is [   ] late.
End   He gets up early [   ].

All three positions	Middle position only (before main verb except *to be*)	Initial/end position only
sometimes, often, occasionally, frequently, generally, normally	*always, never, rarely, hardly ever, seldom, usually*	expressions of exact frequency and other longer expressions: *once a week, every weekend, once in a while*

1   What is the safest position for all one-word frequency adverbs + *hardly ever*?
2   Which frequency expressions cannot occur in that position?

2   Correct any word order mistakes in the sentences below.

1   Never I can remember your address.
2   Normally we take our holiday in August.
3   I go to the gym three afternoons a week.
4   He sleeps hardly ever more than five hours.
5   She never is in her office when I phone.
6   Always you must read the instructions.
7   Once in a while we buy a take-away meal.
8   The company every year holds a staff party.

3   Make true sentences about yourself using frequency expressions and the prompts below.

1   listen/news/radio   3   play tennis   5   tell/joke
2   cook/meal   4   do exercise   6   do nothing

4   Work in pairs. Describe a typical day in your life, either at work or studying. Try to speak for 1–2 minutes. Begin: *I usually get up at …*

Call my bluff

5   Work in groups of 3 or 4. Take it in turns to make three statements about yourself using frequency expressions. Two should be true. One should be false. Your partners can ask you questions about the statements for 2 minutes. They must then decide which statement was false.

Focus on writing 1 *Introduction to Task 1*

> ▶ **EXAM LINK** Writing
>
> The IELTS Writing module takes 60 minutes and includes two tasks, a description and a discursive essay. Task 1 carries one third of the total marks and Task 2 carries two thirds.

SKILLS PRACTICE

1 Describe each type of writing below. Which ones could be required in the Academic module of the IELTS test?

A

Can't remember if I told you but Sam's got a place at Keele University. He's thrilled to bits, needless to say. And what about your news? I'm dying to hear all about the new job. Give me a ring when

B Some people argue that the solution to the drugs problem is education, and while I accept that education has a part to play, I do not agree that it provides the whole answer.

C

Notes

Why? memory aid, use for essays, etc, active learning

When? lectures, seminars, reading, revising, thinking & planning

What? main points *only*. Info that is relevant & impt. (key words)

How?

D Sea water flows through a small canal (A) into a series of basins. The first basins are the largest (B) and each lies a little below the level of the previous one, so that the water moves on by force of gravity. As the water passes through the

F I am very sorry to tell you that I will have to return home one week before the end of term. The reason for this is that my sister is getting married on 15th December, and I will be expected to attend this important family event. I have made arrangements with a friend to copy the notes from the lectures that I miss

E As we can see from the graph, there was a slight decrease in the number of serious road traffic accidents between 1999 and 2001. In 2002, however, the number of accidents

2 Match the statements below to types of writing A–F above. A statement may have more than one correct answer.

1 This type of writing is usually based on a diagram of some kind.
2 You often use incomplete sentences or note form in this type of writing.
3 This type of writing needs to be organised logically, usually in several paragraphs, with a clear beginning, middle and end.
4 It's important that the facts or figures in this writing are absolutely accurate.
5 You usually try to present a balanced point of view in this type of writing.

▶ Task I

▶ EXAM LINK Writing

In Task I of the Writing module, you are given a diagram or table of some kind and you have to present the information in your own words, using at least 150 words.

SKILLS PRACTICE
▶ Reading the data

3 Study tables A and B and say whether the following statements are True or False. Correct the false statements.

1 Americans spend **less time** watching TV than the world average.
2 People in Malaysia spend **fewer hours** watching TV than Italians do.
3 People in Australia spend **exactly the same amount of time** watching TV as British people.
4 *Yomiuri Shimbun* sells **more** copies every day than any other newspaper.
5 *USA Today* has a **slightly smaller** circulation than the *Wall Street Journal*.

A WORLD TV VIEWING

Country	Hours per week
United States	49.35
Italy	28.93
Hong Kong	28.70
Columbia	23.80
United Kingdom	23.80
Australia	21.98
Chile	17.50
China	10.59
Malaysia	10.50
World average	19.67

B

Newspaper	Country	Average daily circulation
Yomiuri Shimbun	Japan	14,500,00
Asahi Shimbun	Japan	12,600,00
Sichuan Ribao	China	8,000,000
Sun	UK	3,273,116
Daily Mail	UK	2,426,533
Chosun Ilbo	S Korea	2,220,000
The Times of India	India	2,144,842
USA Today	USA	2,120,357
Wall Street Journal	USA	1,800,607
Mirror	UK	1,719,743

▶ Describing the data

4 Study the Essential language below, then write three similar True or False statements about tables A and B and exchange with another student. Mark your partner's statements True or False and correct as necessary.

KEY LANGUAGE
Comparison
▶ p. 142

▶ ESSENTIAL LANGUAGE

Comparison

slightly	more		
considerably	less/fewer	+ NOUN	than …
	larger/smaller		
(exactly/approximately)	the same …	+ NOUN	as …
(just) under/over	a quarter/25%		
exactly	a third		
almost/nearly	half/50%		
about/approximately	three quarters/75%		

5 Complete the description using information from diagram C, and using suitable expressions from the Essential language box on page 21.

> The best-selling popular newspaper in Britain is the *Sun*, which has a market share of **1** .... The next most popular paper is the *Mail*, which has a market share of **2** .... The *Mirror*'s market share is only **3** .... than the *Mail*'s at 23%. After these three market leaders, the *Express* and the *Star* have smaller market shares of **4** .... and **5** .... respectively.

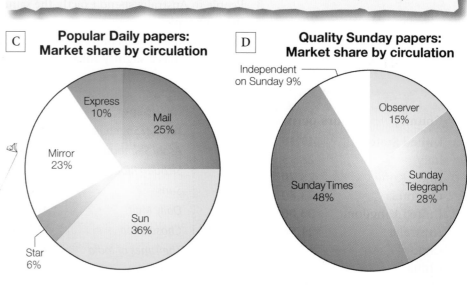

C Popular Daily papers: Market share by circulation

Express 10%
Mail 25%
Mirror 23%
Sun 36%
Star 6%

D Quality Sunday papers: Market share by circulation

Independent on Sunday 9%
Observer 15%
Sunday Times 48%
Sunday Telegraph 28%

6 Write a similar description of diagram D.

DIY Learning strategy *Good learning habits*

1 Work in pairs. Ask questions to find out how often your partner does each of the things below. Use frequency expressions when answering your partner's questions.

- **looks up** a word in an English/English dictionary
- **writes** to someone in English
- **translates** an English text into their own language
- **speaks** English on the telephone
- **revises** something from the coursebook
- **listens** to English on the radio
- **checks** a grammar point in a reference book
- **meets** English speakers
- **makes a note** of useful vocabulary
- **uses** an electronic dictionary
- **asks** a teacher or English speaker a question about grammar
- **plays** a game in English
- **does** extra language practice exercises
- **watches** an English film or video

2 How helpful are these activities in practising and extending your English? Give each activity ticks (✓✓ = very useful, ✓ = useful, no tick = not very useful).

3 Look at the activities you thought were useful. Discuss how you could do these more often.

DIY LEARNING PROJECT

> 1 Choose one of the activities you think would be useful for practising your English.
> 2 Make a definite plan of how you can start doing this on a regular basis.
> 3 Be prepared to tell a partner about what you did and how you got on.

Focus on writing 2 *Task 2*

> ▶ **EXAM LINK** Writing
>
> In Task 2 of the Writing module, you are given a topic and you have to write an essay of at least 250 words. You might have to present and justify an opinion, for example, or to suggest solutions to a problem.

SKILLS PRACTICE

1 To answer a Task 2 question well, you need to express your ideas clearly and logically. Complete each piece of advice below by choosing the best ending a)–d).

Good writers …
1 organise their work in clear …
2 connect sentences and paragraphs using …
3 avoid …
4 use a good variety of …

a) linking expressions
b) paragraphs
c) vocabulary and grammatical structures
d) repetition

▶ Paragraphing

2 In an essay, each main topic should be dealt with in a separate paragraph. Divide Text 1 into three paragraphs, and say what the topic is in each case.

> **Text I**
> At university you will have to write often and in various different formats, depending on the subjects you are studying. The most common form of writing is the essay but reports, case studies, summaries and, on some undergraduate programmes, a dissertation at the end of the year can be
> 5 included. All pieces of writing need to be structured in a particular way, and when your tutor sets you a task he or she will generally advise you about the most appropriate structure to use for it. You need to be clear about this so, if you are at all uncertain, you should always ask the tutor. You will normally be expected to word process your work and you will
> 10 also be told how many words you should write. This is important because if you do not write enough words, you may lose marks. Conversely, if you write too many, the tutor may not mark the extra ones.

From *The International Student's Guide*

▶ Linking expressions

3 Good writers use linking expressions and other signalling words to make it clear to the reader how different parts of a paragraph are connected. Find examples of each type of expression in Text 1 on page 23.

1 Addition: .*and,*...........................
2 Cause/effect: ....
3 Generalisation: ....
4 Contrast/opposite idea: ....

▶ Reference links

4 One way of avoiding unnecessary repetition is by using pronouns like *he, it, this,* etc. Find the following expressions in Text 1 and say what they refer to.

1 *he or she* (line 6)   3 *this* (8)   5 *ones* (12)
2 *it* (7)   4 *This* (10)

5 Text 2 below is not well written because it has too much repetition. Underline any parts which are repeated unnecessarily. How would you replace them?

Text 2

Greenland is situated in the north Atlantic. Greenland has an Arctic climate and much of Greenland's land is permanently covered with ice. Greenlanders are an independent people, and Greenlanders' origins are a mix of Inuit and European. Young people are increasingly rejecting the traditional lifestyle by moving to the towns. The fact that they are rejecting the traditional lifestyle and moving to the towns is becoming a problem for Greenland's welfare system.

6 Read the example question and then choose endings a)–h) to complete each piece of advice on how to answer it. There is a model answer based on this task on page 156.

WRITING PRACTICE
Task 2, Model answer
▶ Practice 1, p. 156

Write about the following topic:

> *Modern communications mean that it's no longer necessary to write letters.*
>
> *To what extent do you agree or disagree?*

How to write a good Task 2 essay:

1 Carefully study …   a) conclusion
2 Underline …   b) grammar, punctuation or spelling mistakes
3 Make a logical …   c) introduction
4 Begin with a clear …   d) key words
5 Divide your answer into … e) paragraphs
6 End with a suitable …   f) plan
7 Write a neat and legible … g) the question
8 Check your work for …   h) answer

IELTS VOCABULARY BUILDER

TV programmes

1 Choose types of programmes from the box to match the definitions below. You do not need to use all the words in the box.

> Chat show   News   Sitcom   Documentary   Quiz show
> Soap opera   Drama   Reality TV   Wildlife programme

1 An amusing programme in which there is a different story each week about the same group of people, e.g. *Friends*.

2 A television or radio story about a group of people and their lives, which is broadcast regularly for many years, e.g. *Neighbours*.

3 A programme which features ordinary people (not actors), who are usually in competition with each other to win money and become famous, e.g. *Big Brother*.

4 A programme in which famous people talk about themselves and answer questions about their lives, opinions, etc.

5 A programme in which people or teams compete to answer questions.

6 A programme that gives you facts and information about a serious subject, such as history, science or social problems.

Word partners: *do, give* and *make*

There isn't always a logical reason for the choice of verb in a phrase. The only way to use many common phrases correctly is to make a point of learning them.

2 Add the correct verb *do, give* or *make* to complete the following expressions.

1 .... a note of/notes	8 .... instructions
2 .... an answer	9 .... an explanation
3 .... an exercise	10 .... an examination/test
4 .... a mistake	11 .... a lecture
5 .... homework	12 .... advice
6 .... some practice	13 .... an announcement
7 .... a plan	14 .... a telephone call

3 Complete the sentences with the correct expression from exercise 2.

1 If you hope to .... the IELTS .... , you'll need to study hard.

2 This book will .... you plenty of helpful .... on exam techniques.

3 If you don't .... a .... before writing an essay, you could easily leave something important out.

4 You can still pass the writing test even if you .... a few minor grammatical ....

5 If you want to progress quickly, it's a good idea to .... some extra language .... outside class.

6 In the listening test the recording will .... you clear .... for each part.

ACADEMIC WORD STUDY 1

In these sections you will meet important vocabulary that you need to understand and learn. All the words come from the Academic Word List (AWL), a list of the most common words in academic texts (see pages 138–139). Increasing your academic vocabulary is a key way of improving your reading and writing in the IELTS test.

When you've completed the exercises, check the answers on page 168 and correct any mistakes so you can use this page as a reference point for revision.

Understanding academic words

1 Academic vocabulary is generally fairly formal. Match these common academic verbs to a less formal verb with the same meaning from the box below.

1	**assist**	He was assisted by a colleague.
2	**construct**	The bridge took 4 years to construct.
3	**indicate**	The graph indicates a rise in sales.
4	**obtain**	You can obtain a visa at the embassy.
5	**purchase**	Tickets may be purchased in advance.
6	**require**	The problem requires careful thought.
7	**respond**	They did not respond to my letter.
8	**select**	You must select an answer A–D.

> *answer   build   buy   choose*
> *get   help   need   show*

2 The examples below come from *Reading academic texts* (page 12). Each one contains an academic word in bold. Study the way the academic word is used and write the correct part of speech, noun (N), verb(Vb) or adjective (Adj), in the right-hand column.

1 *academic fields like computer sciences* (D) ....*Adj*..........
2 *to see if a book is **relevant** or not* (A) ....
3 *to **extract** deeper meaning* (A) ....
4 *there's no **substitute** for careful reading* (A) ....
5 *your short term memory does not **retain** information* (B) ....
6 *short term memory can ... retain only about six **items*** (B) ....
7 *One popular **technique** is to look for signals* (C) ....
8 *the **structure** of a passage of text* (C) ....

3 Study the meanings below and match each one to an academic word 1–8 from exercise 2.

> **Meanings**
> a) relating to education, especially at college or university level ..*1*..
> b) a special way of doing something ......
> c) to keep or store ......
> d) to remove or take ......
> e) a single thing (e.g. on a list) ......
> f) something which can be used instead of another thing ......
> g) the way in which the parts of something are connected together ......
> h) containing information which is useful ......

Using academic vocabulary

4 Complete the following using academic words from exercises 1 and 2. Make any changes necessary.

1 Saccharin is a chemical substance which tastes sweet and is often used as a .... for sugar.
2 A cut in income tax was the most popular .... on the government's agenda.
3 Exam information can be .... from the www.ielts.org website.
4 50% of the patients in this hospital .... long-term care.
5 Scientists are now able to .... DNA from a single hair.
6 New medical .... mean that people spend less time in hospital after an operation.
7 The government is planning to .... 500,000 new homes in the south east.
8 I found several articles on the Internet which are .... to my essay topic.

5 Choose four academic words from this page and write personal examples to help you remember them.

1 ....
2 ....
3 ....
4 ....

REVIEW 1

Grammar

SPOT THE ERROR

1 Each sentence below contains at least one mistake. Make any necessary corrections.

1 He doesn't spend enough time to study for his exam.
2 I enjoy very much listening folk music.
3 She goes once a week to college for study computing.
4 Little more than quarter of university students have part-time jobs.
5 The job requires someone who can speak fluently Russian.
6 Electricity cost exactly the same amount of money than gas.
7 Climbing has fewest participants than skiing.
8 According to my opinion, the government should encourage people save money.

Vocabulary

PREPOSITIONS

2 Fill in the missing prepositions in the following text.

1 How often do you listen .... English .... the radio?
2 It's a difficult expression to translate .... English.
3 .... any one time, there are .... least 250,000 people travelling .... plane.
4 The subject will be discussed .... more detail .... the future.
5 .... average, USA postal services deal .... 520 million items of mail every day.
6 .... university you could be asked to write in different formats, such .... essays or case studies, depending .... the subject you are studying.
7 I asked my tutor .... some advice .... exam techniques.
8 You can buy frozen meals but they're no substitute .... fresh food.

SPELLING

3 Seven of the words below are spelt wrongly. Underline the mistakes and correct them.

1	accurate	7	langauge
2	carefuly	8	pronounciation
3	comunication	9	secretary
4	grammer	10	strength
5	increase	11	sucessful
6	intresting	12	vocabulary

WORD CHOICE

4 Choose the correct answer A–C to complete the following sentences.

1 You can .... any words you don't understand in a dictionary.
   A look out   B look up   C look at

2 What do the letters IELTS .... ?
   A put across   B make up   C stand for

3 A teacher can .... the mistakes in your work.
   A point out   B show up   C clear out

4 I need to .... some extra grammar practice exercises.
   A make   B have   C do

5 Try and .... a note of useful vocabulary.
   A make   B do   C give

Exam skills

5 Answer the following questions. Page numbers are given in brackets for you to check your answers if necessary.

1 Which tenses are especially important for successful speaking and writing in the IELTS test? Why? (7)
2 How long do you have to complete the IELTS Reading module? (10)
3 How many passages do you have to read? (10)
4 How long do you have to complete the IELTS Writing module? (20)
5 How many writing tasks are there? (20)

3 ▶ It goes with the job

In this unit you will practise:

- **Reading skills:** Skimming; scanning; reading for detail; reference links; guessing unknown vocabulary
- **Speaking skills:** Speculating; discussing jobs and careers
- **Grammar:** Past simple; *depend on/if*
- **Vocabulary:** Word partners; pronunciation: word stress

Exam Focus

Reading: Short-answer questions; sentence completion; T/F/NG

Speaking: Parts 1, 2, 3

Lead-in

1   In a recent survey, teenagers in the USA were asked what kind of work they hoped to do for a career. Their top ten choices in alphabetical order were:

Top Career Choices for Teens (Aged 13–17)

- Athlete
- Chef
- Computer specialist
- Doctor/Nurse/Medical worker
- Engineer
- Lawyer
- Musician
- Soldier/Army officer
- Teacher
- Vet

Discuss these questions with another student.

1   Which THREE of the ten careers do you think were the most popular of all?
2   Which THREE careers were much more popular with boys than girls?
3   Which career was much more popular with girls than boys?

2   Study the Essential language below, then discuss which of the top ten career choices would be:

- the best paid
- the most satisfying
- the most stressful
- the shortest

KEY LANGUAGE
Comparison
▶ p. 142

▶ ESSENTIAL LANGUAGE

Speculating

Use this language to give an answer that is a probable (rather than definite).

I think/I suppose ... could/might/would probably ... be/have ... because ...
e.g. *I suppose* a career as a chef **might be** very popular these days.
    I think most lawyers **would probably be** well paid.

Focus on speaking 1 *Discussing jobs and careers*

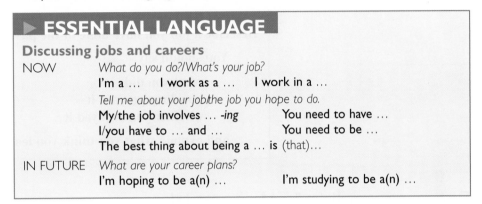

> ▶ **EXAM LINK** Speaking
>
> Work is a common topic in Parts 1 and 2 of the Speaking module. You might have to describe the job you have or would like to have, or you might be asked to talk about your career plans in general.

SKILLS PRACTICE

1 Study the Essential language below.

> ▶ **ESSENTIAL LANGUAGE**
>
> **Discussing jobs and careers**
>
> NOW *What do you do?/What's your job?*
> I'm a …   I work as a …   I work in a …
> *Tell me about your job/the job you hope to do.*
> My/the job involves … -ing   You need to have …
> I/you have to … and …   You need to be …
> The best thing about being a … is (that)…
>
> IN FUTURE *What are your career plans?*
> I'm hoping to be a(n) …   I'm studying to be a(n) …

2 The mindplan below shows several aspects of work. Make notes to help you answer questions on the subject.

- If you have a job, prepare to answer questions from any part of the diagram.
- If you are studying, think about a job you'd like to do and prepare to answer questions from the General section of the diagram only.

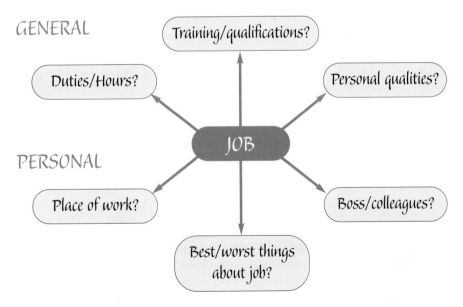

GENERAL

Training/qualifications?

Duties/Hours?

Personal qualities?

PERSONAL

JOB

Place of work?

Boss/colleagues?

Best/worst things about job?

EXAM PRACTICE
▶ Part 1

3 Work in pairs to interview each other on the subject of work. One person should take the role of the examiner each time. Make sure you ask complete, correct questions based on the mindplan above. Answer in as much detail as possible.

► Part 2

4 Read the following task card and think of a job to describe. It doesn't need to be full-time or paid, it could be part-time work, or even something you did as a child. Before you begin, make notes using any relevant ideas from the mindplan and interviews. Try to speak for one to two minutes.

> **Describe a job you have done in the past.**
>
>   **You should say:**
>
>   **what you did**
>   **how long you did it**
>   **whether you enjoyed it**
>
>   **and explain what you think you learnt from this job.**

Focus on reading 1 *My worst job*

SKILLS PRACTICE

► Skimming

1 Read the four texts A–D and then answer questions 1–4. Circle the correct answer A, B, C or D in each case. Which of the jobs involved:

1 working in a factory?	A B C D
2 working in a market?	A B C D
3 being a salesman?	A B C D
4 dealing in scrap metal?	A B C D

A

Nadine Theron, 32
Physiotherapist, Johannesburg, South Africa

When I was 15 I used to have to get up at 5 a.m. and go out on a horse-drawn cart, searching our neighbourhood for people who were throwing away tins, pans and anything else made of metal that could be recycled. We lived in a poor northern shanty town on the outskirts of the city and times were very hard. To make a living we had to collect every bit of scrap metal we could, which we then sold to a factory, who paid a few cents for every kilo. I had to sit on the cart while my father pulled the mule along, and I had to shout out non-stop 'We're buying tins, pots and pans'. There were days when we had to spend hours going through dark alleys to collect enough scrap metal to make even the small amount of money we needed to buy that day's food.

B

Tanja Lindberg, 46
Diplomat, Helsinki, Finland

I was 17 years old and keen to improve both my money situation and my German, so I got a job packing eggs in Lower Saxony for two months. I was there with a friend, which certainly helped, but the really difficult thing was the 6 a.m. start and the subsequent ten-hour day, standing at an assembly line packing eggs into boxes of six or ten. Occasionally, when eggs were out of date or unsold, they were returned to the plant and I would get egg-breaking duty. This involved me standing next to a big metal industrial vat throwing in all these rotten eggs. The smell was absolutely terrible. I had done some agricultural work before, when I was very young – picking out turnips which were too small to be sold. Packing eggs was much, much worse, and for once I was grateful when I went back to school after the holidays.

C

Koshi Domoto, 39
Data Analyst, Tokyo, Japan

I was 18 when I opted out of going to college and started working as a cleaner or 'sanitary worker' in the Tsukiji fish market in Tokyo. My job involved cleaning the area where fish, like tuna, are cut up and auctioned each day. To the outsider, the market is an extremely interesting place because most of Tokyo's fish and sushi are obtained from here, but my memories of my time at Tsukiji are terrible. The smell of fish never seemed to leave my body. The Japanese are generally tolerant people but my family decided that I smelt so bad that I would have to move to the back room of our house, which got very cold in wintertime. Around that time I met a girl who I loved and wanted to marry, but

she could not bear the thought of being married to a fish market cleaner. After a while I found a job as a trainee fishmonger preparing fish for sushi chefs, so things got better. I subsequently studied for a degree at night school and now work for a financial services company. Life is altogether better and I now have some prospects for the future.

D

Chen Liang, 22
Waiter, Shanghai, China

Earlier this year I worked as a sales representative for a transportation company. My work started at 8.30 a.m. and I was expected to spend the whole day travelling around visiting different businesses and trying to convince them to use our transportation services. The only problem was that I was very inexperienced and young, and nobody knew who I was in the companies I visited. Consequently, I would spend whole days without getting any business. I did not enjoy returning to my office at the end of the day, as the boss would give me a hard time. Like any boss he wants to make money and my failures made him pretty unhappy.

▶ **EXAM LINK** **Reading**

Remember that **skimming** and **scanning** are important exam skills. Skimming is the quickest way of finding out what a text, or part of a text is about, and once you know the general subject, it's easier to read for detail. Scanning is the most efficient way of locating the information you need to answer exam questions.

It's important to underline or highlight key words or phrases in the questions. This helps you to focus on the information you need to find in the text.

▶ Scanning

2 **Give brief answers to these questions.**

1 Which country does Tanja Lindberg come from?
2 What is Nadine Theron's present job?
3 Who is the youngest of the four?
4 How did Nadine Theron travel around while she was working?
5 What was Koshi Domoto's first job?
6 Which language did Tanja Lindberg want to practise?
7 What time did Chen Liang begin work?
8 How long was Tanja Lindberg's working day?

▶ Reading for detail

LANGUAGE CHECK
involve + *ing*
This is a way of giving details
about a job, a course, an
examination, etc.
e.g. *My job **involved** clean**ing**
the area where fish are
cut up.*
• Explain some of the things
your current course of
study involves.
• Choose jobs from the box
on page 28 and say what
they involve.

3 Read the four texts more carefully to answer these questions. Circle the correct answer(s) A, B, C or D in each case. There may be more than one correct answer.

1   Who mentions unpleasant smells in the job they did?   A B C D
2   Who needed to travel as part of their work?   A B C D
3   Who worked with a friend?   A B C D
4   Who worked with a member of their family?   A B C D
5   Who was often unsuccessful in their work?   A B C D
6   Who lived at home while they were working?   A B C D
7   Who describes starting work early in the morning as hard?   A B C D
8   Who mentions their present career?   A B C D
9   Who was the youngest at the time of the job they describe?   A B C D
10 Who mentions they had worked before the job they describe?   A B C D

Focus on grammar *Past simple*

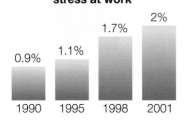

**Illness caused by
stress at work**

0.9%   1.1%   1.7%   2%

1990   1995   1998   2001

▶ **EXAM LINK**

You need the **past simple** tense to describe completed actions in the past, for example to talk about events in your life in the Speaking module.

Around that time I met a person who became my best friend.

You also need the past simple in Task 1 of the Writing module to refer to a date or a period in the past. See bar chart (left).

In 1995, stress caused 1.1% of all illness at work.

1 Study these sentences and cross out the ones which are not in the past simple.

1   The train arrived on time.
2   I didn't enjoy the film very much.
3   Where did you go last night?
4   I've lived here for two years.
5   Did I miss anything at work today?
6   It was raining this morning.
7   By 2005 share prices had fallen 20%.
8   Nobody came to the meeting.
9   Did you have a good journey?
10 He didn't find the test too hard.

2 Now complete these notes:

1   To form the past simple tense of regular verbs we add ....
     e.g. *arrive...*, *miss...*, etc.
2   The only way to know the past tense of irregular verbs is to ....
     one by one.
3   To form the negative, we use .... + infinitive.
4   To form a question, we use .... + ... + infinitive.

3   **Choose verbs to complete the sentences and put them into the past simple.**

> *become   begin   bring   can   catch   cost   fall   find*
> *freeze   go   make   rise   spread   take*

1   The cost of production .... 16% last year, adding to the
    company's problems.
2   Fortunately, the economy .... to recover in spring last year.
3   Many people .... cholera and other diseases from contaminated
    water.
4   Families who .... part in the experiment in July
    .... that eating healthily .... no more than eating
    junk food.
5   In the past, only people who .... afford to pay ....
    to university.
6   The disease .... rapidly in a matter of weeks and soon
    .... a major epidemic.
7   The temperatures .... so low last winter that water in the pipes
    ....
8   Strikes .... chaos to the transport system last month and
    .... many people's journey home a nightmare.

4   **Four of the following sentences are not correct. Underline them and make the
     necessary corrections.**

1   Unemployment decreased last month.
2   Where did you stayed while you were on holiday?
3   It poured with rain all night.
4   He didn't leave a message for me, did he?
5   I'm sorry, I didn't understood the question very well.
6   Manchester United won the Cup Final last night.
7   How much you paid for your course fees?
8   The manager rung the police when he discovered the break-in.

KEY LANGUAGE
Past simple
▶ p. 150

Focus on speaking 2 *Job satisfaction*

SKILLS PRACTICE

In a recent survey, the employees on the left of the table below were found to be the happiest in their work, while those on the right were the least contented.

FUN JOBS	SAD LOT
Medical secretaries	Civil servants
Child carers (e.g. nursery nurses)	Bank managers
Police officers (sergeant and below)	Laboratory technicians
Cleaners and domestic staff	Telephone operators
Farm workers	Authors, writers, journalists
Hairdressers, barbers	Assembly line workers

1 **Work with a partner to discuss these questions.**

1 Can you suggest any reasons why the workers on the left were happier in their jobs than the workers on the right? Make a list of factors that might contribute to job satisfaction, e.g. pay.

2 Considering the factors you have listed, what level of job satisfaction do you think the following workers would have: high (H), medium (M) or low (L), and why? Study the Essential language box before you begin.

- gardeners
- school teachers
- waiters
- airline pilots

> **ESSENTIAL LANGUAGE**

Depend (on/if)
It depends on + noun e.g. *It depends on the kind of school.*
It depends if + clause e.g. *It depends if the pupils are well-behaved.*
It depends + 'wh' word e.g. *It depends who the teacher is.*

EXAM PRACTICE
▶ Part 3

2 **Work with a partner to discuss these questions.**

1 What personal qualities does a person need to be a good boss?
2 Would you prefer to work for an organisation or be self-employed? Why?
3 What are the advantages and disadvantages of working from home, rather than going to an office?

> **EXAM LINK** Speaking

In the third part of the Speaking module, you will have a discussion with the examiner about more abstract issues which are linked to the topic from Part 2. The discussion lasts between four and five minutes.

Focus on reading 2 *Service workers are the happiest staff*

EXAM PRACTICE
▶ Short-answer questions

▶ TIP
These questions are in the same order as information in the text.

1 Study lines 1–24 of the text on page 36 and answer the questions below. Write no more than three words and/or a number for each answer.

1 In which country were workers studied?
2 How many workers were interviewed as part of the research?
3 Who was responsible for organising the study?

▶ Sentence completion

2 Study lines 17–40 on page 36 and complete each of the following sentences with the correct ending A–G from the box.

TASK APPROACH

- Read through the questions and underline key words.
- Skim the text until you find the information you need.
- Study the information and choose the best ending.

▶ TIP
These questions are in the same order as information in the text.

1 According to the report, petrol pump attendants have the advantage of being able to work ....
2 The report suggests that medical secretaries enjoy their work because it is ....
3 The report considers salary and job security to be aspects of ....
4 The report found that prison officers have poor ....

A key role	**E** useful
B long hours	**F** part-time
C material satisfaction	**G** quality satisfaction
D well-paid	

▶ True/False/Not Given

3 Read the whole text again. Look for three True and three False statements. One statement contains information which is not mentioned in the text. Mark this Not Given.

Do the following statements agree with information in the reading passage?

Write

TRUE	*if the statement agrees with the information*
FALSE	*if the statement contradicts the information*
NOT GIVEN	*if there is no information on this*

▶ TIP
These questions are in the same order as information in the text.

1 Some of the people who are happiest in their jobs may be poorly paid. ....
2 Solicitors have a high level of job satisfaction. ....
3 Working without supervision is an important factor in job satisfaction. ....
4 Working as a medical secretary involves long hours and hard work. ....
5 Taxation experts have a high level of quality satisfaction. ....
6 The report does not recommend increasing the number of call centres. ....
7 People working in the computer industry generally enjoy their work. ....

4   Working in pairs, compare your answers and discuss which reading skills you needed to answer exercises 1, 2 and 3.

Service workers are the happiest staff

New research shows that cleaners are some of the happiest workers in Britain, along with child carers, medical secretaries, hairdressers and petrol pump attendants.

5   The study of 35,000 employees found that the highest levels of job satisfaction were among those providing personal service, even if the pay is poor. There are highly paid professional and managerial staff who enjoy excellent pay and conditions, but

10   many of these appear to hate their jobs. Civil servants lie almost at the bottom of the league table, with solicitors and various engineers and scientists not far behind.

Michael Rose of Bath University, who led the

15   study, said a key element of job satisfaction was the potential to work part-time and unsupervised. A cleaner's job may not appeal to all, but it has hidden perks. 'You can trim your hours and you don't have a supervisor breathing down your neck

20   all the time. You can sit in the boss's chair and smoke a cigarette if you feel like it,' he said. Petrol pump attendants, too, had a choice of working part-time shifts with relatively little direct supervision.

25

One explanation offered for the high job-satisfaction rate of medical secretaries – at the top of the league with 75% of them happy in their job is that they are 'doing something useful'. Seeing

30   that you are playing a key role in the delivery of healthcare is very satisfying, despite the low pay scale of £8,000–£15,000.

The study divides overall satisfaction into *Material satisfaction* such as money, promotion and

35   security – and *Quality satisfaction* – which involves the job, relations with the boss and hours. Taxation experts and prison officers score high marks for material satisfaction but low marks for quality satisfaction. The profile of carpenters and

40   ambulance staff is the opposite: high on quality and low on material satisfaction.

The report strongly warns against the rapid growth of telephone call

45   centres, noting that telephone staff register some of the lowest levels of job satisfaction. It also gives a warning that

50   many computer and communications occupations also record 'poor to dismal' levels of job satisfaction.

From the *Times*

SKILLS PRACTICE

▶ Recognising reference links

5   What was the writer referring to when he used the following pronouns?

1   *those* (line 6)   3   *it* (17)   5   *them* (27)
2   *these* (10)   4   *he* (21)   6   *It* (47)

▶ Guessing unknown vocabulary

LANGUAGE CHECK

despite
Despite is followed by a noun or an *-ing* form.
e.g. *The delivery of healthcare is very satisfying despite the low pay scale.*
Despite being late for the interview, he was offered the job.

6   Find the following words in the text and study the context carefully. You will probably need to read at least one sentence before and after the word in question. Then choose the best explanation, A or B.

1   *perks* (line 18)   **A** advantages   **B** disadvantages
2   *trim* (18)   **A** slightly increase   **B** slightly reduce
3   *breathing down your neck* (19)   **A** watching you   **B** talking about you
4   *shifts* (23)   **A** periods of work   **B** uniforms
5   *dismal* (52)   **A** very good   **B** very bad

IELTS VOCABULARY BUILDER

Word partners

1 Match words from columns A and B to make common work expressions.

A		B	
1	self-	a)	pay
2	job	b)	rise
3	work	c)	conditions
4	white-collar	d)	line
5	sick	e)	employed
6	working	f)	experience
7	assembly	g)	satisfaction
8	pay	h)	worker

2 Complete the following sentences with expressions from exercise 1.

1 Bank employees and other .... have less job security now.
2 Although she's well-qualified she has no relevant ....
3 It's great being your own boss as a .... person, but you can't afford to get ill because you won't receive any ....
4 I worked on a(n) .... in a car factory one summer but the heat and noise made the .... terrible.

3 Choose verbs from the box to complete the following sentences. Make any necessary changes.

| do   give   go   hand in   make   meet   take |

1 For years I managed to .... a living as an office temp.
2 I had to .... a day off work to attend a hospital appointment.
3 He's a good person to .... business with – tough but fair.
4 I knew the boss wasn't happy with my work so I decided to .... my notice before he could .... me the sack.
5 The fire fighters have threatened to .... on strike unless their pay demands are ....

Pronunciation: Word stress

4 Practise saying the following two-syllable words according to the stress pattern.

Oo   e.g. MANage, collar, worker, recent
oO   e.g. comPLETE, suggest, decide, correct

5 Match the following words to the correct stress pattern.

afford   although   answer   career   employ   involve   office
person   receive   sentence   stressful   workforce

Oo ....
oO ....

4 ▶ Family values

In this unit you will practise:

- **Listening skills:** Letters and sounds; prediction
- **Writing skills:** Reading and describing data; identifying trends; paragraphs; topic and supporting sentences; reference links
- **Speaking skills:** Discussing relationships; dealing with difficult questions
- **Grammar:** Articles; *depend on/if/how/what/when*
- **Vocabulary:** Family tree; right word/wrong word; word families
- **DIY Learning strategy:** Listen up!

Exam Focus

Listening: Section 1; Note completion
Writing: Tasks 1, 2
Speaking: Parts 2, 3

Lead-in

1 **Work in pairs to discuss these questions. Be prepared to give reasons for your opinions.**

1 What are the advantages and disadvantages of growing up in each of the families below?

2 Which of the following do you think is the best way to live? What are some benefits of the others?

a) living alone
b) sharing with friends
c) married without children
d) married with children
e) living with parents

2 **The words in column A are the first halves of common expressions used in describing families and relationships. Match words from column A and B to make the common expressions. Check meanings in a dictionary if necessary.**

A	B
1 wedding	a) family
2 married	b) status
3 best	c) parent
4 maternity	d) ring
5 extended	e) couple
6 family	f) leave
7 marital	g) friend
8 single	h) tree

3 Choose words from the two columns to answer these questions.

    1 Find at least four words with one syllable.
    2 Find at least four words with two syllables.
    3 Find three words with three syllables.
    4 Find one word with four syllables.

4 Choose three expressions which you think it would be useful to learn/revise and make a note of them. Compare ideas with a partner.

Focus on speaking 1 *Discussing relationships*

> ▶ **EXAM LINK** Speaking
>
> Family and friends is a very common topic in Part 1 of the Speaking module, and it's often appropriate to refer to personal relationships in other parts of the test. So this is a topic area which is well worth preparing for.

SKILLS PRACTICE

1 Study the Essential language below and underline expressions which apply to you.

> ▶ **ESSENTIAL LANGUAGE**
>
> **Discussing relationships**
> FAMILY BACKGROUND
> | | |
> |---|---|
> | I come from | (quite) **a large family**. |
> | I've got | two (older/younger) **brothers** and a(n) (older/younger) **sister**. |
> | I'm | the **oldest**/the **middle child**/the **youngest** of (four). |
> | | an **only child**. |
>
> MARITAL STATUS
> | | |
> |---|---|
> | I'm | **single**/**engaged** (to be married). |
> | | NB married/engaged <u>to</u> a person NOT ~~with~~ a person. |
> | | My **husband's**/**wife's**/**fiancé(e)'s** name is … . |
> | We | **got married**/**engaged** … months/years ago. |
>
> CHILDREN
> | | |
> |---|---|
> | I've/we've got | **a little girl**/**boy** called … . |
> | | two **children**, **aged** … and … . |

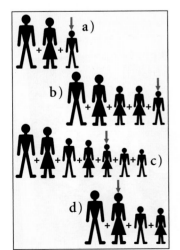

2 Imagine that you are the person indicated with an arrow in each family group on the left. Describe your position in the family.

    e.g. *I'm the eldest of three children. I've got two younger brothers.*

3 Working in pairs, take it in turns to tell each other about your family. Before you start, take a few moments to think about what you're going to say. Try to add extra information about your relations' special skills, work or education.

    e.g. *My brother is very good at sport. He even plays football in the school team.*
           My mother works incredibly hard looking after the family.
           My son is four years old now and he goes to primary school, which he loves.

4 Study the instructions for the task below. Take a few moments to decide on a family and think about what you're going to say, then take it in turns to speak for about a minute.

> **Describe a family, other than your own, that you know well.**
>
> **You should say:**
>
> > **how you know this family**
> > **who the members of the family are**
> > **what they do and what they're interested in**
>
> **and explain how you feel about the family.**

Focus on writing 1 *Task 1: Key skills*

> **▶ EXAM LINK** Writing
>
> In Task 1 of the Writing module, you have to present the information from a graph, table, chart or diagram. To do this well, you have to understand the data, select the most important points to include and identify any significant trends.

SKILLS PRACTICE

The table below gives statistics about the size of US households over a number of years. (Household = all the people living together in one house.) Study the information and answer the questions.

US household by size 1790–1990

Year	Per cent distribution of number of households							Average population per household
	1 person	2 persons	3 persons	4 persons	5 persons	6 persons	7 persons	
1790	3.7%	7.8%	11.7%	13.9%	13.9%	13.2%	35.8%	5.4
1890	3.6%	13.2%	16.7%	16.8%	15.1%	11.6%	23.0%	4.9
1990	24.6%	32.2%	17.2%	15.6%	6.7%	2.3%	1.4%	2.6

LANGUAGE CHECK
A two-person household
When an expression with a number is used as an adjective before a noun, it becomes singular.
e.g. *a two-hour lesson,*
a 100-metre race,
a four-storey house

▶ Reading the data

1 Complete these statements.

1 The table covers a period of .... years.
2 The largest household included in the table consists of .... people.
3 A figure such as 3.7% represents a percentage of the total ....
4 The part of the table which shows average numbers of people in a household is ....

▶ Identifying significant trends

2 a) What is the most common and least common household size for each year?

	Most common	Least common
1790		
1890		
1990		

b) Study the last column. How can you describe the change in the average household size between 1790 and 1990?

▶ Describing the data

3 It's often helpful to describe data in terms of the nearest fraction (half/a quarter, etc). Look back at the Essential language on page 22 and then rewrite these figures in words.

1 49%   2 26%   3 32.5%   4 77%

EXAM PRACTICE
▶ Task I

KEY LANGUAGE
Past perfect
▶ p. 149

WRITING PRACTICE
Task I, Guided practice
▶ Practice 2, p. 157

4 Complete the following model answer.

US households by size 1790–1990

We can see from the table that households in the US have become much smaller over the last 1 .... years. Households in 1790 had an average of 2 .... members but by 1990 the figure had fallen by about half to only 3 .... In 1790 4 .... of all households had seven members. This was still the most common household size in 1890 but the proportion had dropped slightly to 5 .... One-person households were the 6 .... common, representing less than 7 .... of the total in both 1790 and 1890. By 1990, however, there had been a major change. Now only about 1% of households had seven members, while 8 .... of all households consisted of only one or two people.

Focus on listening 1 *Letters and sounds 2*

SKILLS PRACTICE

1 🎧 /aɪ/ is the sound in ice or sky. The sound /ei/ was introduced in Unit 2. Write each word from the following list in the correct box below and then listen and repeat.

| child   height   great   weight   flight   eye |
| quite   break   buyer   neighbour |

/aɪ/ is the sound in *ice* or *sky*.	/eɪ/is the sound in *make* or *day*

2 🎧 /e/ is the sound in red or ten but there are several other possible spellings for the same sound. Circle the word with the sound /e/ in each of the following pairs of words. Then listen to the recording to check your answers.

e.g. wealth/wheat

1 said/paid   5 guess/queue
2 many/lazy   6 leisure/seize
3 reason/measure   7 breathe/breath
4 chief/ friend   8 pretty/plenty

3 🎧 Write down the places that you hear spelt out.

1 ....   3 .... Inn
2 .... Hotel   4 Lake ....

Focus on listening 2 *International Friendship Club*

> ▶ **EXAM LINK** Listening
>
> The Listening module consists of four sections, each with ten questions. The first two sections are concerned with social needs such as finding accomodation or healthy eating. The second two sections are related to educational situations. The recording is played **once** only and **correct spelling** is essential.

EXAM PRACTICE
▶ Section I

You will hear a student telephoning a university friendship club which helps promote understanding between students of different nationalities and cultures. The conversation is in two parts.

▶ Prediction

1 Study questions 1–5.

a) What kind of answer is needed for question 1?
b) What sort of things could be 'packed with useful information' in question 2?
c) What kind of word, e.g. noun, verb or adjective, is needed in question 3?
d) Which figure will be higher: the answer to question 4 or 5?

2 Now listen and complete the advertisement below. Write no more than two words or a number for each answer.

IFC International Friendship Club

Do you want to meet students from all over the world and make new friends?
Come and join our friendly club!

Membership benefits:

Weekly club meetings on **1** .... evenings

Regular **2** .... packed with useful information

Full social programme

Special certificates for **3** .... participation

Membership Fee:

Only **4** £........................... per term or **5** £........................... per year

Call Daisy or Simon now on 2466

▶ Post-listening

3 Compare your answers with another student.

▶ Prediction

4 Study questions 6–10.

a) Which answer(s) will be a number?

b) Which answers might be difficult to spell?

c) What kind of answer is needed for question 10?

▶ EXAM LINK

Listening

By studying the questions in advance and thinking about possible answers, you reduce the options and make the listening task easier.

5 Now listen to the second part of the conversation and complete the notes below. Write no more than two words or a number for each answer.

International Friendship Club

TELEPHONE ENQUIRY

Date: 12th May

Name: Maria **6** ....

Nationality: **7** ....

Address: 47 **8** .... St, Southville

Age: **9** ....

Studying: MA in **10** ....

▶ Post-listening

6 Compare your answers with another student. Did you find any of the ten questions more difficult to answer? Which ones and why?

Focus on grammar *Articles*

1 Read the text and find an example for each of the rules a)–g) below.

> A RECENT STUDY in North America has found that it is much less common for families to eat together than it used to be. Life has become more hectic and people have less time to enjoy a meal nowadays. According to the study, the proportion of teenagers who eat fast food regularly is now 20%.

KEY LANGUAGE
Articles
▶ p. 141

Use *a/an* with singular, countable nouns when you mention:
a) something for the first time
b) something that is one of many

Use *the* when the one you're talking about is clear because:
c) it has been mentioned before
d) it is specific or clearly defined (e.g. with a relative clause)

Use no article to talk about:
e) plural nouns in general
f) uncountable nouns in general
g) most names of people and places

2 Correct the mistakes in these sentences.

1 On average, the women live slightly longer than the men.
2 Drugs are serious problem nowadays.
3 This is my second visit to the Taiwan.
4 The diagram gives information about number of students who entered higher education in 2005.
5 The life in big cities can be lonely.

3 Read the more detailed notes about articles on page 141 and then complete the following text by adding *a/an, the* or – (for no article).

Watching **1** .... television is by far **2** .... most popular leisure activity in **3** .... UK. Nearly all **4** .... households have at least one television set and about 80% of **5** .... teenagers have **6** .... television in their bedroom. In **7** .... recent years, there has been **8** .... increase in **9** .... number of television channels available and more **10** .... people are also taking out **11** .... subscription to **12** .... satellite TV.

Focus on writing 2 *Task 2: Paragraphs*

> **EXAM LINK** **Writing**
>
> In order to communicate your ideas clearly in an essay it's essential to use paragraphs. Paragraphs help the reader to follow your argument by dividing the writing into separate sections, each dealing with one main topic area.

SKILLS PRACTICE
▶ Topic sentences

1 A paragraph is a group of sentences which deal with one main topic area, as we saw in Unit 2. Each paragraph normally contains a <u>topic sentence</u> which states the main idea and <u>supporting sentences</u>, which give information or examples to support the main idea. The topic sentence is usually, but not always, the first sentence of the paragraph.

Underline the topic sentences in these extracts. What additional information do the supporting sentences give?

A A lecture is a talk on a particular topic given to a group of people. The audience is usually quite large and may number as many as several hundred. Sometimes there is time for questions and discussions at the end of the session but generally the role of the lecturer is to present knowledge and information, and the responsibility of the audience is to listen and absorb what is being said.

B Many students feel that once they hand their essay in their task is finished. However, the most important learning can often take place after the work is returned to them. By studying the feedback from your teacher, you can learn a lot about your strengths and weaknesses in writing and about how far you meet the requirements of your university.

C Learning another language is not just a question of learning language but also of discovering how another society communicates. As we learn how people express beliefs, customs, ideas, etc, we are also becoming familiar with a different cultural system. If there are any gaps in our knowledge of that system, this may cause problems in understanding. Humour is a good example. Even if we understand every word in a joke, we may not see what is funny if we lack the necessary cultural knowledge.

Adapted from
The International
Student's Guide

▶ Reference links

2 To avoid repeating a word or phrase in a paragraph good writers often use another expression with a similar meaning. What do the following refer to?

1 *The audience* (extract A)   4 *the work* (B)
2 *the session* (A)   5 *becoming familiar with* (C)
3 *the responsibility* (A)

▶ Supporting sentences

3 Complete each paragraph below by writing at least two supporting sentences. Remember to try and avoid repeating words.

1 In many countries, schools are facing increasing problems with pupils' behaviour. …
2 Obesity is a major health problem in many countries and children are just as much at risk as adults are. …

4 Write two paragraphs on the following topic.

> *Which is more important in your opinion: family or friends, and why?*

Focus on speaking 2 *Dealing with difficult questions*

SKILLS PRACTICE
▶ Part 3

1 Sometimes it's hard to give a simple answer to a question, because there are many possibilities, depending on the situation. Study the language in the box.

> ▶ **ESSENTIAL LANGUAGE**
>
> **Dealing with difficult questions**
> It's hard to say …
> It (really) **depends on** + NOUN; It (really) **depends if/how/what/when** + CLAUSE
> How long does the journey take? *It's hard to say. It really depends on the traffic.*
> What's the best restaurant? *It's hard to say. It depends what kind of food you like.*

2 Answer these questions using language from the box above.

1 What clothes should I pack for a holiday in your country?
2 Which hotel would you recommend?
3 How long does it take to learn a language?

EXAM PRACTICE

3 Discuss these topics in pairs.

1 What is the ideal age to get married, for men and for women?
2 What should happen to elderly people in society?
3 Which three of these qualities are most important in a friend?

| brave | generous | honest | fun-loving | intelligent |
| kind | loyal | reliable | warm | |

DIY Learning strategy *Listen up!*

English (Australian/Canadian, etc.) people speak too fast.

It's much harder to follow a recording than a 'live' speaker.

I understand my teacher but other people often have strange accents.

It's important to practise your listening skills outside class. Listening to different voices in different situations will increase your confidence and ability. You can listen to spoken English on TV, DVD or radio, for example, and if you're in an English-speaking country, why not practise by socialising with native speakers?

Remember these rules:

- Try to listen to lots of DIFFERENT types of spoken English including monologues and dialogues, 'live' and recorded speech.
- Build your confidence STEP BY STEP! Start with shorter, easier pieces.
- Don't try to understand every word. Listen for the GENERAL MEANING.
- MAKE A NOTE OF any interesting words or expressions you hear.

DIY LEARNING PROJECT

> 1 Choose one way of practising listening from the ideas above, and make arrangements to borrow/rent the CD/DVD, etc.
> 2 Spend at least ten minutes listening – longer if possible.
> 3 Only use a dictionary to check words or phrases you really need to know.
> 4 Be prepared to describe your listening experience and also to explain one thing you've learnt from the experience.

IELTS VOCABULARY BUILDER

Family tree

1 Complete Mark's family tree.

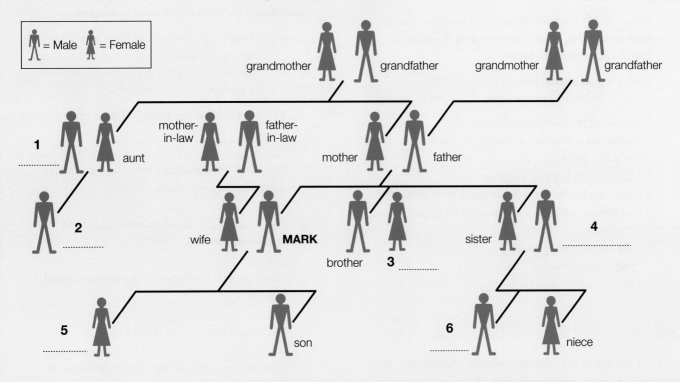

Right word/wrong word

2 Complete the sentences by choosing one word from each pair in the box. Check the meanings of any words you don't know in a dictionary.

1 In Greece, it's traditional for wedding guests to pin paper money to the (bride's/groom's) dress.
2 After their wedding, they left for a ten-day (reception/honeymoon) in the Caribbean.
3 When their marriage ran into trouble, they decided to (divorce/separate) for a while.
4 He's stayed good friends with his (widow/ex-wife) since the divorce.
5 Everyone was invited to bring their (partner/fiancé) to the office party.

Word families

3 Make nouns from the following adjectives. Use a dictionary to check your answers.

1	brave	....	6	kind	....
2	engaged	....	7	loyal	....
3	generous	....	8	reliable	....
4	high	....	9	responsible	....
5	honest	....	10	warm	....

ACADEMIC WORD STUDY 2

NOUN SUFFIXES

1 You probably know more common academic words than you realise. Write a noun ending in *-ation* to match each definition below.

Example Exchanging ideas or information
by writing or speaking   *communication*

1 showing how something works
2 a statement that two amounts are equal
   (e.g. $E = mc^2$)
3 picture in a book or magazine
4 entering another country to make your home there
5 an official attempt to find out the truth (e.g. about a crime)
6 the act of making laws
7 place or position
8 taking part in an activity

Using academic vocabulary

It's not enough to understand academic vocabulary – you also need to know how to <u>use</u> some of the most common expressions: for example, which word partner to choose, or which grammatical pattern should follow.

WORD PARTNERS

2 In each sentence ONE of the words in brackets cannot be used. Cross out the incorrect word in each group.

1 A (big/high/large) **proportion** of people voted in the election.
2 It is (fairly/clearly/perfectly) **obvious** that we need to make changes.
3 The (great/vast/big) **majority** of people know little about science.
4 The graph (covers/lasts/represents) a **period** of five years.
5 It needs a brave person to (perform/undertake/make) such a dangerous **task**.
6 You have to (do/meet/satisfy) the entry **requirements** of the university.

GRAMMATICAL PATTERNS

3 Rewrite the following sentences, using the academic word in brackets, so that the meaning is the same. Do not change the form of the word in brackets.

Example People have a choice of three methods of payment. (**select**)
People can select from three methods of payment.

1 There are only two or three people in most families. (**consist**)
   ....
2 The company introduced pay cuts even though there were angry protests. (**despite**)
   ....
3 The police still don't know who carried out the crime. (**established**)
   ....
4 There are various things the government could do. (**options**)
   ....
5 The data is not correct. (**error**)
   ....
6 In recent years people have begun to marry later. (**trend**)
   ....
7 You should start by saying what you mean by 'success'. (**definition**)
   ....
8 It's difficult to find accommodation. (**available**)
   ....

4 Choose four academic words from this page and write personal examples to help you remember them.

1 ....
2 ....
3 ....
4 ....

Check your answers on page 168 and use this page as a reference point for revision.

REVIEW 2

PAST SIMPLE

1   Write the past simple of the following verbs in the spaces provided.

1	become	....	9	know	....
2	bring up	....	10	make	....
3	can	....	11	pay for	....
4	catch	....	12	rise	....
5	cost	....	13	set up	....
6	fall	....	14	spread	....
7	freeze	....	15	take	....
8	go	....	16	think	....

ARTICLES

2   Complete the **Article Wheel** below by putting the letters A–H into the correct sections, then complete sentences 1–5 below.

A   … Equator, … IELTS test
B   … hunger, … technology
C   … man, … town
D   … man I spoke to, … town where I live
E   … New Zealand, … President Kennedy
F   … United Kingdom, … Atlantic
G   … computers, … years
H   … best solution, … easiest question

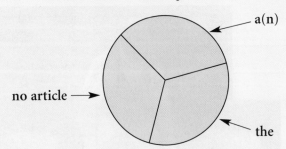

1   .... children generally enjoy playing .... games on .... Internet.
2   .... tiredness kills! Take .... break. (Sign on .... M4 motorway.)
3   There has been .... increase of 39% in .... number of .... traffic accidents over .... last ten years.
4   .... women took .... increasingly important role in .... labour market during .... 20th century.
5   .... Spain is .... most popular holiday destination for .... UK residents, followed by .... USA.

WORD BUILDING

3   Use the word given in capitals at the end of each line to form a word that fits the space. Make sure your answer fits grammatically as well as logically.

Example
There have been great advances in the ..*treatment*.... of cancer.   TREAT

1   She has a recognised .... in accountancy.   QUALIFY
2   More than 75% of the country is .... land.   AGRICULTURE
3   Fortunately, my parents were .... of my taste in music.   TOLERATE
4   He began his career as a .... chef.   TRAIN
5   .... drivers have to pay more for insurance.   EXPERIENCE
6   The manager has overall .... for staff welfare.   RESPONSIBLE
7   He couldn't give any .... for his behaviour.   EXPLAIN
8   You need to be a minumum .... to work as a stewardess.   HIGH

4   Write up to three words or a number to complete the following sentences. Page numbers are given in brackets for you to check your answers if necessary.

1   You have one minute to .... before Part 2 of the Speaking module and you can make .... if you wish. (30)
2   It's a good idea to .... key words or phrases in reading questions. (31)
3   The third part of the Speaking module is a .... lasting between .... and .... minutes. (34)
4   To do well in Task 1 of the Writing module, you have to .... the data and .... the key points to include. (40)
5   Answers in the Listening module need correct information <u>and</u> correct .... (42)

5 ▶ A sporting chance

In this unit you will practise:

- **Reading skills:** Predicting; skimming; parallel expressions
- **Speaking skills:** Discussing sports and hobbies; describing a person; agreeing/disagreeing
- **Grammar:** Present perfect
- **Vocabulary:** Sports and games; *do*, *play*, *go*; pronunciation: word stress

Exam Focus

Reading: Short-answer questions; classification; T/F/NG; summary completion; matching

Speaking: Parts 1, 2, 3

Lead-in

1   If you take part in a strenuous sport, your heart becomes larger according to the level of effort you need to use. Complete the following table by filling in the remaining sportspeople according to how strenuous you think their sports are.

Athletes with the Largest Hearts
1
2
3   Rowers
4
5   Sprint cyclists
6   Middle distance runners
7
8
9   Sprinters
10

Weightlifters
Decathletes
Swimmers
Boxers
Tour de France cyclists
Marathon runners

You can check the answers on page 168.

2   Discuss these questions in pairs.

1   What is the most strenuous sport or activity that you have ever done? Tell your partner what you did and how you felt.

2   What are the advantages of taking part in sport? Are there any dangers?

Focus on speaking 1 *Discussing sports and hobbies*

1 **Seven of these sentences contain common errors. Identify and correct them.**

1 My brother makes several different sports.
2 I'm not very good at the sport.
3 My favourite play is netball.
4 I'm not really very sporty but I enjoy an occasional game of tennis.
5 We usually play a match of football at the weekend.
6 They belong to the local sports club.
7 I took place in a half marathon last year.
8 Most of my friends are supporting Manchester United.
9 He's very good at swimming.
10 We are running once a week.

2 **Work in pairs. Take it in turns to take the role of the examiner and interview each other on the following topics. Try to add a few follow-up questions, e.g.** *When … ? Where … ? How often … ?*

- Do you take part in any sport regularly?
- What sport(s) did you do at school? Did you enjoy it? Why/Why not?
- Which sporting events do you enjoy watching on TV?

> ### ▶ ESSENTIAL LANGUAGE
>
> **Discussing sports and hobbies**
>
> | | |
> |---|---|
> | go + *-ing* | *I **go swimming** (at least) once a week.* |
> | enjoy + noun/*-ing* | *I really **enjoy playing** tennis.* |
> | be interested in/keen on + noun/*-ing* | *(I'm afraid) **I'm not** (very/really) **interested in** sport.* |
> | prefer + *-ing* to + *-ing* | *I **prefer watching** football **to** playing it.* |
> | | *(Actually,) **I'm not very sporty**.* |

3 **Work in pairs. Discuss whether you agree or disagree with the following opinions. Before you start, study the Essential language in the box below.**

- There isn't enough sport on TV.
- Sports stars get paid too much money.
- It's good for children to take part in competitive sports.

> ### ▶ ESSENTIAL LANGUAGE
>
> **Agreeing and disagreeing with a point of view**
>
> **Agreeing**
> (Yes,) **I agree** (with that).
> (Yes,) **I think that's** (quite) **true**.
>
> **Partly agreeing**
> **I agree up to a point but** …   **I think/in my opinion** …
>
> **Disagreeing**
> (No,) **I don't** (really) **agree** (with that).
> (No,) **I don't think that's true** (at all).

Focus on reading 1 *The Boys of Summer, the Men of Fall*

SKILLS PRACTICE
▶ Predicting

1 Read just the title and subtitle from the text opposite, then say in your own words what you think the text will be about.

> ▶ **EXAM LINK** Reading
>
> Always study the title and the subtitle, as well as any pictures or diagrams first. Try and predict what the text will be about and think of anything you know about the subject. This will help you to 'tune in' to the topic and to read more efficiently.

▶ Skimming

2 Read through the text quickly to answer these questions. Before you begin, underline the key words or phrases in each question.

1 What three ingredients are needed for excellence in sport?
2 Find one sport where sportsmen and women have a long career.
3 Find one sport where sportsmen and women have a short career.
4 What provides energy for the muscles in sporting events?

▶ Parallel expressions

3 a) Exam questions often use different words from a text. They may use a word with a very similar meaning or they may use a phrase which summarises part of a text. Answer the following questions about 1–4 above.

1 Which question has key words which are **exactly the same** in the text?
2 Which question has a key phrase which **has a similar meaning** to a word in the text?
3 Which two questions have key phrases which **summarise** sections of the text?

b) Match the words 1–8 with meanings a)–h).

1	component	a)	need
2	crucial	b)	speed
3	deteriorate	c)	become weaker
4	power	d)	depend
5	rate	e)	study
6	rely	f)	part (of a system)
7	require	g)	very important
8	research	h)	strength

EXAM PRACTICE
▶ Short-answer questions

4 Answer the questions below. Write no more than three words or a number for each answer.

1 What is Waneen Spirduso's special field of study?
2 At what age does the oxygen capacity of the lungs become smaller?
3 Which components of the body become less effective between the ages of 20 and 30?

The Boys of Summer, the Men of Fall

Why some athletes improve with age and some don't.

'Ageing is sports-specific,' says **Waneen Spirduso**, *a researcher in human movement at the University of Texas, because excellence in any sport depends on three ingredients – power, endurance and good nerves – and these components deteriorate at different rates.*

Weightlifting, rowing and wrestling all require short bursts of great strength, the ability least affected by ageing. The muscle cells which make up the tissue responsible for strength die off with the passing years but so slowly as to make little difference until the age of 50 or beyond. Forty-year-old rowers can therefore remain competitive with 25-year-olds.

To fuel muscles for longer events, the body relies on oxygen. The sooner oxygen reaches muscles, the better the performance. But with age, the lungs lose elasticity and take in less oxygen. Beginning at 30, oxygen capacity decreases 5–10% per decade. This makes a major difference to cyclists, swimmers, and runners.

The third of the athletic skills, good nerves, underlies gymnastics and field events, which require perfect balance. Because neurons start to deteriorate in the 20s, you don't see many world-class gymnasts over 25. Nerves are also crucial in sprints, triple jump and hurdles. That's why most track stars are past their prime by their mid-to-late-20s. Ageing takes its biggest toll in the sprints and jumps where you need a quick reaction time.

Adapted from Newsweek

▶ Classification

5 Classify the following sports (1–5) by the skills A–C they require according to the text.

1	cycling	....
2	hurdles	....
3	rowing	....
4	running	....
5	wrestling	....

> A power
> B endurance
> C good nerves

▶ True/False/Not Given

6 Do the following statements agree with the information in the text?

Write

TRUE	if the statement agrees with the information
FALSE	if the statement contradicts the information
NOT GIVEN	if there is no information on this

1 The muscle cells responsible for strength begin to die off when we are 50.
2 A 40-year-old rower is just as likely to win a race as a younger rower.
3 According to research, the best anti-ageing tonic is in the mind.
4 The oxygen capacity of the lungs is reduced by 5–10 per cent every year.
5 Athletes in sprints and jumps events are worst affected by ageing.

Focus on grammar *Present perfect*

1 The extracts below illustrate three important uses of the present perfect. Underline examples of the present perfect in each one. Then choose the TWO statements A–C which correctly describe that use of the present perfect. Cross out the incorrect statement.

1

Japanese researchers have found a cheap, convenient and drug-free way for diabetics to lose weight and improve their insulin sensitivity. It is called walking.

2

In the 11 months I have been here I have learnt so much and I have also made friends from all over the world.

3

Following yesterday's earthquake, the president has declared a state of emergency.

> **► EXAM LINK**
>
> The **present perfect** tense is useful in the Speaking module for talking about your life and experiences. It's also needed in certain Writing tasks, particularly for describing changes and developments in Task 2.

1 In extract 1 the present perfect tense is used to talk about:
   A an action/event which happened in the past.
   B when the action/event happened.
   C an action/event which has a present result.

2 In extract 2 the present perfect tense is used to talk about:
   A a situation which began in the past.
   B a situation which continues up to the present.
   C a situation that finished in the past.

3 In extract 3 the present perfect tense is used to talk about:
   A an action/event that happened some time ago.
   B an action/event that happened recently.
   C an action/event which has a present result.

KEY LANGUAGE
Present perfect
► p. 151
Adverbs
► p. 140

2 We use the present perfect when there is a strong link between the past and the present. Complete these sentences using *just, already, never, yet* and a suitable verb in the present perfect tense.

1 I'm not hungry. I …
2 I'm afraid I can't tell you anything about New York. I …
3 My brother is having a big celebration tomorrow. He …
4 'Did you pass the exam?' 'I don't know. I …'
5 It's too late to board the plane. The check-in desk …

3 Write true sentences about yourself, using the present perfect and including the words: *never, since, for many years, recently.*

4 Complete these texts using either a past simple or a present perfect tense.

In the early Olympic Games, judges **1** (have to) .... use their own watches to time events. Then in 1932, the Swiss company Omega **2** (supply) .... 80 stop-watches, which **3** (be) .... accurate to a tenth of a second. Since then technology **4** (improve) .... enormously.

At the beginning of the 20th century, pole vaulters **5** (use) .... bamboo poles. However, the introduction of metal and other materials like glass fibre in the 1950s **6** (make) .... poles much stronger, and the pole vault record **7** (increase) .... by 53% since the first official record in 1912.

People first **8** (play) .... golf in Scotland in the 15th century. There **9** (be) .... huge international growth in the game in the last 20 years and it **10** (become) .... a status symbol in many countries.

Focus on reading 2 *The curse of the referee*

SKILLS PRACTICE
▶ Predicting

1 Read the headline on the following page and discuss these questions.

1 What does a referee do?
2 How many sports or games with a referee can you think of?
3 A 'curse' is something which causes trouble or harm. What are some of the problems a referee has to face?

EXAM PRACTICE
▶ Summary completion

TASK APPROACH

▶ TIP
The items **may not** be in the same order as information in the text.

2 In this task you have to complete a summary of part or all of a text by choosing answers from a list of words. Read the following advice.

- Look through the summary fairly quickly so you know what it's about.
- Read it again more carefully, stopping at each gap and thinking about the missing word. Is it a noun, verb or adjective? What is the general meaning?
- Go back to the text to check the information.
- Choose a suitable answer from the box. Make sure your answer means exactly the same as the text and fits grammatically.

▶ TIP
This task is based on lines 1–24.

3 Complete the summary below by choosing words from the box.

People who want to become referees must be prepared to face **1** .... or even physical abuse in the course of their work. They must also accept that the **2** .... they receive will be fairly poor. In order to qualify as a football referee, applicants have to take various **3** .... and they also need excellent **4** .... They will be expected to maintain a high level of **5** .... throughout their career, and both this and their performance will be **6** .... checked. It's a very strenuous job, **7** .... for someone who's over forty, as many referees are.

especially	*even*	*examinations*	*fitness*	*healthy*	*hearing*
interviews	*pass*	*pay*	*receipt*	*regularly*	*salary*	*sometimes*
standard	*verbal*	*violent*	*vision*		

The Curse of the Referee

» IT'S NOT EASY TO UNDERSTAND why people become referees. From American football to baseball, from ice hockey to polo, referees have
5 been shouted at, sworn at, spat at, pushed, punched and kicked. They have had their eyesight questioned, and their dressing rooms damaged. Certainly, nobody becomes a referee to win a popularity contest.

10 And yet most of them continue to tolerate the abuse along with their small financial reward, and give up their spare time entirely for the love of the game. To get to the top as a football referee – and qualify for an allowance of around £300 for each
15 Premiership match – takes at least 15 years.

It's not an easy job to excel at. Referees have to take written and oral examinations and they also have to pass stringent eyesight and colour tests. Their performance and fitness are constantly
20 monitored. Because it takes so long to rise through the ranks most of the top referees are in their forties, but they will run between 10 km and 15 km in the course of a 90-minute match, much of it backwards.

25 Cricket umpires don't require the fitness of football or rugby arbiters, but their task is no less arduous. They have to stand for hours in blazing sunshine, and make instant decisions on something that happens 20 m away as a consequence of a ball
30 hurled at 145 km an hour. It requires an experienced eye to achieve that.

Tennis umpires face similar problems, although they have the advantage of being able to carry out their duties while they are seated. Furthermore, at
35 the top level, they now have the help of modern technology in the form of 'Cyclops', the electronic eye on the service line.

Unlike cricket umpires, tennis umpires also have to keep the score and run several stopwatches
40 simultaneously. There are now limits for the length of time between games, points, first and second

services, and for injury assessment and treatment. In addition, they have to adjudicate for 'racket abuse' (in other words outbursts of bad temper)
45 and issue periodic warnings against the use of mobile phones or flash photography by spectators. Their only reward is a brief handshake at the end of the match.

All sports present certain problems for the
50 referees. The rules for American football run to 250 pages and this is the only sport where referees use microphones to explain their decisions to the crowd. Water polo referees suffer a particular disadvantage in that they stand beside the pool, though 75 per
55 cent of fouls are committed under water.

Bowls referees have to ensure that none of the players are wearing jeans. The use of talcum powder on the soles of shoes, to facilitate a smooth slide of the foot when releasing the ball, is also
60 forbidden.

Referees of physical sports, especially rugby, boxing and ice hockey, must be brave. A boxing referee has to protect the losing fighter from further punishment and be prepared to throw himself into
65 the fight. Consider, too, the Sumo wrestling judges who must get close enough to recognise a legitimate hold and be quick enough not to get crushed underneath a 300 kg man mountain.

Refereeing is a dirty (and sometimes dangerous)
70 job. Referees and umpires will never be loved. As football manager Ron Atkinson said after his team were knocked out of a European Cup tie in controversial circumstances: 'I never comment on referees and I'm not going to break the habit of a
75 lifetime for that twerp.'

Adapted from *Focus*

▶ Matching
TASK APPROACH

▶ **TIP**
This task is based on lines 25–75 of the text.

▶ **TIP**
In exam matching tasks, the items in the list to choose from always appear in the same order in the text.

4 In this task you have to match sports to their descriptions. Read the following advice.

- In the text, underline or highlight the eight sports (A–H) from the box below so they are easy to find.
- Study each question and underline or highlight key words. The first has been done as an example.
- Read the information in the text about each sport and then look for a match in the notes.
- Look for parallel expressions in the text which match expressions in the questions.

Look at the following statements about sports referees and umpires (1–7) and the list of sports (A–H). Match each statement 1–7 with a sport in A–H below.

NB There are more sports than descriptions.

1 The referee has to <u>give</u> the <u>spectators</u> <u>reasons</u> for his <u>decisions</u>.
2 The weather conditions may make the umpire uncomfortable.
3 The referee may ask to examine players' footwear.
4 There's a danger that the referee could be injured by a heavy contestant.
5 The umpire may have to warn spectators about their behaviour.
6 The referee may get involved in the action to prevent injury.
7 It's especially difficult for the referee to see when rules are broken.

LIST OF SPORTS	
A Cricket	E Bowls
B Tennis	F Ice hockey
C American football	G Boxing
D Water polo	H Sumo wrestling

Focus on speaking 2 *Describing a person '20 questions'*

SKILLS PRACTICE

1 Work in pairs. Think of a well-known sportsperson. He or she can be from the present or past but make sure it's someone your partner is likely to have heard of. Don't tell your partner who you've chosen.

Take it in turns to ask questions to find out the name of your partner's sportsperson.

Rules: You can only ask 20 questions each.
           You can only answer *Yes* or *No.*

Examples: *Is the person alive now? Yes*
           Do they play a team sport? No

2 a) Study the following task card.

Describe a sportsperson that you admire.

You should say:

who the person is
what their sport is
how you know about them

and explain what you admire about them.

b) Remember that you have one minute to think about what you're going to say.

1 Think of a sportsperson to talk about. It doesn't have to be anyone famous – you could choose a sports coach you had at school, or a friend who is a keen amateur. Just decide on someone you have plenty to say about!

2 Prepare a mindplan based on the one below. Aim to spend about a minute on this. You don't need to include all the branches but try to think of at least four. Adapt the mindplan as necessary to suit your choice of sportsperson.

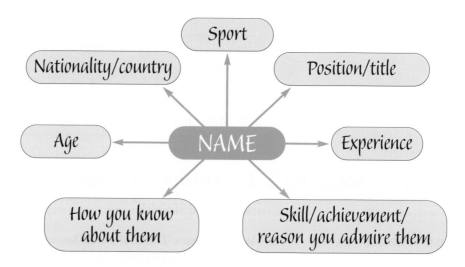

Sport

Nationality/country

Position/title

Age

NAME

Experience

How you know about them

Skill/achievement/ reason you admire them

3 Work in pairs. Take it in turns to describe your sportsperson. Try to speak for about two minutes. After that, your partner can ask one or two questions.

▶ **ESSENTIAL LANGUAGE**

Describing a person you admire
The person I **admire most is** …
What I (really) **admire about him/her is** … his/her dedication to the sport.
the fact that he/she is so dedicated.

He/she has …		He/she is …	
real	skill, ability	really	skillful, able
incredible	dedication, commitment	incredibly	dedicated, committed
fantastic	courage, leadership	fantastically	courageous.

IELTS VOCABULARY BUILDER

1 Use words from the box to complete the sentences below.

> amateur coach compete course court event goals pool
> professional record spectators stadium supporters teams train

1 If you want to .... in a marathon, you'll need to
  .... for at least six months beforehand.

2 He won his first ever golf tournament while he was still a(n) ....
  but he went .... shortly after that.

3 He holds the .... for the highest number of ....
  scored in a single football season.

4 Over 20,000 .... are expected to attend the match, and
  .... of the two .... will occupy seperate areas of the
  ....

5 The sports centre has an Olympic-sized swimming .... , an
  18-hole golf .... and a squash ....

6 Working with a new .... improved her technique and helped her
  to win a silver medal in the women's 200m .... in the last
  Olympics.

Word partners: *do, play, go*

2 Which verb is needed to complete the following expressions?

1 .... exercise   4 .... sport

2 .... baseball   5 .... karate

3 .... running   6 .... climbing

Pronunciation: Word stress

3 Practise saying the following words according to the stress pattern:

Oo   e.g. HELmet, courage, fitness, cyclist

oOo   e.g. kaRAte, equipment, condition, fantastic

ooO   e.g. JapanESE, underneath, disagree, overcharge

4 Match the following words to the correct stress pattern.

athletics	supporter	football
referee	understand	contest
umpire	athlete	entertain
disappear	spectator	gymnastics

Oo   ....

oOo   ....

ooO   ....

6 ▶ Animal rights and wrongs

In this unit you will practise:

- **Listening skills:** Recognising numbers and abbreviations
- **Writing skills:** Stages in writing a Task 2 answer, giving reasons/arguments
- **Speaking skills:** Expressing personal reactions; discussing moral issues
- **Grammar:** Review of present tenses; comparison
- **Vocabulary:** Prepositions; word families; right word/wrong word
- **DIY Learning strategy:** Make a note of it

Exam Focus
Listening: Sections 2, 3; Note completion; sentence completion; table completion
Writing: Task 2
Speaking: Parts 1, 3

Lead-in

1   Discuss these questions.

1   Why do people keep pets?
2   How do people think of their pets?
3   What kind of lives do some pets lead?

2   One word does not fit in each group below. Which is it, and why?

1   sheep, cow, dog, cat, wolf
2   veterinary surgeon, botanist, marine biologist, zoologist, zoo keeper
3   stable, nest, aquarium, cage, bowl
4   spider, bat, beetle, butterfly, ant
5   breeding, hunting, fishing, poaching, trapping

Focus on speaking 1 *Discussing animals*

SKILLS PRACTICE

1   Work in pairs to interview each other using the questions below. Try to build a short conversation by finding out a few more details. Before you start, study the Essential language below.

- Are there any animals you particularly like? (If so, find out why.)
- Are there any animals you can't stand? (If so, find out why.)
- Have you ever kept a pet? (If so, find out more.)
- Which animals are popular as pets in your country? (Find out more.)

> ▶ **ESSENTIAL LANGUAGE**
>
> **Expressing personal reactions**
> I find …   (quite/very/really)   interesting/attractive/enjoyable, etc.
>   annoying/unpleasant/noisy/dirty, etc.
>   (absolutely)   fascinating/horrible/disgusting, etc.

2   **Discuss these questions.**

1   The following animals are the top five most popular pets in the UK . Which do you think is the most popular of all?

2   Which of the animals would be most suitable as a pet for the following people, and why?
   a) an elderly person living alone
   b) a seven-year-old only child living in a house with a small garden
   c) a single professional person living in a city apartment

Focus on grammar 1 *Review of present tenses*

> ▶ **EXAM LINK**
>
> Present tenses are at the heart of successful IELTS Speaking and Writing. You need the **present simple** to talk about your life and interests in the interview, or to state facts and make general observations in the Writing module. The **present progressive** is important in describing situations which are developing or changing. If you know which present tense to use, and when, you'll avoid making basic mistakes.

1   **Look through the extracts below and then answer the questions. Which extract A–E mentions:**

1 criminals looking after animals?	A B C D E
2 how looking at animals can affect us?	A B C D E
3 the way dogs and humans think of each other?	A B C D E
4 that pets are becoming more popular?	A B C D E
5 why dogs make good companions?	A B C D E

A We are keeping more pets than ever before. Times are harder and feeding more expensive, yet the number of cats and dogs we keep is increasing each year.

B In most cases, the relationship between human and dog is based on a misunderstanding. Dogs see us as pack leaders or top dogs; we think of them as furry people.

C Pets are helping to rehabilitate prisoners in many countries. Inmates are forming bonds they have never formed before; a kidnapper cares for a gerbil, a murderer feeds a pigeon.

D A dog never says 'Who were you with last night?' or 'Why don't you love me?' What is more, he loves you. He needs you. He makes you take exercise and he makes you laugh.

E According to research carried out in a dental hospital, watching fish in an aquarium before your treatment significantly lowers your heart rate and makes you more relaxed.

KEY LANGUAGE
We cannot use the progressive tense with verbs like *know* or *understand*, which belong to a group known as 'stative' verbs.

• There is for a list of common stative verbs on page 153.

2 Find examples in the extracts to match each of the uses below.

Tense/Use	Extract	Examples
Present simple		
1 A regular action or event in the present	D	A dog never says
2 A scientific fact or a general truth	....	....
3 A mental or emotional state	....	....
Present progressive		
4 Something happening or developing at the present time	....	....

3 Look at the facts about the animals below. Use the information to complete the description of the Lowland gorilla. Then write a similar description of the Greater one-horned rhinocerous.

Lowland gorilla

Size:	Height: 125–175 cm
	Weight: 135–275 kg in males
Found in:	West Africa and Eastern Zaire
Habitat:	Forest
Diet:	A leaf-eater
Status:	Numbers declining
Threats:	Forest clearance

Greater one-horned rhinoceros

Size:	Length: 412 cm
	Weight: 1,600–2,000 kg
Found in:	NE India and Nepal
Habitat:	Grasslands in swampy areas
Diet:	Principally grass
Status:	Endangered but numbers now increasing following intensive conservation programmes
Threats:	Habitat loss and poaching

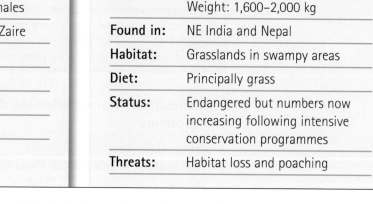

- The Lowland gorilla lives in the forests of West Africa and Zaire and eats a diet of .... It has a height of .... and males weigh between .... and ....:...... kg. Numbers are currently declining as a result of ....
- The Greater one-horned rhinoceros ...

KEY LANGUAGE
Present simple
▶ p. 153
Present progressive
▶ p. 152

▶ ESSENTIAL LANGUAGE

Describing dimensions

It	has a **height/weight/length** etc. of	approximately...
	weighs	up to...
		between ... and ...
	is (approximately) ... **high/long/wide**, etc.	

Focus on listening 1 *Wildlife Film Festival*

SKILLS PRACTICE
▶ Recognising numbers and abbreviations

1 🎧 Listen carefully and circle the numbers you hear.

1	A 23.65%	B 2.365%		C 236.5%
2	A 1,100	B 11,000		C 110,000
3	A 6.15	B 6.50		C 5.45
4	A 572204	B 577204		C 572404
5	A 01628 340951	B 01628 341950		C 01628 351940

▶ **EXAM LINK**

Listening

Look out for symbols like **$** or **%**, or abbreviations like **max** or **mins** in note completion tasks. They give advance warning that you need to listen for a number, and help you listen more effectively.

2 Practise reading aloud the following numbers.

1	2006	4	17/5/05	7	142.4
2	78.23%	5	3/4	8	1,142.5
3	0207 431559	6	2/3	9	1,140,142.8

3 What do the following abbreviations stand for?

1	a.m.	4	#	7	mins	10	dep.
2	arr.	5	Tel	8	kph	11	sq. m.
3	°	6	max.	9	no.	12	%

EXAM PRACTICE
▶ Section 2 Preparation

4 You will hear part of a radio programme giving information about a festival of wildlife films. Before you listen, study the task and answer these questions.

a) Which answers require numbers?
b) Which answers require the names of countries?
c) Try and think of possible answers for questions 2, 5 and 9.

5 🎧 Listen and complete the notes below. Write one word and/or a number for each answer.

Wildlife Film Festival

Day/Time	Title and notes	Country of film-maker
Sat. 1	**My Life as an Ant** Hero is only 1 cm long! Learn about his world as he travels around in search of 2	3 ....
Sat. 7.00 p.m.	4 .... **Oasis** Experience the life and colour of coral reefs off Mexican coast. Watch 5 .... swimming with giant mantas and whales.	USA
Sun. 11 a.m.	**The Mystery of Yunnan Snub-nosed Monkey** Film took 6 .... to make. Highly-endangered animals (less than 7 .... remaining). Winner of TVE award.	China
Sun. 3.30 p.m.	**Riverhorse** Film follows family of hippos over two-year period. Winner of Animal 9 .... category of film award.	8 ....
For information call the Box Office on Tel: 10		

DIY Learning strategy *Make a note of it*

Look at these ways of recording language. What is each one most useful for?

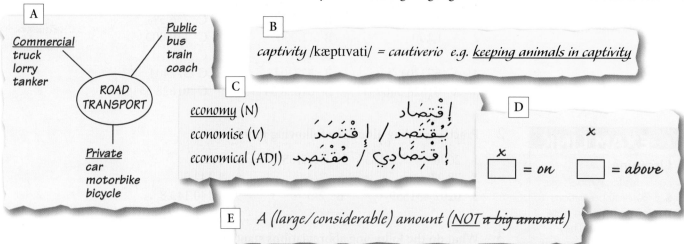

A

Commercial
truck
lorry
tanker

Public
bus
train
coach

ROAD
TRANSPORT

Private
car
motorbike
bicycle

B

captivity /kæptɪvati/ = cautiverio e.g. keeping animals in captivity

C

economy (N)
economise (V)
economical (ADJ)

إقْتِصَاد
يَقْتَصِد / إقْتَصَد
إِقْتِصَادِي / مُقْتَصِد

D

x
☐ = on   ☐ = above
x

E

A (large/considerable) amount (NOT a big amount)

Remember these rules:

- Choose a permanent place to make a note of useful language, such as a notebook.
- Give a brief example of the expression in context.
- Include any useful information, e.g. related noun or adjective, dependent preposition(s), opposite, pronunciation, etc.
- Revise regularly!

DIY LEARNING PROJECT

1 Find out how other students in the class record useful language.
2 Start experimenting with at least one new way of recording vocabulary.
3 Ask your teacher to check your new vocabulary records after a week.

Focus on speaking 2 *Discussing moral issues*

EXAM PRACTICE

▶ Part 1

▶ Part 3

Work in pairs. Discuss these questions.

1 When did you last visit a zoo or wildlife park? Describe the visit.
2 Do you enjoy visiting zoos or wildlife parks? Why/Why not?
3 Should animals be allowed to perform in circuses? Why/Why not?
4 Should scientists experiment on animals in order to develop new drugs? Why/Why not?

▶ ESSENTIAL LANGUAGE

Discussing moral issues

I feel strongly about …

AGAINST	FOR
I'm (totally) against …	I'm (all) in favour of …
I think it's (cruel/immoral, etc.) (to …)	I think … is/are useful/educational, etc.
There's no justification for …	I don't see a problem with …

Focus on listening 2 *The right to roam*

EXAM PRACTICE
▶ Section 3
Preparation

You will hear part of a seminar in which a student called Lisa discusses the problems of keeping animals in captivity.

Before you listen, study the task carefully. Make sure you know how the table is organised. Identify questions which need numbers for answers and think about possible answers.

Questions 1–3.
Complete the sentences below.
Write NO MORE THAN TWO WORDS for each answer.

1   The institution which carried out the research was ....

2   A journal called .... published the results of the research.

3   Large animals often don't breed well in captivity because of ....

Questions 4–10.
Complete the table below.
Write NO MORE THAN THREE WORDS AND/OR A NUMBER for each answer.

ANIMALS THAT DO BADLY IN CAPTIVITY		Animal	ANIMALS THAT DO WELL IN CAPTIVITY	
Polar bear	**4**	**Animal**	**Grizzly bear**	**Snow leopard**
5 .... sq km	148 sq km	**Average territory**	182 sq km	38.9 sq km
1,200 sq km	19.7 sq km	**6** .... **territory**	**7** .... sq km	
8.8 km	11 km	**Average distance travelled 8**	**9** .... km	1.3 km
65 per cent	42 per cent	**Infant mortality rate**	0 per cent	**10** .... per cent

WRITING PRACTICE
Task 1, Guided practice
▶ Practice 3, p. 159

Focus on grammar 2 *Comparison*

1 The bar chart shows what percentages of five species of animals are endangered. Study the examples and then make two more sentences about the bar chart.

1	adj + *er* + **than**
	more/less + adj/adv + **than**

e.g. *Fish are **more endangered than** any other species.*

2	**as** + adj/adv + **as**
	not as/so + adj/adv + **as**

e.g. *Mammals are **just as endangered as** amphibians.*
*Birds are **not so endangered as** mammals.*

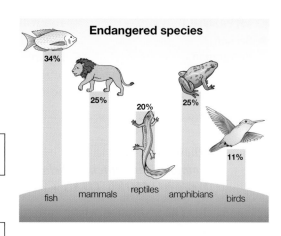

Endangered species

34% fish
25% mammals
20% reptiles
25% amphibians
11% birds

2 Discuss these questions, then underline the comparative or superlative adjectives and adverbs.

1 Which is the largest animal in the world?
2 Which land animal can move the fastest?
3 Which snake is the most venomous?
4 Which group of animals have the best eyesight?
5 Do you think animals can make people more relaxed and happier?

3 Underline the comparative and superlative adverbs in the sentences below.

Some large animals, such as grizzly bears and snow leopards, adapt more successfully to captivity than others. Large predators that roam across hundreds of miles in the wild suffer most severely in captivity.

4 Find examples from the sentences in exercises 1–3 above to illustrate these rules for forming comparatives and superlatives in English.

- **Adjectives and adverbs of one syllable** add *-(e)r* to form the comparative and *-(e)st,* to form the superlative, e.g. 1 ....
- **Adjectives ending in** *-y* change to *-ier* or *-iest*, e.g. 2 ....
- **Most other adjectives and all adverbs of two or more syllables** take *more* and *most*, e.g. 3 ....

Can you complete this list of irregular comparative and superlative forms?

Good/well	4	....	....
Bad/badly	5	....	....
Little	6	....	....
Much	7	....	....

5 Use the superlative forms of suitable adjectives to complete these sentences.

1 Howler monkeys of Central and South America are .... creatures on Earth. Their calls can be heard up to 16 km away.

2 .... fish in the world is a species of piranha. In 1981 they reportedly killed 300 people when a passenger boat capsized in Brazil.

3 .... altitude recorded for a bird is 11,300 m for a vulture which collided with a commercial aircraft in 1973.

4 The world's .... snake is the anaconda. A female shot in Brazil in 1990 was estimated to weigh around 227 kg.

5 Koko, a gorilla born in San Francisco zoo, could be the world's .... animal. She has a vocabulary of over 1,000 signs and understands around 2,000 words of spoken English.

<table>
<tr><td>KEY LANGUAGE
Comparison
▶ p. 142</td></tr>
</table>

6 Work in pairs.

a) Choose two or three adjectives from the following box and make **true** sentences containing **comparative** forms.

tidy	boring	attractive	healthy	useful	rich	easy	important

b) Choose one of these phrases and tell your partner a true story about yourself. Try to talk for about two minutes if you can.

the best teacher   the worst food
the biggest mistake   the most exciting experience

Focus on writing *Task 2: Presenting and justifying an opinion*

EXAM PRACTICE
▶ Task 2

Study this exam topic and follow the four stages in writing a Task 2 answer.

> *'Keeping <u>animals</u> in captivity is cruel. There is no reason for <u>zoos</u> to exist in the 21st century.'*
>
> *How far do you agree or disagree with this opinion?*
>
> Give reasons for your answer and include any relevant examples from your own knowledge or experience.

▶ Analyse the question

1 Two key words in the question have been underlined. Both are used very generally.

1 Is keeping ALL animals in captivity cruel?
If not, which animals do badly in captivity, and why? (Think about the information in *Focus on listening 2*.) Which animals do better?

2 Do ALL zoos have poor conditions?
If not, what improvements have there been to modern zoos (or wildlife parks)? Can you mention any examples you've visited?

▶ Plan your answer

2   Work in pairs to discuss ideas for your essay.

| Introduction ? |

| Arguments FOR zoos | Arguments AGAINST zoos |

Arguments FOR zoos
- Easy life for animals!
  why?
- Education
  especially for?
- Research
  e.g. ?
- Conservation
  e.g. breeding programmes
  for endangered species

Arguments AGAINST zoos
- Cruel
  why?
- People visit zoos for entertainment
  not education
- Research possibilities limited
  animals in unnatural conditions
- Breeding not always successful
  e.g. polar bears

| Conclusion ? |

▶ Write your answer

3   Complete this introductory paragraph with a suitable word or phrase and then write three more paragraphs based on the notes below.

INTRODUCTION
Most people who have seen a lion or tiger in a cage have felt **1** ....
that such a magnificent beast is unable to **2** .... Those who feel
strongly about animal rights go further and argue that there is no justification
for keeping animals **3** .... **4** .... , it is important to
look at both **5** .... of the argument .

ARGUMENTS FOR
Supporters of zoos would argue that there are many benefits to keeping animals
in captivity. One of the most important of these is that …

ARGUMENTS AGAINST
On the other hand, those who oppose zoos would would argue that …

CONCLUSION
On balance, I feel that zoos …
However, they need to …

WRITING PRACTICE
Task 2, Model answer
▶ Practice 4, p. 159

▶ **ESSENTIAL LANGUAGE**

Giving reasons/arguments:	**One of the** (main/most important) **arguments is** …
	Some people (would) **argue that** …
Giving more reasons/arguments:	**Another/A further argument** (for/against) **is** …
	In addition, Furthermore, …
Giving an opposite argument:	**On the other hand, By contrast,** …

▶ Check your answer

4   Once you've finished, check your essay carefully for mistakes. Look especially
for subject/verb agreement and for your 'favourite' spelling mistakes.

IELTS VOCABULARY BUILDER

Prepositions

1 Add suitable prepositions to complete the following sentences.

1 Zoos need to concentrate ...... education and conservation.
2 What do the letters *TVE* stand ...... ?
3 There are plenty of courses to choose ....
4 In most cases, the relationship ...... humans and animals is based ...... a misunderstanding.
5 Taking a dog ...... a walk every day helps you keep fit.
6 I'll take care ...... the finances if you look ...... advertising.
7 It's important to look ...... both sides of the argument.
8 The bald eagle is endangered ...... a result of hunting.

Word families

2 Fill in the missing words to complete the table. You can check your answers in a dictionary.

Verb	Noun	Adjective
capture	a)	b)
behave	c)	
	extinction	d)
conserve	e)	
	zoology	f)
migrate	g)	h)
enclose	i)	j)
survive	k)	

Right word/wrong word

3 Choose the correct word from each pair to complete the sentences. Check the meanings of any words you don't know in a dictionary.

1 He didn't (speak/talk) very good English when he arrived.
2 The only radio programme I (hear/listen to) is the morning news.
3 Cats can (see/look) better in the dark than humans.
4 Few people think that politicians always (say/tell) the truth.
5 A knee injury (avoided/prevented) the horse from racing.

ACADEMIC WORD STUDY 3

Understanding academic vocabulary

1 The following words come from the reading texts in Unit 5. Decide what part of speech each word is, noun (N), verb (Vb), adjective (Adj) or adverb (Adv), then match to the correct definition from the list a)–h). If necessary, go back to the passage to see how the word is used in context.

First passage (*page 53*)

1 components (paragraph 1)   *...N (plural), c)...*
2 affect (2)   ....
3 decade (3)   ....
4 crucial (4)   ....

Second passage (*page 56*)

5 constantly (line 19) ....
6 monitor (20)   ....
7 consequence (29)   ....
8 achieve (31)   ....

Definitions

| A Nouns |

a) result
b) period of ten years
c) parts (that make up a whole system)

| B Verbs |

d) succeed in doing something
e) make a change in something
f) check regularly

| C Adjectives |

g) very important

| D Adverbs |

h) very regularly

Using academic vocabulary

2 Complete the following extracts with the correct academic word from exercise 1. You may need to make small grammatical changes.

The course has two main 1 ....: literature and language, and your tutor will 2 .... your progress throughout the year. It's important that you complete all the assignments because your marks 3 .... your final grade. If you miss an assignment, the 4 .... could be that you fail the course.

The forests where the gorillas live are 5 .... threatened by timber companies and others, but if we want to save these fascinating animals, it's 6 .... that we preserve their habitat. That's what the Gorilla Trust has been working to 7 .... over the last 8 ....

WORD PARTNERS

3 Choose the correct verb from the box to combine with academic words in the sentences below. Make sure the verb fits grammatically.

| *do   face   give   have   play   reach* |

1 The president is .... a **challenge** to his leadership.
2 The committee has not .... a **conclusion** yet.
3 He .... an **indication** of his intention to resign.
4 An increase in the price of fuel will .... **consequences** on the economy.
5 He's .... **research** into the subject.
6 Diet can .... a **role** in preventing some diseases.

4 Choose a suitable adjective from the box to go before each academic word in exercise 3.

| *clear   crucial   fascinating   final   important   in-depth   major   serious   significant* |

5 Choose four academic expressions from exercises 3 and 4 and write personal examples to help you remember them.

1 ....
2 ....
3 ....
4 ....

Check your answers on page 168 and use this page as a reference point for revision.

70

REVIEW 3

Grammar

IRREGULAR VERBS

1 Write the past and past participles of the following verbs in the spaces provided.

1 begin ....
2 buy ....
3 choose ....
4 do ....
5 eat ....
6 find ....
7 give ....
8 lose ....
9 make ....
10 put ....
11 see ....
12 speak ....
13 stand ....
14 tell ....
15 understand ....
16 win ....

SPOT THE ERROR

2 Not all the following sentences are correct. Underline all the mistakes and correct them. Page numbers are given in brackets for you to check your answers if necessary.

1 *I have arrived two weeks ago.* (54)
2 *The results haven't been announced yet.* (54)
3 *I find the subject absolutely fascinating.* (60)
4 *The lorry is containing toxic chemicals.* (62)
5 *The Florida panther live in the Florida. It length between 210 and 270cm.* (62)
6 *The number of eagles is reducing due to being shooted.* (66)
7 *I have never seen a more happier child.* (66)
8 *His work is still more careless than it should be.* (66)
9 *She is the taller in the class.* (66)
10 *It is the least pleasant job I can think of.* (66)
11 *There is nothing better as home cooking.* (66)
12 *The government told that it would improve health care.* (69)

Vocabulary

SPELLING

3 Seven of the words below are spelt wrongly. Underline the mistakes and correct them.

1 *achievement*
2 *aproximately*
3 *arguement*
4 *behaviour*
5 *commitment*
6 *dissappear*
7 *extinct*
8 *furthermore*
9 *heigth*
10 *imoral*
11 *responsable*
12 *spectater*

PREPOSITIONS

4 Fill in the missing prepositions.

1 .... balance,
2 .... comparison,
3 .... contrast,
4 .... addition,
5 .... the other hand,
6 .... a result of
7 be .... favour of
8 be keen ....
9 be interested ....
10 concentrate ....
11 prefer (one thing) .... (another)
12 rely ....

WORD CHOICE

5 Choose the correct answer A–C to complete the following text.

1 .... of zoos believe that there are many
2 .... to keeping animals in captivity. One of the
3 .... ones is to help in the conservation of
4 .... species. Other people would 5 ....
that there's no 6 .... whatsoever for keeping
animals in zoos and that this 7 .... particularly
to large species like polar bears or lions, which have
large territories in their natural 8 ....
9 .... , it's important to look at both
10 .... of the question.

	A	B	C
1	A Visitors	B Followers	C Supporters
2	A reasons	B benefits	C possibilities
3	A main	B great	C front
4	A dangerous	B endangered	C risky
5	A tell	B believe	C argue
6	A justification	B right	C point
7	A applies	B appeals	C approves
8	A country	B area	C habitat
9	A By contrast	B However	C Furthermore
10	A opinions	B ideas	C sides

7 ▶ Appropriate technology

In this unit you will practise:

- **Reading skills:** Forming a general picture; finding specific information
- **Speaking skills:** Describing places
- **Grammar:** Passive
- **Vocabulary:** Environment; word families; pronunciation: sounds

Exam Focus

Reading: Sentence completion; matching; labelling a diagram; locating information; multiple choice

Speaking: Part 2

Lead-in

1 A British newspaper recently carried out a survey to find out which inventions its readers thought were the most important. Their top four choices are listed below but they are NOT in the correct order. Match each invention to a section of the pie chart to show the result of the survey.

- Vaccination
- Electricity
- Computer with World Wide Web
- Bicycle

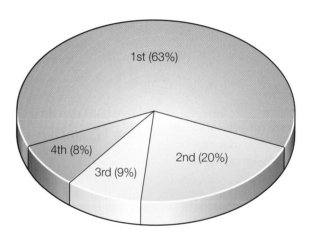

2 Check the actual result on page 168 and say whether you agree with it or not and why.

3 Discuss which of the four inventions:

- was developed earliest.
- made the biggest difference to people's lives when it was first introduced.
- would be the best way of helping a poor community in the less economically developed world.

Focus on reading 1 *Changing lives*

SKILLS PRACTICE
▶ Introduction

1 Each picture 1–4 on the opposite page represents a simple technological solution to a problem in a less economically developed country. Discuss what the problem might be in each case, and how the solution works.

1 Fish cage

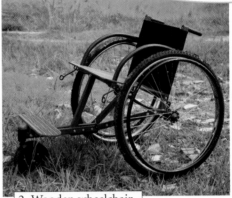

2 Wooden wheelchair

3 Tsetse fly trap

4 Bicycle ambulance

▶ Forming a general picture

2 **Match each text A–D below to one of the inventions above. Look through just the first few lines of each text to find clues to the topic. Write the name of the invention at the beginning of each text.**

A

Without suitable transport, villagers of the terai, or plains, of Nepal had no way of taking sick or injured people to the nearest health centre. However even the poorest villages had bicycles. The charity Practical Action was already working with the villagers to build bicycle trailers to take goods to market, and the next step was to adapt them to become ambulances. The two-wheel trailer is made from moulded metal with standard wheels with rubber tyres. The bed section can be padded with cushions to make the patient comfortable, while the 'seat' section allows a family member to attend to the patient during transit. In response to user comments, a cover has been designed that can be added to give protection to the patient and attendant in poor weather. Made of treated cotton, the cover is durable and waterproof. The total cost of a complete bicycle ambulance is £150.

▶ **EXAM LINK**

Reading
Together these four texts contain about 675 words. A typical reading passage in the exam will be slightly longer. Remember that with long texts, you need to use skimming skills to find out the main topic in each section.

B

Across Africa, the tsetse fly threatens a staggering 55 million people and their livestock. The insect sucks blood and in doing so may pass on rabies or the deadly parasite that causes *trypanosomiasis*, sometimes known as sleeping sickness. Infected animals suffer from poor growth, weight loss and low milk yield, They may also become infertile and die. An estimated 500,000 people are also affected by the disease each year, and most of them will die.

Tsetse fly traps are a simple but effective solution. They are built using blue cloth spread between three poles, which looks like a cow to the hungry insect, while bottles containing a mixture of cows' urine and acetone are placed below. Attracted by the smell, the tsetse fly settles on the cloth but is unable to get a bite and falls into the trap. One tsetse fly trap costs only £20 to build but tests have shown that a single trap is ineffective. For this reason it's important that farmers build a number of traps across an area.

C

In Bangladesh, some 56 per cent of the under-fives are malnourished because their families don't have the land, the resources or the money to get them the food they need. However, there is a simple invention, costing only £5, that is helping children and their families to thrive. The 'hapa' is a fish cage which allows villagers to 'grow' fish in their local ponds by feeding them on nothing more than scraps and waste. The 'hapas' provide vitamin and protein-rich food all year round, as well as a little extra money to pay for healthcare and school fees.

A few young fish are put in each 'hapa', which acts as their home, floating just below the surface of the pond. With a little food – oil cakes, kitchen waste and snails – fish grow to full size and in just a few months begin to produce young.

The cages are made using a few cheap materials. Bamboo poles form the outer frame and these are secured with string. This is then covered in netting and floats made of cork are added at the corners. With a capacity of one cubic metre, the cage can hold up to 300 fish at a time.

KEY LANGUAGE
Relative clauses
► p. 154

D

In 1993, the charity Motivation was asked to address the desperate need for wheelchairs in Cambodia, where thousands are disabled by mines every year. A team then carried out a 12-month project to set up production of the Mekong wheelchair, which had to be suitable not only for people who had lost both legs but also for the needs of people with other disabilities. A lack of steel tubing in Cambodia and the country's predominantly rural environment convinced the wheelchair designers that the Mekong should be a wooden frame chair with three wheels to make it more stable and manoeuvrable in rough conditions. The wheelchair packs flat into rice bags, making transport of the vehicle very efficient, and takes approximately two hours to assemble. The workshops are capable of producing the Mekong at a rate of more than 800 a year and at a cost of £40 each. A child's version is also available.

► Finding specific
   information

3 You should now know which part of the text you need to study to find specific information. Use scanning skills to answer these questions quickly.

1 Complete this table.

Invention	Cost
Wooden wheelchair	a)
Fish cage	b)
Bicycle ambulance	c)
Tsetse fly trap	d)

2 Write short answers to these questions. Remember to underline key words.
   a) How many wooden wheelchairs can the workshops make in a year?
   b) What is the capacity of the fish cage?
   c) How many Africans are estimated to catch *trypanosomiasis* each year?
   d) What proportion of Bangladeshi children under the age of five suffer from malnourishment?
   e) How long did Motivation spend preparing to produce its wheelchair?

EXAM PRACTICE

▶ Sentence completion

▶ EXAM LINK

Reading
You don't need to answer exam questions in order. Answering easy questions first makes the task simpler by reducing the possible options.

4 Now complete Exam questions 1–15 below.

Questions 1–4
Complete the sentences below. Choose ***NO MORE THAN TWO WORDS*** *from the passage for each answer.*

1 The word 'terai' in the Nepali language means …

2 A more common name for *trypanosomiasis* is …

3 In Bangladesh, the local word for a fish cage is …

4 The charity Motivation called their wooden wheelchair …

▶ Matching

In this task you have to match a number of descriptions to the correct inventions in the text. Before you start, study the following advice.

TASK APPROACH

- Study the questions and underline key words or phrases.
- Start with any questions that look easier!
- Skim read to find the right section of text and then search for words or phrases with the same meaning as the expressions you underlined.

Work individually to complete the task. When you've finished, compare your answers with your partner's.

Questions 5–10
Look at Questions 5–10 and the list of inventions below.
Match each statement with the correct inventions, A–D.
NB You may use any letter more than once.

Example	*Answer*
Blue cloth is used in its construction.	**B**

5 It can be put together in a couple of hours. ....

6 It was developed from an earlier invention. ....

7 People can use left-over food in this. ....

8 This is specially designed to be easy to transport. ....

9 This doesn't work well on its own. ....

10 An extra part was added after users made some suggestions. ....

A	The bicycle ambulance	**C**	The fish cage
B	The tsetse fly trap	**D**	The wooden wheelchair

▶ Labelling a diagram

In this task you have to label the parts of a diagram using information from a text. In this example, there's a list of answers to choose from. Before you start, study the following advice.

TASK APPROACH

▶ **EXAM LINK**

Labelling tasks in the IELTS exam do not have a list of answers to choose from.

- Find the part of the text where the object is described.
- Read this section carefully, underlining any key words or phrases.
- Study the diagram, then check the text to find the correct answers.
- Make sure your spelling is correct!

Follow these steps to answer questions 11–15 below. When you've finished, compare your answers with another student.

Questions 11–15
Label the diagrams below.
Choose your labels from the list below the diagrams.

There are more answers to choose from than questions, so you will not need to use every label.

Fish cage

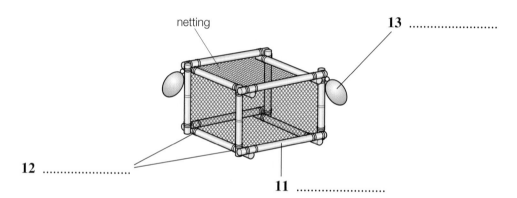

netting

13 ....

12 ....

11 ....

Bicycle ambulance

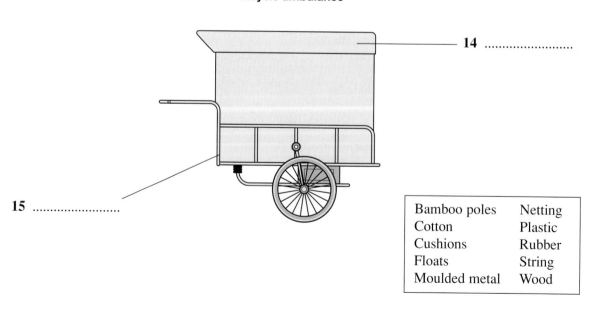

14 ....

15 ....

Bamboo poles	Netting
Cotton	Plastic
Cushions	Rubber
Floats	String
Moulded metal	Wood

Focus on grammar *Passive*

The passive is most common in written English but there are also times when it's natural to use the passive in speaking.

e.g. *I **was born** and **brought up** in Sydney.*
*In the end, our flight **was delayed** by more than four hours.*

1   Study the passive structures printed in bold in the examples above, then underline all the passives you can find in reading texts A–D on pages 73–74.

2   Complete this table to show how the passive is formed. Use passive structures you underlined in texts A–D to complete the Example column.

Passive	Form	Example
Present simple	am/is/are + past participle	1 ....
Past simple	was/were + past participle	2 ....
Present perfect	has/have been + past participle	3 ....
4	5 .... + past participle	*The company **had been established** for 20 years.*
6	7 .... + past participle	*The new airport **will be completed** next year.*
Modals (present) e.g. *can, may, must*	modal + be + past participle	8 ....
Modals (past) e.g. *could, had to, etc.*	modal + have been + past participle	*The problem **could have been solved**.*

KEY LANGUAGE
Passive
▶ p. 148

3   Decide whether the following sentences are True or False and then make any corrections necessary.

1   The passive is mostly used in informal writing.
2   The passive is used when the subject is not known or is not important.
3   The passive sounds more formal and impersonal.
4   It's important to say who or what does the action in passive sentences.
5   The passive can only be formed with the verb *to be*.

4   Use the following prompts to make sentences using passive structures.

Tickets ...   The latest information ...
The exam results ...   A new species of tiger ...
The election ...   No sharp objects ...

Focus on reading 2 *The price is wrong*

EXAM PRACTICE

▶ Locating information

TASK APPROACH

In this task you have to identify sections of the text which contain specific information. Before you start, complete these guidelines.

- Read the questions and .... key words or phrases.
- Study the .... one or two sentences of each section to find the topic.
- Use .... skills to read through the rest of the section.

▶ **EXAM LINK** Reading

Locating information and **Matching headings** tasks are similar. In both you have to match information to sections of a text. The difference is that headings generally *summarise information* in a section while locating information questions usually *pick out a key point.*

Questions 1–5
The reading passage has six sections, A–F.
Which section contains the following information?

Example	*Answer*
the importance of technology for developing countries.	**A**

1	a country which benefits from a successful solar power industry	....
2	where financial contributions should come from	....
3	how major drug companies could help developing countries	....
4	two developments that could make a big difference in poor countries	....
5	how many useful technologies are too expensive for poor people	....

▶ Matching

Questions 6–10
Look at the following statements and places.
Match each statement with the correct place, A–E.

6	There has been little or no development in this location in recent years.	....
7	Schoolchildren now have access to the Internet using radio links here.	....
8	An inexpensive medical treatment has saved many children's lives here.	....
9	Cheap computers are produced here.	....
10	This country made use of certain laws to obtain important drugs.	....

PLACES	
A Bangladesh	**D** Brazil
B Kenya	**E** Sub-Saharan Africa
C South Africa	

▶ Multiple choice

Question 11
Choose the correct letter **A**, **B**, **C** *or* **D**.

11 According to a UN report, genetically modified crops

   A should not be sold in poor countries.

   B should not be used anywhere.

   C should be available in poor countries

   D should be produced more cheaply

THE PRICE IS WRONG

A In a world where 2 billion people live in homes that don't have light bulbs, technology holds the key to banishing poverty, according to a major United Nations report. Even the simplest technologies can transform lives and save money. Vaccines, crops, computers and sources of solar energy can all reduce poverty in developing countries. For example, cheap oral-rehydration therapy developed in Bangladesh has dramatically cut the death toll from childhood diarrhoea.

B But even when such technologies exist, the depressing fact is that we can't make them cheap enough for those who most need them. Solar panels, batteries and light bulbs are still beyond the purse of many, but where they have been installed they change lives. A decent light in the evening gives children more time for homework and extends the productive day for adults.

C Kenya has a thriving solar industry and six years ago pioneers also started connecting schools to the Internet via radio links. These people were fortunate in being able to afford solar panels, radios and old computers. How much bigger would the impact be if these things were made and priced specifically for poor people?

D Multinationals must become part of the solution, because although they own around 60 per cent of the world's technology, they seldom make products for poor customers. Of 1,223 new drugs marketed world wide from 1975 to 1996, for example, just 13 were for tropical diseases.

According to the main author of the report, Sakiko Fukuda-Parr, 'It's the big corporations that really should read this report. We're asking them to be more socially responsible.' They could do more to provide vital products such as medicines at different prices around the world to suit what people can afford. Alternatively, they could pay a percentage of their profit towards research and development for the poor.

E Governments from rich countries should contribute more too. They and other sources such as the World Bank and international institutes could provide as much as $10 billion. Developing countries should also make better use of intellectual property laws that entitle them to vital medicines, just as South Africa did with AIDS drugs.

F Controversially, the report backs genetically modified (GM) crops despite the widespread opposition to them among Western environmentalists and non-governmental organisations. 'To reject GM crops entirely is to give up a huge opportunity,' says Fukuda-Parr. 'If they're so good for multinationals, why shouldn't they be used by poor farmers' she says.

Computers could also revolutionise the lives of poor people, allowing them to benefit from a global wealth of free information that could help solve local problems. But they would need to be cheap and wireless. Fukuda-Parr says that Brazil and India have already developed cheap computers, proving what countries can do for themselves.

But the objectives will be difficult to achieve. Time has stood still in many areas such as sub-Saharan Africa, where there has been no increase in tractor use in a decade.

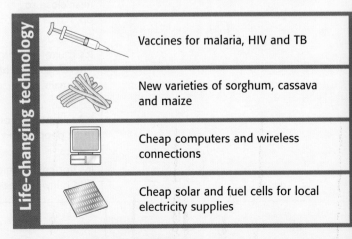

Life-changing technology

	Vaccines for malaria, HIV and TB
	New varieties of sorghum, cassava and maize
	Cheap computers and wireless connections
	Cheap solar and fuel cells for local electricity supplies

From *New Scientist*

Focus on speaking *Describing places*

EXAM PRACTICE
▶ Part 2

LANGUAGE CHECK
In the north describes a place within a larger area. *Delhi is **in the north** of India.* **To the north** describes a place outside another area. *Nepal is **to the north** of India.*
• Describe the location of places in or near your country.

1 Before you practise the following exam task, study the task card and think about a place to describe. Don't only consider your own area or country – it may be easier to find things to say about another place you have lived in or visited. Study the whole question before deciding.

> **Describe a country or state that you have lived in or visited.**
>
> **You should say:**
>
> > **what its main features are (e.g. cities, landscape)**
> > **what the climate is like**
> > **what it has to offer visitors**
>
> **and explain how you feel about the country or state.**

2 Look at the following example mindplan and answer these questions.

1 Which headings are definitely relevant to the question?
2 Which heading(s) are not relevant? Cross these out.
3 Which heading(s) may be relevant to the question?

WRITING PRACTICE
There is an optional task with guided practice based on climate on page 160.
▶ Practice 5, p. 160

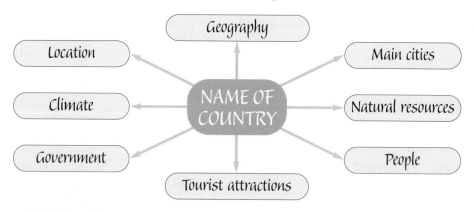

Geography · Location · Main cities · Climate · NAME OF COUNTRY · Natural resources · Government · Tourist attractions · People

▶ ESSENTIAL LANGUAGE

Describing places

LOCATION

in + geographical area	*in the north/south/centre (of the country)*
next to/bordered by	*Nepal is next to/bordered by China.*
near/close to	*close to the Himalayas, near the Equator*
on + river/sea/coast	*on the coast, on the river Seine, on the Red Sea*

GEOGRAPHY

It's (quite) mountainous/hilly/flat, etc.
There's an area of mountains/lakes/desert/rainforest/marsh, etc.
The main towns/tourist areas, etc. are …

PEOPLE

It has a population of (approximately) …
Most people/The majority of the population … live in …/speak French, etc.

CLIMATE

It's hot/cold/humid/wet in summer/winter, etc.
The rainy/dry season (usually) begins in …/lasts from … to …

IELTS VOCABULARY BUILDER

Environment

1   Put the following words or phrases into the right category A–C. There are six
    words in each.

bay coastline cyclone drought estuary flooding forest humidity mineral deposits monsoon natural gas oil reserves plain rubber showers timber valley water

A Climate/Weather	B Geography	C Natural resources

Word families

2   The nouns below can be used in describing areas of a country. What are the
    corresponding adjectives?
    * These adjectives are completely different from the nouns.

1 agriculture	4 countryside*	7 industry
2 town/city*	5 forest	8 marsh
3 coast	6 hill	9 mountain

Pronunciation: Sounds

3   /aʊ/ is the sound in *how* or *shout*.
    Which TWO words in the following list do **not** have this sound?

brown   crowd   drought   grow   house   loud   plough   sound   tough

4   /ɔː/ is the sound in *law* or *door*.
    Which TWO words in the following list do **not** have this sound?

bought   cough   caught   fought   four   ought   raw   shore   though

5   Practise these sounds. If you can work with a partner, take it in turns to say one of
    the words below. Your partner must say which column the word was from.

A	B	A	B	A	B
torn	town	all	owl	floor	flower
fall	foul	nor	now	lord	loud
bought	bout	core	cow	short	shout

8 ▶ Communications

Lead-in

1 **Work in pairs to answer these questions.**

1 What do these signs and symbols below mean?
2 Which were easy, which more difficult to interpret, and why?

A B C D E

F G H I J

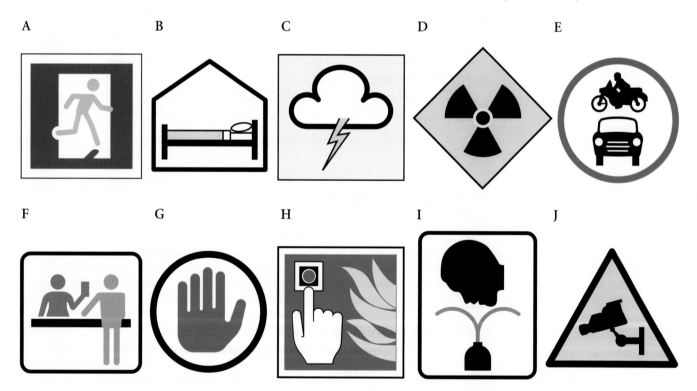

2 Think of at least THREE more examples of signs or symbols used in everyday life, e.g. a teacher's ✓ for 'correct', or picture instructions for setting up a computer.

3 What are the advantages of using signs and symbols instead of words? What problems can you think of?

Focus on grammar *Permission, prohibition and obligation*

1 Complete the table by filling in the following headings in the correct places.

| *Formal*   *Obligation*   *Prohibition*   *Informal*   *Permission* |

	1	2 ....
3	You **can** use a dictionary. You**'re allowed** to use a dictionary.	The use of dictionaries **is permitted**.
4	You **must/have to** wear a crash helmet.	It is **compulsory** to wear a crash helmet.
5	You **can't** smoke in class. You **mustn't** smoke in class. You**'re not allowed to** smoke in class.	Smoking in class is **forbidden/ prohibited**.

> ▶ **EXAM LINK**
>
> This language is useful for discussing many common topics in the Writing and Speaking modules, e.g. for talking about customs or laws in your country or for suggesting ways of solving a problem.
> *Everyone has to carry an identity card.*
> *The speed limit should be reduced.*

KEY LANGUAGE
Modal verbs
▶ p. 146

2 Correct the mistakes in these sentences.

1 You can't to park here.
2 When we agreed to rent the flat, we must pay a deposit of one month's rent.
3 He didn't could take the bicycle on the train.
4 In a few years' time students can use dictionaries in the exam.

3 Complete these rules.

> 1 **Must** and **can** are modal verbs and are followed by .... without *to*.
> 2 **Can/can't:** Only use *can* and *can't* in the present tense. When talking about permission in the past use *could/couldn't* or .... When talking about permission in the future use .... or ....
> 3 **Must:** Only use *must* in the present tense. The past tense of *must* is .... The future tense of *must* is ....

4 Discuss the following points with a partner.

1 Say what people in your country *can, can't* and *must* do when visiting a friend's house for a meal.
2 Say what you *had to* do and *were not allowed to* do at school.

5 Complete the following sentences.

1 If you can't drive to work, you .... go by bus.
2 No dogs .... inside the shop.
3 Carrying sharp objects inside your hand luggage ....
4 1994 was the first year students .... pay tuition fees.
5 Students who fail the exam .... re-sit until June.

Focus on listening 1 *Mobile phone safety*

SKILLS PRACTICE
▶ Prediction

You will hear a talk about mobile phone safety. Look through questions 1–10 and try to predict the correct answers. Compare your ideas with another student.

EXAM PRACTICE
▶ Section 2

Questions 1–3
*Listen to the first part of the talk and choose the correct letters **A–C**.*

1 The first commercial mobile phone network opened in 1979. In which country?

   A Japan   **B** the USA   **C** Norway

2 Which diagram shows the percentage of people in the EU who own a mobile phone?

   A   **B**   **C**

Key
□ owners of mobile phones

3 How do mobile phones transmit messages?

   A by infrared   **B** by radio waves   **C** by microwaves

Questions 4–10
*Complete the notes below. Write **NO MORE THAN TWO WORDS** for each answer.*

DO'S	DONT'S
Only use phone when necessary.	Don't buy phone with a **7** .... 'SAR' value.
Keep calls **4**	Don't buy phone with an **8** .... aerial.
Carry phone away from **5** .... when it's on standby.	Don't use phone when reception is **9** ....
Buy phone with long 'talk time'. It gives out emissions which are **6**	Don't buy protective gadgets that haven't been independently **10** ....

Focus on speaking 1 *Discussing communications*

SKILLS PRACTICE

'It's me – I'm on the throne.'

1 Work in pairs to answer these questions. Find out as much as you can about your partner's habits and preferences and be prepared to report back on them.

1 How do you communicate with people most?

A letter
B email
C talking on a mobile phone
D talking on a fixed-line phone
E texting

2 Where do you get most of your information a) for studying b) about the news?

A the Internet   B reference books   C TV   D the radio

3 How do you prefer to spend your personal leisure time?

A at a computer   B reading   C watching TV

4 Which, if any, of the following could you NOT bear to be without, and why?

• access to the Internet
• email
• mobile phone
• satellite/cable TV

Find out how young people in Britain responded on page 168.

EXAM PRACTICE

▶ Part 3

2 Discuss these questions with a partner. One person should take the role of the examiner each time. Before you begin, study the Essential language below.

1 In what ways were communications different in your parents' day?
2 What are some of the advantages and disadvantages of mobile phones?
3 What do you think the next big development in communications will be?

> ## ▶ EXAM LINK
>
> **Speaking**
> You could be asked to talk about the **past, present** or **future** in the Speaking module. Make sure you use appropriate tenses or other verb forms in your answers.

> ## ▶ ESSENTIAL LANGUAGE
>
> **Comparing past and present**
>
> | | | |
> |---|---|---|
> | Years ago … | people **used to** … | But/whereas now(adays) … |
> | In the past, … | everybody **had to** … | |
> | When I was younger, … | I remember …**ing** | |
> | In my parents' day, … | hardly anybody **had** … | |

Focus on writing 1 *Task 1: Describing a diagram*

▶ Reading the diagram

1 **Study diagram A and answer these questions.**

1 How many types of communication equipment were included in the study?
2 Why are there two bars for each piece of equipment?
3 What do the figures at the end of each bar represent?
4 Which equipment was most popular in 2001–2?
5 Which equipment was least popular in 1998–9?

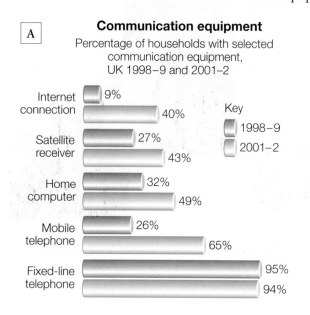

A **Communication equipment**
Percentage of households with selected communication equipment, UK 1998–9 and 2001–2

Internet connection 9% / 40%
Key
1998–9
2001–2
Satellite receiver 27% / 43%
Home computer 32% / 49%
Mobile telephone 26% / 65%
Fixed-line telephone 95% / 94%

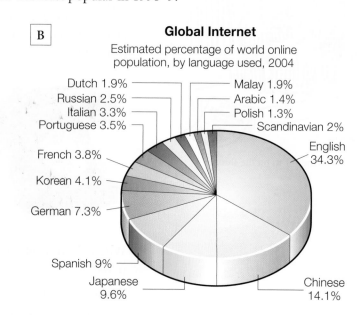

B **Global Internet**
Estimated percentage of world online population, by language used, 2004

Dutch 1.9%
Russian 2.5%
Italian 3.3%
Portuguese 3.5%
French 3.8%
Korean 4.1%
German 7.3%
Spanish 9%
Japanese 9.6%
Malay 1.9%
Arabic 1.4%
Polish 1.3%
Scandinavian 2%
English 34.3%
Chinese 14.1%

▶ Selecting key information

2 **Find three interesting things to say about diagram A. Compare your ideas with a partner. Now answer these questions.**

1 Which equipment was most popular in both periods?
2 Which two types of equipment increased in popularity most over the period? How much did their popularity increase respectively?
3 Which equipment actually decreased in popularity? How much did its popularity decrease?

▶ Describing the data

3 **Study diagrams A and B and say whether the following statements are True or False. Correct the false statements.**

A Communication equipment
1 In 1998–9 **just over a quarter** of all households in the UK had a satellite receiver.
2 **More than two thirds** of UK households had a computer in 2001–2.

B Global Internet
3 **Almost a third** of the online population is English-speaking.
4 The **second largest** section of the online population is Chinese-speaking.
5 There are **slightly more** Japanese speakers than Spanish speakers.
6 The **percentage of** Russian and Dutch speakers is **exactly the same.**
7 There are **almost twice as many** German speakers **as** Portuguese speakers.
8 The **smallest** group of language speakers on the chart is Scandinavian.

KEY LANGUAGE
Comparison
▶ p. 142

4 Write five more true or false sentences about diagrams A and B using language from the box below. Exchange sentences with another student and mark the sentences True or False, correcting as necessary.

> ### ▶ ESSENTIAL LANGUAGE
>
> **Numerical comparisons**
>
> | | | |
> |---|---|---|
> | almost/nearly/(just) under | half | as much/many + noun as … |
> | about/approximately | twice | |
> | exactly | three/four times | as tall/popular + noun as … |
> | (just) over/more than | | |

▶ Introducing the report

▶ **EXAM LINK**

Writing
If you introduce your answer using exactly the same words as the question, the examiner won't count these as part of the words you need to write.

5 It's important to write a brief introduction to your description but try to think of slightly different ways of expressing the information in the question.

1 Study the following examples to see how information in the question can be rephrased in your answer.

Question		Answer
*The **amount** of leisure time …*		*how many hours of leisure*
*unemployment **figures** …*	*or*	the **level** of unemployment
		the **number** of unemployed people

2 Think of another way to express the following information.

Question	Answer
a *the **number** of PCs per 100 people …*	…………………………………
b *the **amount** of money spent …*	…………………………………
c *the **figures** for imprisonment …*	…………………………………
d *between 2000 and 2005 …*	…………………………………

> ### ▶ ESSENTIAL LANGUAGE
>
> **Introducing the report**
> The chart/table **shows/gives** information about/**provides** a breakdown of …
>
> **Beginning the analysis**
> Overall we can see …
> As we can see from …/According to … the chart/table/data/information.

6 Write a paragraph describing some interesting information from diagram C. Answer the following questions first to give you ideas.

C **Number of PCs per 100 people, 2001**

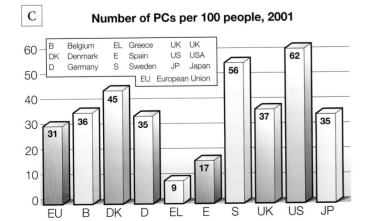

1 What is the average percentage of PCs in the EU as a whole?
2 Which countries have the highest and lowest percentages of PCs?
3 Compare US and EU average percentages.

Begin: *The bar chart shows* …………………………………
in (places) ………………………………… *in (year)*
…………………………………

Focus on speaking 2 *Internet activities*

SKILLS PRACTICE

1 Work in pairs to discuss the following questions.

a) Which THREE of the following Internet activities are most popular across all age groups?

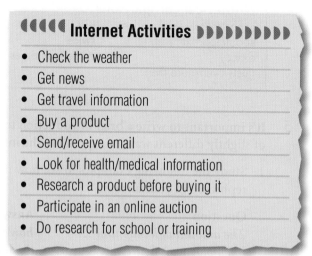

◀◀◀◀◀ Internet Activities ▶▶▶▶▶▶▶▶▶

- Check the weather
- Get news
- Get travel information
- Buy a product
- Send/receive email
- Look for health/medical information
- Research a product before buying it
- Participate in an online auction
- Do research for school or training

You can check the results according to a computer industry survey on page 168.

b) What other Internet activities can you think of, especially ones which would be popular with young people?

EXAM PRACTICE
▶ Part 1

2 Interview your partner about their personal use of the Internet. Ask about these points, and be prepared to ask follow-up questions to find out more.

- activities you most use the Internet for, and why
- time you spend on the Internet each week
- the best thing about the Internet
- the most annoying thing about the Internet
- people you email most often, and why

▶ Part 2

3 Study the following exam topic individually and take a few moments to make notes, perhaps in the form of a mindplan.

> **Describe your favourite website.**
>
> **You should say:**
>
> **what the website is**
> **what it offers**
> **how often you visit it**
>
> **and explain why you like it so much.**

4 Work in pairs. Take it in turns to speak on the topic for about two minutes. Your partner should keep an eye on the time and let you know after two minutes if necessary.

Focus on writing 2 *Task 2: Presenting and justifying an opinion*

EXAM PRACTICE
▶ Task 2

1   Remember that there are four stages in answering a Task 2 question. Complete the table below. Refer to pages 67–68 if necessary.

1	.... the question
2	.... your answer
3	.... your answer
4	.... your answer

2   Study the following exam topic and underline the key words. Some of the terms in the question are rather general, so before planning your answer, you need to think about how to interpret them. Discuss ideas in pairs.

> *Computers are not necessarily the best way for children to learn. In many areas of education a teacher can be more effective in helping pupils to gain new skills and knowledge.*
>
> *To what extent do you agree or disagree with this point of view?*

- **children:** What age group(s) should you consider? Is there a difference between younger and older children or not?
- **areas:** Which areas of education are best learnt with a teacher, and which by computer?
- **more effective:** What techniques can a teacher use that a computer doesn't offer? Why are these more effective?

3   The boxes below represent the four main sections of your essay. Work in pairs to decide on headings for each box, then discuss ideas for each section. Compare the skeleton plan on page 68 if necessary.

1

↓

2

↓

3

↓

4

WRITING PRACTICE
There is an optional task with practice on selecting information for a Task 2 question.
▶ Practice 6, p. 162

▶ EXAM LINK

Writing
Remember that Task 2 carries **two thirds** of the total marks in the Writing module. You are advised to spend 40 minutes on this task in the exam so you will need to plan your time carefully.

4   Now write your answer. You will find useful language for giving reasons and arguments, and also for putting an opposite argument on page 68. Check your essay carefully when you have finished.

Focus on listening 2 *Txt don't talk*

SKILLS PRACTICE
▶ Prediction

EXAM PRACTICE
▶ Section 3

You will hear a conversation between two students. Look at the questions and think about possible answers. Check any vocabulary you don't know.

Questions 1–4
Choose the correct letters A, B, C.

1 Which diagram shows the percentage of young people who use a mobile phone at least once a day?

A   B   C   **Key**
% of young people who use mobile at least once a day

2 Which diagram shows the recent growth in text messaging?

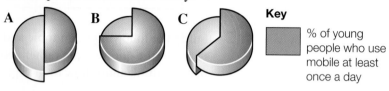

A 2 billion   B 2 billion   C 2 billion
  1 billion   1 billion   1 billion
  0   0   0

3 The peak period for text messaging is between
  A 10.30 a.m. and 11.00 a.m.
  B 7.30 p.m. and 8.00 p.m.
  C 10.30 p.m. and 11.00 p.m.

4 Most British teenagers would never carry their mobile phones
  A on their belt   **B** in their bag   **C** in their pocket

Questions 5–7
Choose THREE functions A–F. Which THREE mobile phone functions will Mary talk about in the presentation?

A taking photos   **C** text messaging   **E** playing games
B sending photos   **D** voicemail   **F** video recording

Questions 8–10
What information is true about the following people?
Write the correct letter, A, B or C, next to each question.

Write   **A** if it is true about Cindy
         B if it is true about Michael
         C if it is true about Linda

Example	*Answer*
He/she always has the latest mobile phone.	**B**

8 He/she uses a mobile phone to remember appointments.   ....
9 He/she sleeps with their mobile phone very close to them.   ....
10 He/she has a limit on their mobile phone bill each month.   ....

IELTS VOCABULARY BUILDER

Computer terms

Answer the clues below to complete this crossword.

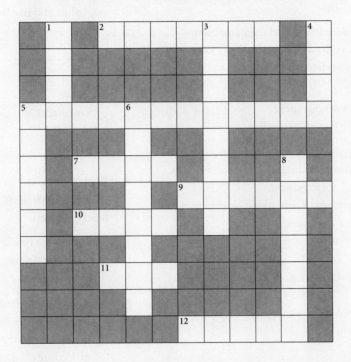

Across

2 When your computer is *on* .... it is saving energy. (7)

5 You use a .... like Yahoo or Google to find the site or information you want. (2 words) (6, 6)

7 Junk email that arrives in your mail box without your permission. (4)

9 Someone who can get into another person's computer system to use or change the information there. (6)

10 To wander from site to site on the Internet, looking for something to interest you. (4)

11 When you .... *on* you connect your computer to a computer system so you can start work. (3)

12 The term *cyber*............................... describes the world that exists only on computers. (5)

Down

1 This is an electronic document stored on your computer. (4)

3 To transfer information from the Internet to your computer, you need to .... it. (8)

4 When you are *on*............................... you are connected to the Internet. (4)

5 You use a mouse wheel to .... *up* or *down* a page on your computer. (5)

6 This is a place you can go to 'talk' to Internet users from around the world. (2 words) (4, 4)

8 A set of pages of information on the Internet about a particular subject. (7)

ACADEMIC WORD STUDY 4

Understanding and using academic vocabulary

VERBS ENDING IN -ise/-ize

1 Study the following definitions and then complete each example with a verb ending in -ise. NB These words are sometimes spelled -ize, especially in American English.

Example complete an arrangement,
    e.g. *We can't <u>finalise</u> the booking.*

1 examine carefully, e.g. *to .... the evidence.*
2 give a short account including only the main points, e.g. *to .... an argument.*
3 give special importance to something or stress, e.g. *to .... the financial benefit.*
4 make as small as possible, e.g. *to .... the risk.*
5 make as large as possible, e.g. *to .... the company's profits.*
6 be a sign or symbol of something, e.g. *Kangaroos .... Australia.*

GRAMMATICAL PATTERNS

2 Rewrite the following sentences, using the academic word in brackets, so that the meaning is the same. Do not change the form of the word in brackets.

1 The maximum temperature is about 40°C and the minimum is about 10°C. (**varies**)

....

2 You're not allowed to use a calculator in the exam. (**prohibited**)

....

3 I can't connect to the Internet on my present computer. (**access**)

....

4 Low-cost flights have played a part in the growth of tourism. (**contributed**)

....

5 The sports facilities will be useful for the whole community. (**benefit**)

....

6 Most people live by the coast. (**majority**)

....

OPPOSITES

3 Choose the correct prefix to form the opposite of the following adjectives. When you've finished, choose 5 opposites and use them in sentences of your own.

il-	in-	ir-	un-

1 accurate   6 predictable
2 aware   7 relevant
3 consistent   8 reliable
4 flexible   9 secure
5 legal   10 significant

4 Replace the parts in italics in the following sentences with academic words from earlier Academic Word Study sections.

Example She finally *got to* her goal of becoming a professor.
Answer achieved

1 The report is based on very detailed scientific *facts and figures.*
2 It's *very, very important* that everyone follows safety procedures.
3 Researchers who tested the drug over a three-month *length of time* say that the results they have *got* so far are positive.
4 Your password should *be made up of* four letters and a number.
5 The Student Services department can *lend you a hand* with finding accommodation.
6 Your tutor will *keep an eye on* your progress during the course, and discuss the various *things you could choose* for your case study.

5 Make personal examples to illustrate four of the opposites in exercise 3 above.

1 ....
2 ....
3 ....
4 ....

Check your answers on page 168 and use this page as a reference point for revision.

REVIEW 4

Grammar

SPOT THE ERROR

1 Each sentence below contains at least one mistake. Make the necessary corrections.

1 *The graph describes us the different of male and female wages.*
2 *About 80% of men and less 20% women enjoy to watch football.*
3 *Electricity use in winter was nearly twice higher than electricity use in summer.*
4 *In 1999 there was a little increase of the number of visitors.*
5 *There are about twice as much Korean speakers than Dutch speakers.*
6 *From overall we can see that most of electricity used for heating rooms.*
7 *Women earn very low wages comparing with men.*
8 *If the price of tickets is increase any more, people might cannot buy them.*

PREPOSITIONS

2 Complete the **Preposition Wheel** by putting the letters A–L into the correct section.

A midday
B Tuesday morning
C two weeks' time
D winter
E the evening
F the weekend
G the centre of town
H the south coast
I the north
J the North Pole
K the right-hand side
L the back of the class

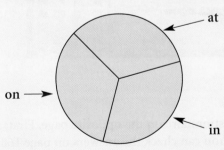

3 Make true statements about yourself with similar expressions of time and place, using prompts 1–6.

1 eat lunch
2 would like to live
3 prefer working
4 finish studying
5 see friends
6 take a holiday

Vocabulary

WORD CHOICE

4 Choose the correct word from each pair to complete each sentence.

1 The (most/majority) of people drive to work.
2 There were only two TV channels in my parents' (day/year).
3 A huge (number/amount) of money is wasted.
4 There is a(n) (area/place) of rainforest in the west.
5 The country has a tropical (weather/climate).

PRONUNCIATION: WORD STRESS

5 Put the following words in the correct box according to how they are pronounced.

analysis	development	industry
appropriate	diagram	Internet
benefit	estimate	majority
bicycle	geography	medical
community	humidity	mountainous
countryside	industrial	technology

Ooo as in *Canada*	oOoo as in *Australia*

Exam skills

6 Say whether the following statements are True or False, and make any corrections necessary.

1 Find out the main topic in each section of a reading text by skimming.
2 Always answer reading questions in the order they appear on the paper.
3 You are more likely to find the passive in the Reading module than in the Listening module.
4 The two writing tasks carry equal marks.
5 It's best to use the same words as the question in your introduction to a Task 1 answer.

9 ► Earth matters

In this unit you will practise:

- **Reading skills:** Prediction; scanning; forming a general picture
- **Speaking skills:** Discussing environmental matters; speculating; softening phrases; expressing degrees of agreement
- **Grammar:** Cause and effect; -ing v infinitive
- **Vocabulary:** Word partners; word families; nouns with general meaning

Exam Focus

Reading: Sentence completion; summary completion; multiple choice; T/F/NG

Speaking: Parts 1, 3

Lead-in

1   What environmental problems do these pictures illustrate?

2   Which do you think is the most serious?

3   Have you ever experienced any of the problems?

Focus on speaking 1 *How green are you?*

SKILLS PRACTICE

1   Work in pairs to complete the questionnaire on the opposite page. First, study the Essential language box below. You can check the answers on page 168.

> ► **ESSENTIAL LANGUAGE**
>
> **Speculating**
> Use this language when you're less than 100% sure of a fact.
> I'm not (really/completely) sure but …
> (I think) it could/may/might/must be …/it's (probably) …
> *What's your country's main industry? **I'm not sure, but I think** it's probably tourism.*

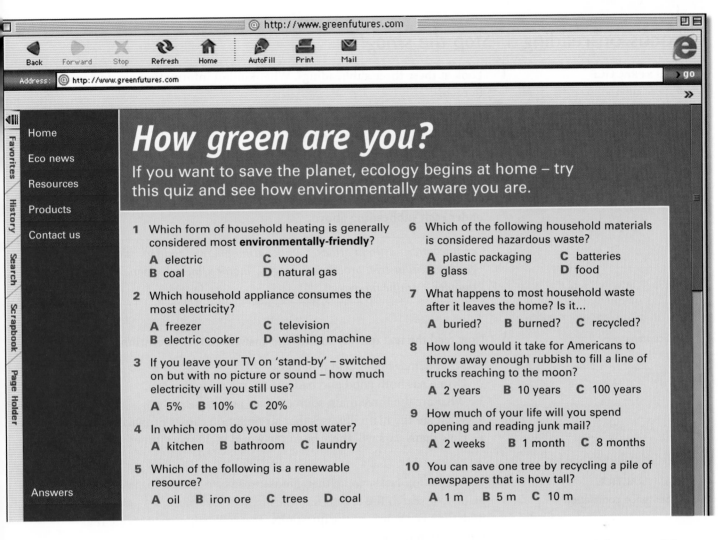

Address: @ http://www.greenfutures.com

Home

Eco news

Resources

Products

Contact us

How green are you?

If you want to save the planet, ecology begins at home – try this quiz and see how environmentally aware you are.

1 Which form of household heating is generally considered most **environmentally-friendly**?

   A electric   C wood
   B coal   D natural gas

2 Which household appliance consumes the most electricity?

   A freezer   C television
   B electric cooker   D washing machine

3 If you leave your TV on 'stand-by' – switched on but with no picture or sound – how much electricity will you still use?

   A 5%   B 10%   C 20%

4 In which room do you use most water?

   A kitchen   B bathroom   C laundry

5 Which of the following is a renewable resource?

   A oil   B iron ore   C trees   D coal

6 Which of the following household materials is considered hazardous waste?

   A plastic packaging   C batteries
   B glass   D food

7 What happens to most household waste after it leaves the home? Is it...

   A buried?   B burned?   C recycled?

8 How long would it take for Americans to throw away enough rubbish to fill a line of trucks reaching to the moon?

   A 2 years   B 10 years   C 100 years

9 How much of your life will you spend opening and reading junk mail?

   A 2 weeks   B 1 month   C 8 months

10 You can save one tree by recycling a pile of newspapers that is how tall?

   A 1 m   B 5 m   C 10 m

Answers

EXAM PRACTICE
▶ Part 1

2 Work in pairs to discuss the questions below. Try to answer as fully as possible, giving reasons. Before you begin, study the Essential language box below.

1 How do you get about mostly? by bus/by bicycle/by car/on foot
2 Where do you do most of your shopping? in an out-of-town hypermarket/in local stores/in a supermarket/on the Internet
3 Which of the following do you recycle regularly? newspapers/bottles/ aluminium cans/none of these

> **▶ ESSENTIAL LANGUAGE**
>
> **Softening phrases**
>
> **I'm afraid/to be honest**
> We use these expressions in spoken English to talk about something we're not very proud of, or to admit to a failure of some kind. You can give a reason by adding:
> **I know ... but ...**
> *I'm afraid I nearly always go by car because the buses are so unreliable.*
> *I know I should recycle more, **but, to be honest**, it's too much trouble.*

▶ Part 3

3 Work in pairs to discuss these questions.

1 How much interest in environmental matters is there in your country?
2 What are the main environmental problems in your country?

Focus on reading 1 *Stop the smog!*

SKILLS PRACTICE

▶ Prediction

1 Look at these three subheadings. What kind of information would you expect in each?

1 What's in the air?
2 Where pollution comes from
3 How it affects your body

2 Choose THREE words or phrases from this list that you might expect to find under each subheading above.

> architecture   asthma attack   upper atmosphere   cycling   doctors   gases
> geology   industrial processes   lungs   motor vehicles   ozone   sports
> thunder   traffic fumes

▶ Scanning

3 Now read the text quickly to find the answers to these questions.

1 What damage does acid rain cause?
2 Ozone has both good and bad effects. What are they?
3 What are the three main sources of air pollution?
4 What are the main illnesses that air pollution causes or makes worse?
5 How many cars will there be in the world in 20 years' time?

EXAM PRACTICE

▶ Sentence completion

4 In completion tasks, you either choose words from a list (as in Questions 1–4 below), or search the text to find the answer (Questions 5–7 opposite). First, underline key words in the questions. This will help you to locate the information quickly.

▶TIP
Read the first section of the text with the title *What's in the air?*

> *Questions 1–4.*
> *Complete each sentence 1–4 with the best ending, A–I below.*
>
> **1**   Carbon monoxide levels are at their highest during ....
> **2**   .... is a gas which is commonly present at petrol filling stations.
> **3**   Ozone is most likely to be produced during ....
> **4**   .... can exist in both solid and gaseous form.
>
> | | |
> |---|---|
> | **A** | acid rain |
> | **B** | benzene |
> | **C** | carbon monoxide |
> | **D** | hydrocarbons |
> | **E** | motor vehicles |
> | **F** | ozone layer |
> | **G** | smog |
> | **H** | rush hours |
> | **I** | warm weather |

▶ **EXAM LINK**

Reading
Don't rely on memory or guesswork. Always go back to the text to find the information you need.

STOP THE SMOG!

WHAT'S IN THE AIR?

Sulphur dioxide contributes to acid rain, which contaminates rivers, streams and lakes, causes serious erosion of buildings and endangers wildlife. It also makes breathing problems worse by tightening the tubes which carry air to the lungs.

Nitrous oxides (nitrogen dioxide and nitric oxide gases) cause acid rain and smog[1].

Carbon monoxide reduces the amount of oxygen that can be carried by the blood. Peaks occur during rush hours, and high levels are found inside cars.

Hydrocarbons are released when fuel is not completely burned. They can be gases or solids.

Volatile Organic Compounds (VOCs) are gases which form smog. Benzene escapes from the exhaust pipes of cars and from petrol tanks when cars are filling up.

Ozone is a gas produced naturally in the upper atmosphere. A thin layer of ozone helps to shield the Earth from the Sun's damaging rays. At ground level, ozone is the main enemy for people with breathing problems. It is created by the effect of sunlight on smog, a reaction which occurs most easily when weather conditions are calm and warm.

WHERE POLLUTION COMES FROM

Motor vehicles are the fastest-growing source of air pollution today, pumping out a toxic mixture of health-threatening pollutants. Traffic fumes are largely responsible for the increasing number of smogs which pollute our towns, cities and rural areas.

Industry A lot of pollutants are released into the atmosphere by industrial processes. For example, when coal is burnt in power stations to generate electricity, sulphur dioxide and nitrous oxides are produced. These are the two major gases which cause acid rain.

Waste disposal When rubbish is burned, the smoke and gases produced often contain pollutants such as dioxins, which are a threat to human health and the environment.

HOW IT AFFECTS YOUR BODY

High concentrations of ozone and the chemicals released by motor vehicles can lead to serious health problems including irritation of the lungs and a reduced resistance to infection. They also aggravate bronchitis and may even cause cancer. Many pollutants can trigger an asthma attack. During levels of peak pollution, doctors advise sufferers to stay indoors and avoid exercise.

GRIM FACTS

- Cars produce 15 per cent of worldwide greenhouse gases.
- Car ownership is rising in every country. There are now more cars than adults in the USA.
- It is estimated that the number of cars on the world's roads will rise to 1.5 billion in the next 20 years.
- The number of children admitted to hospital with asthma in the UK has more than doubled since 1980.

[1] smog: air pollution, especially in cities, which looks like a mixture of smoke and fog

▶ Summary completion

> **▶ TIP**
> Read the second section of the text *Where pollution comes from.*

Questions 5–7.
Complete the sentences below. Choose NO MORE THAN TWO WORDS from the text for each answer.

One of the main sources of air pollution mentioned in the text is industry. Electricity generation is a typical example, as coal-burning power stations release gases which cause **5** .... Burning rubbish is another source of pollutants like **6** .... which can be harmful to health and the environment. However, the cause of pollution which is increasing most rapidly today is **7** ....

▶ True/False/Not Given

> ▶ **TIP**
> Read the last two sections of the text.

Questions 8–12
Do the following statements agree with the information given in the passage?

Write

TRUE	*if the statement agrees with the information*
FALSE	*if the statement contradicts the information*
NOT GIVEN	*if there is no information on this*

8 Pollution can make people less resistant to infection.

9 Medical advice for people with asthma is to rest during periods of high pollution.

10 Cars produce the majority of worldwide greenhouse gases.

11 The USA has more cars than any other country in the world.

12 Fewer children are admitted to hospital with asthma now than in 1980.

> **LANGUAGE CHECK**
> *-ed* participle clauses
> *Acid rain, **caused by** gases from power stations, can endanger wildlife.*
> *'caused by'* is short for the full relative clause *which is caused by* …
> *-ed* participle clauses like this are common in written English in general, and academic English in particular. It is important to be aware of them as you read, or you may miss part of the meaning.

Focus on grammar 1 *Cause and effect*

> ▶ **EXAM LINK**
> The language of **cause and effect** is common in reading passages in the IELTS exam. It is also important for many topics in the Writing module.

1 Underline the expressions that describe cause and effect in the following sentences from the text.

1 Sulphur dioxide contributes to acid rain, which contaminates rivers, streams and lakes …
2 Nitrous oxides cause acid rain and smog.
3 Traffic fumes are largely responsible for the increasing number of smogs which pollute our towns …
4 High concentrations of ozone and the chemicals released by motor vehicles can lead to serious health problems…
5 Many pollutants can trigger an asthma attack.

2 Which expressions suggest that:

1 this is one of several factors (not the only one)?
2 this makes something happen very quickly?
3 the effect may happen after some time (not immediately)?

3 a) Write the answers to questions 1–3 in Exercise 2 in the box below.

cause	....	as a result of
be responsible for	....	caused by
account for	....	

b) Complete sentences 1–5 with a suitable expression of cause and effect.

1 Research suggests that just 17 per cent of all vehicles .... 50 per cent or more of the pollution from road vehicles.

2 Carbon dioxide is one of the main factors which .... to global warming.

3 If not disposed of properly, waste oil .... serious pollution.

4 The whole province is suffering drought .... the constant high temperatures this summer.

5 Global warming over the last 40 years has .... a dramatic change in the Atlantic Ocean's salt balance.

Focus on speaking 2 *Expressing degrees of agreement*

SKILLS PRACTICE

You may often need to express degrees of agreement or disagreement with a point of view. Study the Essential language below.

> ## ▶ ESSENTIAL LANGUAGE
>
> **Expressing degrees of agreement (spoken English)**
>
> **Agreeing**
> (weakly)   I **agree up to a point**, but …
>   I **agree** (with that point of view, etc) **on the whole**.
> (strongly)   I **completely/totally agree** (with that point of view, etc).
>   I **couldn't agree more**!
>
> **Disagreeing**
> (weakly)   I'm **not really sure about** that …
>   I **don't** (really) **agree** (with that point of view, etc).
> (strongly)   I **completely/totally disagree** (with that point of view, etc)
>   (I think) **it's ridiculous to say** …

Work in pairs to say how far you agree or disagree with the following opinions, and why.

> *People should have to pay for every bag of rubbish they dispose of. That's the only way to make them more careful about what they buy and what they throw away.*

> *Roads are too crowded and exhaust fumes are causing major pollution problems in many cities. The only answer is for governments to make it so expensive to run private cars that people are forced to use public transport.*

> *People are more important than trees. It's nonsense to preserve forests when people have no land to live on. Natural resources like forests are there for human beings to exploit, in order to improve their lives.*

Focus on reading 2 *How children saved the river*

SKILLS PRACTICE

▶ Forming a general picture

1 Read the first two paragraphs to answer these questions.

1 Which river? Where?
2 Which children?
3 Why did the river need 'saving'?

EXAM PRACTICE

2 Look through the rest of the text fairly quickly before starting the exam practice tasks.

Before you begin to answer the questions:
- underline key words in the question (there is an example in Questions 1–3)
- complete the Tips in the margin

▶ Multiple choice

▶TIP
Read sections ... and ... of the text.

Questions 1–3
*Choose **THREE** letters A–F.*
*Which **THREE** of the following did the schoolchildren do?*

A They <u>visited</u> other <u>primary schools</u>.

B They went swimming in the river.

C They wrote a letter to the mayor.

D They praised the local media.

E They spent a day studying the river.

F They asked the people of Chengdu to keep the river clean.

▶ True/False/Not Given

▶TIP
Read section ... of the text.

Questions 4–8
Do the following statements agree with information in the text?
Write

TRUE	*if the statement agrees with the information*
FALSE	*if the statement contradicts the information*
NOT GIVEN	*if there is no information on this*

4 Xiong Xiaoli worked as a journalist.

5 Xiong became ill after visiting the Funan River.

6 His doctor had no idea what had caused the illness.

7 The weather was unusually hot at the time.

8 Xiong spent two weeks studying the river.

▶ **EXAM LINK** Reading

Multiple choice and T/F/NG

In both these tasks, you have to say whether a number of statements are accurate or not, according to the text. Be careful! The wrong statements are designed to catch careless readers, so make sure you check the text very carefully before deciding on your answers.

How children saved the river

By Ma Guihua

Funan River after its revitalization

A The Funan River flows through Chengdu City, a cultural and economic centre in southwest China with a population of 3 million. In the 1950s the water had been so clear that
5 fish could be seen from the bank; it was also an area where people could enjoy swimming and angling. By the 1980s the water in the river was too dirty for washing, and it was giving off a foul smell.

10 **B** The first call to do something about the pollution came from pupils at Chengdu's Longjianglu Primary School in 1985. After a one-day field study of the river, they sent a letter to the (then) mayor, describing how they had seen people dumping dirty water and
15 rubbish into the river. Waste was also discharged into the river from a paper mill, a hospital and strongbox factory.

C The children appealed to all city residents to stop dumping garbage in the river and to treat industrial
20 waste before discharging it into the water. In reply, the children received a hand-written letter from the mayor, who spoke highly of their love for, and care of the river. Local media published their letter, accompanied by a commentary praising the pupils' initiative.
25 Students from other schools followed their example.

D Further encouragement for change came two years later when Xiong Xiaoli, a correspondent of Xinhua News Agency, prepared an in-depth report. That summer he had taken his six-year-old son to the
30 river. Afterwards the child developed a high fever and had a rash all over his body. The doctor blamed the polluted water that might contain parasites. Deeply shocked, Xiong immediately started a two-week investigation, bicycling along the entire length of the
35 river within the city limits. His report went direct to the leaders of the central government.

E In 1992 the city government acted. It invested 2.7 billion yuan ($320 million) in a 5-year comprehensive revitalization project for the Funan
40 River. A total of 488 polluting factories were closed down while 478 others were ordered to update their waste disposal technology. The remaining 40 were moved to an industrial park in a suburban area. A 16-kilometre river course was dredged[1] and nearly all
45 the banks were rebuilt or consolidated[2]. Shanty towns[3] along the river were all pulled down to make way for grassland.

F To remind people of environmental protection, white stones were placed on the grassland with
50 carved characters reading 'Don't hurt me' or 'You protect me, I protect you, we protect the Earth'. A Flowing Water Garden was set up by the river to give visitors a demonstration of how water from the Funan River is cleaned through the presence of healthy
55 vegetation. Now with clean water, tidy dams, green lawns and open parks, the Funan River has been acclaimed a 'green necklace around the neck of Chengdu'. The riverside is a new attraction for sightseeing, recreation, wedding ceremonies and
60 morning exercises.

G Having come this far, the city government now has more ambitions for the Funan River. To save precious water resources, the construction of a large water-treatment project of 200 million yuan
65 ($24 million), which will channel the water upstream for reuse, has started. Longjianglu Primary School has also launched its own environment education programme, which encourages students to participate regularly in activities to monitor the pollution of the
70 river and campaign for keeping it clean.

---

1 dredge: to dig up mud from the bottom of a river
2 consolidate: to make stronger or more effective
3 shanty town: a very poor area where people live in small houses they've built from waste materials.

Adapted from *New Internationalist*

► Multiple choice

►TIP
Read sections ... and ... of the text.

►TIP
Read section ... of the text.

Questions 9–11
*Choose **THREE** letters A–F.*
*Which **THREE** of the following did the city government do?*

A It removed the shanty towns beside the river.

B It invested 2.7 billion yuan in an education programme.

C It cleaned a long section of the river and repaired most of the banks.

D It closed down all the factories along the river.

E It placed advertisements for environmental protection in the papers.

F It created a water garden near the river.

Question 12
Choose the correct letter A–D.

12 What additional project has the city government recently begun?

    A a new primary school.

    B a new environment education programme

    C a new water-treatment works

    D a new campaign to keep the river clean

Focus on grammar 2 *-ing v infinitive*

► **EXAM LINK**

You can improve your language accuracy if you know whether to use the *-ing* or **infinitive** form of a verb. Study the notes below.

- Some verbs are followed by *-ing* forms while others are followed by infinitive forms. Try to learn the most common of these.
  e.g. *People **enjoyed swimming** and **angling** in the river.*
     *Doctors **advise** sufferers **to stay** indoors.*
- All prepositions are followed by *-ing* forms.
  e.g. *It makes breathing problems worse **by tightening** the tubes which carry air …*

Put the verbs in brackets into the correct form.

1 The water in the Funan River was too dirty for (wash) in.
2 They failed (treat) industrial waste before (discharge) it into the river.
3 Xiong's son became ill after (visit) the river.
4 The problem appears (get) worse during warmer weather.
5 She decided (raise) money by (sell) her car.
6 When I finish (write) my dissertation, I want (take) a holiday.
7 There was a campaign which encouraged people (give up) (smoke).
8 The course I'm planning (do) involves (spend) a year abroad.

IELTS VOCABULARY BUILDER

1   The words in column A are the first half of common expressions connected with
environmental problems. Choose words from column B to complete each
expression.

A	B
1 global	a) station
2 renewable	b) fuels
3 air	c) pollution
4 greenhouse	d) rain
5 environmentally-	e) fumes
6 ozone	f) warming
7 power	g) gases
8 acid	h) energy
9 exhaust	i) layer
10 fossil	j) friendly

2   Make a note of THREE expressions you could easily make a spelling mistake with
and THREE expressions that would be useful in an essay on world traffic
problems. Check the meanings of any expressions you're not sure about in a
dictionary.

3   Make adjectives from the following words.

Example industry → industrial

1 atmosphere	4 comparison	7 economy	10 science
2 benefit	5 culture	8 effect	11 suburbs
3 commerce	6 democracy	9 resist	12 technology

4   Which general terms can be used to include the following words in groups?

Example cabbage, cauliflower, potato: ....*vegetable*...........

1   saw, hammer, drill, screwdriver: ....
2   bronchitis, asthma, pneumonia, cancer: ....
3   car, lorry, van, tanker: ....
4   oven, refrigerator, washing machine, freezer: ....
5   TV, radio, newspapers, magazines: ....
6   school, college, university, academy: ....
7   dictionary, grammar book, lexicon, thesaurus: ....
8   park, library, museum, swimming pool: ....
9   Boeing 747, helicopter, glider, jet fighter: ....
10   leather, wood, plastic, steel: ....

10 ▶ Health check

In this unit you will practise:

- **Listening skills:** Prediction
- **Writing skills:** Improving your style; preparing your answer; reading and describing the diagram; selecting information
- **Speaking skills:** Discussing various health issues; reflecting; balancing the argument
- **Grammar:** Quantifiers; comparing and contrasting
- **Vocabulary:** Healthcare and medicine; prepositions; register
- **DIY Learning strategy:** Spot the mistake

Exam Focus

Listening: Sections 2, 4; Table and note completion; multiple choice

Writing: Tasks 1, 2

Speaking: Part 3

Lead-in

1   Match facts and figures to make ten correct statistics about the human body. Remind yourself about the language for speculating (page 94) if necessary.

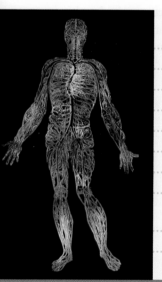

Body Count

1	The percentage of water in the human body:	10 million
2	The number of nerve cells in the brain:	
3	The number of hairs on your head:	300,000 100,000
4	The number of main blood groups:	
5	The percentage of body weight accounted for by muscle:	230
6	The number of joints in the body:	
7	The volume of blood in litres in an average-sized adult:	70% 40%
8	The number of different shades of colour the human eye can distinguish:	37 20
9	The age at which brain cells start to die:	5 4
10	Normal body temperature in degrees Celsius:	

You can check your answers on page 168.

2   Remind yourself about the use of softening phrases to admit a failure (page 95) if necessary. Work in pairs. Tell your partner:

- one thing you do which is good for your health
- one thing you do which is bad for your health
- how much attention you pay to your diet
- how often you take vigorous exercise (brisk walking/jogging/cycling, etc.)

Focus on grammar 1 *Countability*

Choosing the right quantifier depends on meaning, grammar and also formality. Test yourself with the following questions then refer to the Key language bank on page 144 to check your answers.

▶ Spot the mistake

► **EXAM LINK**

The correct use of **quantifiers** such as *all*, *any*, *both*, *each*, *few* and *many* contributes to the clarity and accuracy of your writing and speaking in the exam.

KEY LANGUAGE
Quantifiers
▶ p.144

TWO of the following sentences are correct. Tick (✓) these and correct the mistakes in the other sentences.

1 There aren't sports facilities in my town.
2 Children have far too much toys these days.
3 They'll accept either cash or a cheque.
4 Both of Apple and IBM make computers.
5 The test only takes few minutes.
6 I don't know if they have some children.
7 I like all the kinds of music.
8 Few people can afford to have a personal trainer.
9 He earns much money as a lawyer.
10 Every hotel room in the town are full.

Focus on speaking 1 *Facts about smoking*

SKILLS PRACTICE

1 How much do you know about cigarettes and smoking? Work in pairs to answer the following questions. Check your answers on page 168.

How much do you know about smoking?

1 What proportion of the male adult global population smokes?

A a quarter   B almost half   C over half

2 Which region of the world has the highest smoking rate?

A USA   B East Asia   C Europe

3 In what year was smoking linked to lung cancer?

A 1851   B 1901   C 1951

4 How many toxic chemicals are there in cigarette smoke?

A 50   B 1,000   C 4,000

5 How many smokers in the UK want to quit?

A one in ten   B one in three   C two in three

6 Which substance in cigarettes causes addiction?

A nicotine   B tar   C carbon monoxide

7 The tobacco industry in the USA spends about $5 million on advertising.

A a day   B a month   C a year

8 How many young teens (13–15) smoke worldwide?

A one in ten   B one in five   C one in three

9 Of 1,000 young Australians who smoke, one will be murdered and fifteen will be killed on the road. How many will die from smoking?

A 50   B 150   C 250

10 How many people could be fed by food crops grown instead of tobacco?

A 1–2 million   B 5–10 million   C 10–20 million

EXAM PRACTICE
▶ Part 3

2 Discuss the following questions in pairs.

- What's the best way to stop smoking?
- Should smoking be banned in public places like trains, buses and restaurants? Why/Why not?
- How can young people be discouraged from taking up smoking?

Focus on listening 1 *Countdown to a healthier life*

SKILLS PRACTICE
▶ Prediction

1 You will hear a talk about the effects on the body of giving up smoking. Before you listen read through the notes below and think about possible answers. Discuss your ideas with another student.

EXAM PRACTICE
▶ Section 2

2 Now listen and answer Questions 1–10.

Questions 1–10
Complete the notes. Write **NO MORE THAN THREE WORDS AND/OR A NUMBER** *for each answer.*

Time Stopped	Benefits
1	Blood pressure and pulse return to normal. Circulation improves, especially for **2** .... and ....
8 hours	**3** .... in blood returns to normal.
24 hours	Carbon monoxide leaves body. **4** .... start to clear.
48 hours	There is no nicotine left in the body. Senses of **5** .... and .... improve.
72 hours	**6** .... becomes easier. Energy levels rise.
2–12 weeks	Circulation improves throughout the body. Walking and **7** .... become easier.
3–9 months	Breathing problems such as coughing and shortness of breath improve. Lung efficiency increased by up to **8** ....
9	Risk of heart attack falls to about half that of a smoker.
10 years	Risk of cancer falls to about half that of a smoker. Risk of heart attack falls to same as someone who **10** ....

▶ **EXAM LINK**

Listening
It's a good idea to underline the word limit in the instructions. **Any answer with more words than this will be marked wrong.**

Focus on writing 1 *Task 2: Presenting the solution to a problem*

SKILLS PRACTICE

▶ Improving your style

1 Compare these two pieces of writing. Which is in a more suitable style for exam or academic writing, and why? Compare your ideas in pairs.

A

There are lots of health problems in the world. I can think of two examples. AIDS, which is pretty new, is one, and malaria, which has been around for ages, is another. Thank goodness we can cure most diseases with drugs now. But there's a problem! These drugs are very pricey, so poor countries can't afford to use them.

In my opinion, drug companies must make drugs cheaper for poor countries. I also think they should let poor countries make the drugs themselves. That would cost less.

B

There are many serious health problems facing the world today. Some of these are relatively new, like AIDS, while others such as malaria have been in existence for centuries. Fortunately, most diseases can be effectively treated with drugs today. However, such drugs are often too expensive for use in poor countries.

Many people argue that drug companies should reduce the price of drugs they sell in poor countries. After all, why should they make a profit out of people's suffering? Another solution might be for these companies to allow their drugs to be manufactured locally, which would result in cheaper prices.

---

2 Answer these questions, giving examples. Which piece of writing:

1 has shorter sentences?
2 contains passive structures?
3 contains informal expressions?
4 uses more linking expressions?

3 These informal expressions are from Text A. How is the meaning expressed in Text B?

1 lots of
2 pretty
3 has been around
4 ages
5 Thank goodness
6 pricey

4 Rewrite these sentences in a more formal style, linking the parts appropriately.

1 Technology is going incredibly fast. No wonder older people can't cope with all the new gadgets! Begin: *Technology is progressing so fast that …*
2 People sell almost all food in plastic containers now. It isn't necessary and it makes a lot of rubbish. Begin: *Almost all food …*
3 Loads of people have moved to the city recently. They all need a job and a place to live. It's a pity that a lot of them are disappointed.
Begin: *Unfortunately, most of the people …*

5 Rewrite these sentences in a more impersonal and formal style.

1 In my opinion, we should blame TV for falling standards of literacy.
2 As far as I'm concerned, it's up to the government to pay the damages.
3 I feel sure that global warming is behind all the extreme weather we've been having lately.

▶ **ESSENTIAL LANGUAGE**

Impersonal expressions

It seems/appears (that) …
It is generally **agreed/accepted** (that) …
Many/Most people **believe/say/argue** (that) …

EXAM PRACTICE
▶ Task 2
Preparing your answer

6 Study the following exam task.

> *Despite health warnings, a large number of people continue to smoke all over the world.*
>
> *Why should we be concerned about this?*
>
> *What solutions would you suggest?*

7 The quiz on page 105 contains a number of facts about smoking. Highlight any questions that contain information which might be relevant to this task.

8 Use these headings as a paragraph plan and make notes by each heading, including information from the quiz questions that you highlighted.

- <u>Introduction: The scale of the problem</u>

Mention one or two facts about the number of smokers and/or deaths from smoking.

You could also mention why the tobacco industry would like to keep us all smoking.

- <u>The effects of smoking</u>

Think about the various health risks to the individual and also the cost to society.

How could the money which is spent on treating smokers' diseases be better used?

- <u>Possible solutions</u>

Think why people smoke in the first place (e.g. advertising/peer pressure) and why they continue to smoke. Then consider how to deal with these problems. Suggest 2–3 solutions.

- <u>Conclusion ???</u>

9 Write your answer to the question, in four clear paragraphs, using the notes you have made.

Remember:
- keep language fairly formal
- avoid making your writing too personal
- link ideas and sentences appropriately

WRITING PRACTICE
Task 1, Model answer
▶ Practice 7, p. 163

Focus on listening 2 *Milestones of medicine*

SKILLS PRACTICE
▶ Preparation

1 You will hear a student giving a presentation about about some key medical discoveries over the centuries. Before you listen, look through questions 1–10.

- Think about the kind of information that is needed for each question.
- Study the timeline (Questions 2–6) and notice that there are two pieces of information about each discovery. What are they?

EXAM PRACTICE
▶ Section 4

2 Now listen and answer Questions 1–10.

Question 1
Choose the appropriate letter A–C.

1 What problem did Sara have in preparing the presentation?
- **A** She couldn't find enough books on the subject.
- **B** She didn't have access to the Internet.
- **C** She couldn't decide what subjects to choose.

Questions 2–6
*Complete the timeline below using **ONE WORD AND/OR A NUMBER** for each answer.*

Milestones in medicine

Invention	First thermometer (2 ....)	Blood circulation (UK)	Blood 4 .... (UK)	5 .... anaesthetic (USA)	X-rays (6 ....)
Place					
Year	1600 / 1615	3	1700 / 1733	1800 / 1846	1895

Questions 7–10
What information is given about each type of drug?
Write the correct answer, A, B or C, next to Questions 7–10.

> **A** produced from a plant
> **B** had bad side-effects
> **C** tested on animals first

Example	Answer
Penicillin	**A**

7 Aspirin ....
8 Beta blockers ....
9 Insulin ....
10 Cortisone ....

Focus on speaking 2 *Discussing medical developments*

EXAM PRACTICE
▶ Part 3

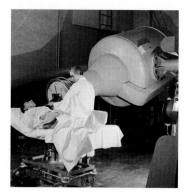

Work in pairs to discuss this question. Before you start, study the Essential language in the box below.

Which of the following is the most important medical development, in your opinion?

x-rays   laser surgery   contact lenses   hip replacement

> ▶ **ESSENTIAL LANGUAGE**
>
> **Reflecting**
> If/when you think about it, …
> *When you think about it, almost all of us have had an X-ray at some time.*
>
> **Balancing the argument**
> But …   On the other hand, …
> *I think contact lenses are a fantastic invention.* **On the other hand**, *they don't save lives!*

DIY Learning strategy *Spot the mistake*

Don't be afraid of making mistakes. They're an essential part of learning. But if you don't learn from your mistakes, you'll be missing a golden opportunity!

Match each mistake below to the correct category. Do you make any of these mistakes regularly?

> 1 The bar chart <u>give</u> information about <u>number</u> of students at UK universities.
>
> 2 In 1999 there <u>is</u> a slight increase <u>of</u> foreign visitors.
>
> 3 Life is easier if you <u>have always</u> good <u>helth</u>.

A Articles   Sp Spelling   G   Subject/verb agreement
T Tenses   P   Preposition   WO Word order

- Study your teacher's corrections carefully. They're valuable personal feedback on your work.
- Take the time to correct your work carefully. Ask if you're unclear about anything.
- Be aware of your 'favourite' mistakes and try to eliminate them, one by one.

DIY LEARNING PROJECT

> 1 Look through some marked homework and identify a 'favourite' mistake.
> 2 Revise this area of language. Use a grammar book or ask your teacher.
> 3 Make notes to remind yourself about the key points. Do some practice exercises if possible.
> 4 Check carefully for your 'favourite' mistake before you hand in your next piece of written work.

Focus on grammar 2 *Comparing and contrasting*

1   a) Work in pairs to discuss which three animals you think kill most humans every year.

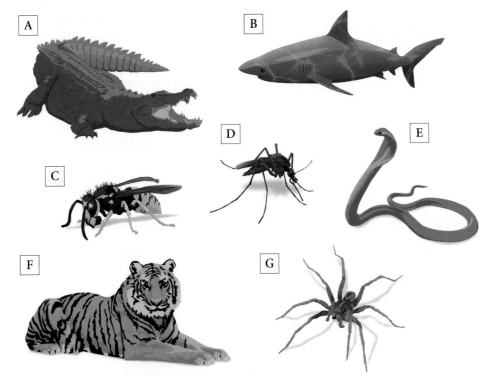

b) Check your answers on page 168 and write the number of deaths per year next to each animal.

2   Study the following language and then answer the questions.

> ▶ **ESSENTIAL LANGUAGE**
>
> **Comparing and contrasting**
> ... **while / whereas** ... + clause
> *Xs are responsible for the deaths of ... people each year* **while / whereas** *Ys only kill about ...*
>
> **By comparison, / contrast,** ... + clause
> *Xs only kill about ... people each year.* **By comparison, / By contrast,** *Ys cause the deaths of ...*

1   Which two expressions are normally used at the beginning of a sentence?
2   Which two expressions are normally used in the middle of a sentence, to link two clauses?
3   Which expression suggests a fairly big difference between two things?
4   We usually avoid using the same verb in both parts of a comparison. Which two expressions are used to avoid repeating the verb 'kill'?

3   Make sentences comparing or contrasting the different animals. Before you begin, look back at the cause and effect expressions on page 99.

Focus on writing 2 *Task 1: Describing data*

SKILLS PRACTICE
▶ Reading the diagram

1 **Study the diagram below and answer these questions.**

1 How many disease groups does the diagram show?
2 What do the figures in the left- and right-hand columns represent?
3 Write an introductory sentence. Begin: *The diagram shows …*

▶ Selecting key
information

2 **Answer the following questions.**

1 Which disease group kills most people in the more economically developed world?
2 Which disease group kills most people in the less economically developed world?
3 In which disease group is there the biggest difference between the two areas?

▶ Describing the data

3 **Complete the extracts using information from the diagram below.**

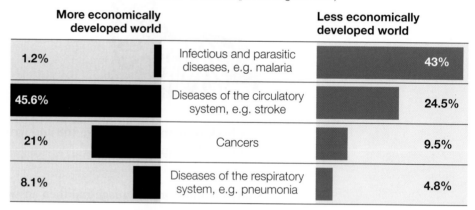

Causes of death (percentage of total)

More economically developed world		Less economically developed world
1.2%	Infectious and parasitic diseases, e.g. malaria	43%
45.6%	Diseases of the circulatory system, e.g. stroke	24.5%
21%	Cancers	9.5%
8.1%	Diseases of the respiratory system, e.g. pneumonia	4.8%

WRITING PRACTICE
Task 1, Guided practice
▶ Practice 8, p. 164

a) Infectious and parasitic diseases cause 1 ....
50% of deaths in the less economically developed countries.
2 .... , these diseases account for only
3 .... of deaths in the more economically
developed world.

b) Diseases of the circulatory system are the biggest killers in the more
economically developed world 4 .... infectious
and parasitic diseases 5 .... the majority of
deaths in the less economically developed world.

4 **Now write two more sentences comparing the effect of the other two disease groups in the more economically developed and less economically developed world.**

IELTS VOCABULARY BUILDER

1 Complete the following sentences with suitable words. The first letters have been given to help you.

1 He received t........................ for a broken ankle in the C........................ Department of the local hospital.
2 Fortunately the passengers suffered only minor i........................ in the accident.
3 As yet there is no c........................ for AIDS.
4 You need a doctor's p........................ to obtain these painkillers.
5 Her doctor arranged for her to see a skin s........................ for further tests.

2 Complete the table by writing the correct branch of medicine in each space.

Cardiology   Neurology   Physiotherapy   Psychiatry

Branch of medicine	What it deals with
1	Brain and nerves
2	Heart and arteries
3	Exercise and massage of the body
4	Mental illness

Prepositions

3 Fill in the missing prepositions. Use a dictionary to check your answers.

1 The human skeletal system is made .... 206 individual bones.
2 The ear canal is about 2.5 cm .... length.
3 Hormones in the blood can have powerful effects .... the body's systems.
4 The spinal column consists .... 26 separate bones called vertebrae.
5 Your brain sends messages .... a rate of 386 kph.
6 The thickness of the skin varies .... 5 and 6 millimetres, depending .... the area of the body.
7 The circulation pumps blood around the body .... means of the heart.
8 She suffers .... very severe headaches.

Register

4 The expressions on the left below are formal or technical. Match them to the non-specialist expressions on the right.

1 undergo surgery   a) heart attack
2 fracture   b) jab
3 cardiac arrest   c) have an operation
4 injection   d) break

ACADEMIC WORD STUDY 5

ADJECTIVES ENDING IN -ical

1 Write an adjective ending in -ical to match each definition below.

Example related to a subject of present interest:
   a topical joke

1 not costing a lot of money:
   a(n) .... *way to travel*

2 seeming reasonable and sensible:
   a(n) .... *solution*

3 relating to the treatment of disease:
   The .... *Faculty*

4 relating to the body:
   a(n) .... *examination*

5 relating to the way the mind works:
   a(n) .... *thriller*

6 connected with knowledge of how machines work:
   free .... *support*

7 connected with machines:
   a(n) .... *failure*

8 exactly the same:
   .... *twins*

RIGHT WORD/WRONG WORD

2 Circle the correct word in brackets in each sentence below.

1 The country is facing an (economic/economical) crisis.

2 Water is the country's most valuable natural (source/resource).

3 It is (estimated/predicted) that one in ten people are colour blind.

4 The college has (acquired/required) an excellent reputation.

5 Public protests were a major (factor/sector) in the government's decision to cancel plans for a new power station.

6 The company has (transformed/transferred) its head office to Rome.

7 On a clear night the moon's craters are (visual/visible) from Earth.

8 The most important (aspect/prospect) of my job is dealing with people.

PREPOSITIONS

3 Complete the following sentences by adding the correct preposition

1 There's no **alternative** .... the present system.

2 The minister refused to **comment** .... the situation.

3 The firm **compensated** workers .... loss of earnings.

4 We need to **concentrate** .... the key issues.

5 The problem is how to **dispose** .... toxic waste.

6 Some important data was **excluded** .... the study.

7 The substance was **identified** .... poison.

8 Every student can **participate** .... the election.

WORD BUILDING

4 Complete the table by writing the nouns formed from the verbs 1–8.

Verb	Noun
1 contribute	
2 dispose	
3 erode	
4 exclude	
5 identify	
6 react	
7 remove	
8 substitute	

5 Choose four academic words from this page and write personal examples to help you remember them.

1 ....

2 ....

3 ....

4 ....

Check your answers on page 168 and use this page as a reference point for revision.

REVIEW 5

Grammar

GRAMMATICAL PATTERNS

1 Complete the second sentence, using the word given, so that it means the same as the first sentence. **Do not change the word given.**

1 Most people think that carbon emissions cause global warming
   agreed
   It .... carbon emissions cause global warming.

2 The river was so dirty that people couldn't swim in it.
   too
   The river was ....

3 The trade in animal skins continues even though it is illegal.
   despite
   The trade in animal skins continues .... illegal.

4 The lake used to be so clear that you could see the bottom.
   enough
   The lake used to be .... the bottom.

5 Today you are very likely to survive a heart attack.
   chance
   Today you have .... a heart attack.

6 Women earn much less than men.
   comparison
   Womens' wages are low .... men's wages.

7 The illness was caused by a virus.
   responsible
   A virus .... the illness.

8 She sold her car in order to raise money.
   by
   She managed .... her car.

Vocabulary

WORD CHOICE

2 Choose the correct answer A–C to complete the following sentences.

1 When you .... about it, it would be difficult to cope without antibiotics.
   A consider   B discuss   C think

2 A cooker is an essential household ....
   A instrument   B appliance   C agent

3 How much time do we all waste dealing with .... mail?
   A junk   B waste   C rubbish

4 I know I should take more exercise but, to be ...., I'm too lazy!
   A accurate   B true   C honest

5 I agree with you up to ....
   A a part   B a point   C a place

6 You can contact me by .... phone or email.
   A either   B both   C any

WORD BUILDING

3 Use the word given in capitals at the end of each line to form a word that fits the space. Make sure your answer fits grammatically as well as logically.

Example

There have been great advances   TREAT
in the *treatment* of cancer.

1 Air pollution can be .... to health.	HARM
2 It won't be easy to find a .... to the problem.	SOLVE
3 .... production has risen by 6 per cent since May.	INDUSTRY
4 Police have begun an .... into the accident.	INVESTIGATE
5 Tests revealed the .... of dangerous chemicals in the water.	PRESENT
6 The government is putting extra money into .... research.	SCIENCE
7 We're carrying out an in-............... study into students' needs.	DEEP
8 Large areas of rainforest are now .... with destruction.	THREAT

11 ▶ Science of happiness

In this unit you will practise:

- **Reading skills:** Identifying the topic; reference links; linking expressions
- **Speaking skills:** Discussing future plans; answering difficult questions; playing for time
- **Grammar:** Present tenses with future reference; articles
- **Vocabulary:** Opposites; word families; expressions with *self-*

Exam Focus

Reading: Short-answer questions; summary completion; matching headings; T/F/NG; multiple choice

Speaking: Parts 1, 3

Lead-in

Work in pairs to discuss these questions.

1. Which of these things is most likely to make you happy?
2. What other things are important to people's happiness?

Shopping

Socialising

Success of sports team

Holidays

Being with family

Success at work

Focus on reading 1 *The formula for happiness*

EXAM PRACTICE
▶ Short-answer questions

1 Skim the text below to find out more about the heading. Answer the questions below. Choose NO MORE THAN THREE WORDS AND/OR A NUMBER from the passage for each answer.

1 How many researchers were responsible for writing the report?
2 How many people did they interview?
3 What does the letter H in the equation represent?
4 What is Dr Rothwell's profession?
5 What was the minimum age of the people interviewed?

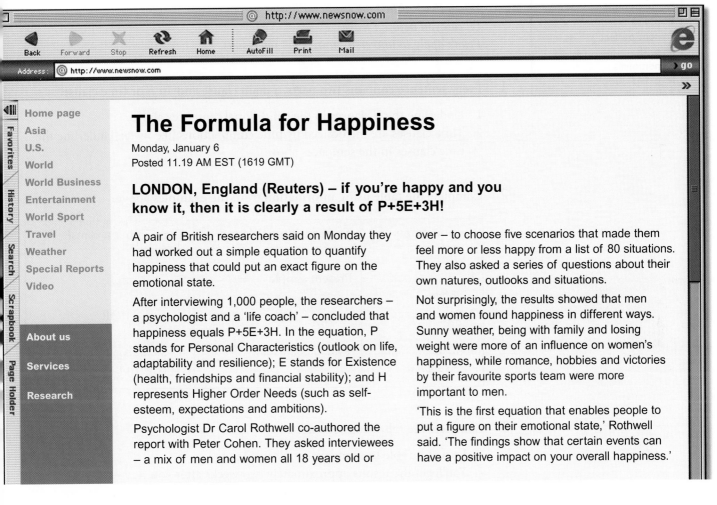

http://www.newsnow.com

Address: http://www.newsnow.com

Home page
Asia
U.S.
World
World Business
Entertainment
World Sport
Travel
Weather
Special Reports
Video

About us
Services
Research

The Formula for Happiness

Monday, January 6
Posted 11.19 AM EST (1619 GMT)

LONDON, England (Reuters) – if you're happy and you know it, then it is clearly a result of P+5E+3H!

A pair of British researchers said on Monday they had worked out a simple equation to quantify happiness that could put an exact figure on the emotional state.

After interviewing 1,000 people, the researchers – a psychologist and a 'life coach' – concluded that happiness equals P+5E+3H. In the equation, P stands for Personal Characteristics (outlook on life, adaptability and resilience); E stands for Existence (health, friendships and financial stability); and H represents Higher Order Needs (such as self-esteem, expectations and ambitions).

Psychologist Dr Carol Rothwell co-authored the report with Peter Cohen. They asked interviewees – a mix of men and women all 18 years old or over – to choose five scenarios that made them feel more or less happy from a list of 80 situations. They also asked a series of questions about their own natures, outlooks and situations.

Not surprisingly, the results showed that men and women found happiness in different ways. Sunny weather, being with family and losing weight were more of an influence on women's happiness, while romance, hobbies and victories by their favourite sports team were more important to men.

'This is the first equation that enables people to put a figure on their emotional state,' Rothwell said. 'The findings show that certain events can have a positive impact on your overall happiness.'

▶ Summary completion

2 Complete the summary below. Choose NO MORE THAN ONE WORD from the text for each answer.

The results of a survey which aims to identify what makes each of us happy have just been published. Researchers asked people to look through a list of **1** .... and select the ones which made them feel happy. Interviewees were also questioned about their natures, situations and **2** .... The research showed that things which affect women's happiness include good **3** .... and spending time with **4** .... , while what mattered more to men were **5** .... by the sports team they supported, along with romance and their various pastimes.

Focus on grammar 1 *Present tenses with future reference*

▶ **EXAM LINK**

Both 'real' conditionals and **time clauses** are very useful for talking about future plans and arrangements in the interview.

KEY LANGUAGE
Present simple
▶ p. 153
Present perfect
▶ p. 151
Conditionals
▶ p. 143

'Real' or Type 1 conditionals and time clauses can both be used to refer to possible events in the future. As the grammar is the same, it makes sense to learn them together. Study these examples and answer the questions below.

'Real' conditionals:
*If I **pass** my exams, I'**ll go** to university.*
*If you **haven't arrived** by six, we'**ll go** without you.*
*I'**ll be** very disappointed if I **don't get** this job.*

Time clauses:
*When I'**ve finished** my studies, I'**ll start** work.*
*I'**ll call** you **before** I leave.*
*I **can't apply** to university **until** I get my results.*

1   Every sentence contains two parts, a main clause and an *if* or time clause.

     1   Underline the *if* clauses in the conditional sentences above.
     2   Time clauses are introduced by time conjunctions like **when**. Underline the time clauses in the sentences above.

2   Complete the table using information from the examples above.

Conjunction	Tense in *if*/time clause	Tense in main clauses
If 1 .... *After* 2	Present simple OR	5 .... OR
3 .... *As soon as*	4	6 .... (e.g. *can, should*, etc.)

3   Complete the following sentences.

     1   I won't be able to send any emails until … .
     2   You'll get the results approximately two weeks after you … .
     3   If I don't pass the exam first time, … .
     4   I'll give him the message as soon as … .
     5   … my parents will be delighted.

4   Make four true sentences about yourself or someone you know, using clauses introduced by *if, when, until* and *as soon as*.

Focus on speaking 1 *Discussing future plans*

SKILLS PRACTICE

1 Look at the eight possible goals in life below. Choose four and put them in order of importance 1–4 (1 = most important).

- be famous
- be financially secure
- be happy/enjoy life/have fun
- be successful in a sport
- finish school/college/university
- make a difference/help people
- get married/have a family
- get a good job/career

2 In pairs, compare your results and discuss any differences. Can you think of any other significant goals which aren't included?

EXAM PRACTICE
▶ Part I

3 a) Discussing your future plans is a common interview topic. Study the Essential language below.

> ▶ **ESSENTIAL LANGUAGE**
>
> **Discussing future plans**
> To express definite intentions you can say:
> **I'm planning to** … or **I'm intending to** … + infinitive
>
> To express less definite intentions you can say:
> **I'm hoping to** … or **I'd like to** …+ infinitive
> *When I finish my degree **I'm planning to** work in my father's company. After that, **I'm hoping to** do a PhD.*

b) Work in pairs to interview each other about your future plans. Try to mention one definite and one less definite intention. The interviewer should ask:

- What are you doing for your next holiday?
- What will you do when you complete your studies/pass the exam?
- Do you have any other goals for the future?

LANGUAGE CHECK
Present progressive for future
e.g. *I'm taking the exam next month.*
The **present progressive** is often used to talk about future events which have already been arranged.
- Make true sentences about any arrangements you have for this evening/weekend.

Focus on reading 2 *The pursuit of happiness*

INTRODUCTION

1 **Look at Figure 1 and answer the following questions:**

1 Which countries report the highest happiness levels (red bars)?
2 Which countries report low happiness levels but high satisfaction levels (green bars)?
3 How is happiness different from satisfaction? Think about what makes you feel happy or satisfied and which feeling changes more quickly.

Fig. 1

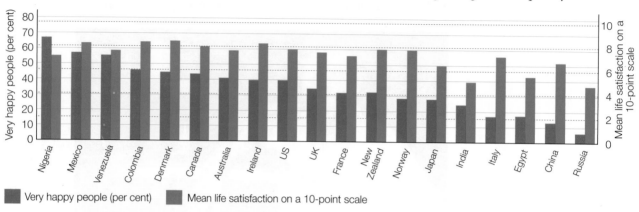

2 **Look at Figure 2 and answer these questions.**

1 What does the diagram show?
2 Describe the development in income.
3 Describe the development in happiness.
4 What can you say about the relationship between income and happiness? Can you suggest any reasons for this?

Fig. 2

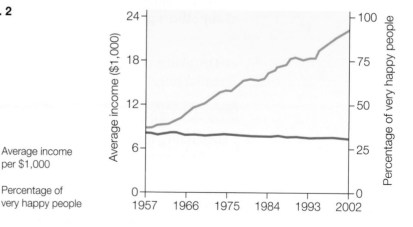

SKILLS PRACTICE
▶ Identifying the topic

3 **Study the text on the opposite page and choose the best answer to complete the headings for sections A–C.**

1 Section A:
   A disappearance   B development   C difficulty
2 Section B:
   A research topics   B research scientists   C research grants
3 Section C:
   A in the past   B now   C now and in the future

The pursuit of happiness

A The .... of happiness studies

Over the past decade, the study of happiness has become an accepted academic discipline. You can find 'professors of happiness' at leading universities and thousands of
5 research papers. The subject even has its own journal, the *Journal of Happiness Studies*.

B Research methods and ....

What has made the systematic study of happiness possible is data gathered from hundreds of surveys of
10 happiness across different cultures, professions, religions, social and economic groups. These surveys use different methods, such as asking people how happy they feel at a particular moment, or at random times over a few weeks, or even asking their family and friends. In this way

15 researchers can investigate, for example, how much difference money makes to a person's happiness; whether happy people are more likely to be leaders or to live longer; and whether inequality in wealth and status is an important source of dissatisfaction or not.

20 ## C The benefits of research ....

'It is an exciting area,' says Ruut Veenhoven, Professor of Social Conditions for Human Happiness at Erasmus University, Rotterdam, 'We can now show which behaviours are risky as far as happiness goes, in the same
25 way medical research has shown us what is bad for our health. We should eventually be able to show what kind of lifestyle suits what kind of person.'

EXAM PRACTICE
▶ Matching headings

In this task, you have to choose suitable headings for sections of a text.
The correct heading will accurately summarise the information in a section.
Before you start, read this advice.

TASK APPROACH

- Study the list of headings and underline key words.
- If there's an example, skim-read that section to see how the heading matches the information.
- Study the first section, thinking about the topic as you read. Look for expressions or information that match key words in the headings.
- Cross out each heading as you choose it.

Questions 1–5
The second part of the text on page 122, has six sections D–I.
Choose the correct heading for paragraphs D and F–I from the list below.

List of headings
i Happiness and health
ii A difficulty for researchers
iii Sources of happiness in the US and Japan
iv Advice to governments
v Attitudes to happiness in different countries
vi Happiness and money

Example	*Answer*
Section **E**	**v**

1	Section **D**
2	Section **F**
3	Section **G**
4	Section **H**
5	Section **I**

D

However, Veenhoven admits that interpreting the data can be a problem because the word 'happiness' has no precise equivalent in some languages. Even in English it means different things to different people, and he has recorded 15 different academic definitions.

E

One interesting result from the surveys is that Asian countries such as Japan and South Korea tend to report lower levels of happiness than many western countries. So are westerners happier than Asian people? Not necessarily. Different cultures value happiness in very different ways. In individualistic western countries, it is often a reflection of personal achievement. Being unhappy suggests that you have not made the most of your life. Meanwhile in nations such as Japan, China and South Korea, people have a more fatalistic attitude towards happiness. According to Eunkook Mark Suh at Yonsei University in Seoul, 'They believe it is very much a blessing from heaven'. One result of this attitude is that

you don't have to feel inferior or guilty about not being happy, since happiness does not reflect your ability.

F

Furthermore, the things that give people happiness, satisfaction and meaning in their lives vary considerably between cultures. In the US, satisfaction comes from personal success, self-expression, pride, a high sense of self-esteem and a distinct sense of self. In Japan, on the other hand, it comes from fulfilling the expectations of your family, meeting your social responsibilities, self-discipline, co-operation and friendliness. So, while in the US it is perfectly appropriate to pursue your own happiness, in Japan you are more likely to find happiness by not directly pursuing it.

G

One of the most significant observations is that in industrialised nations, average happiness has remained almost the same since the Second World War, despite a considerable rise in average income. A growing number of researchers are blaming consumerism for this trend. Study after study has shown that the desire for material goods increases hand in hand with average income.

H

Research by Tim Kasser at Knox College, Illinois, also found that young adults who focus on money, image and fame tend to be more depressed, have less enthusiasm for life and suffer more physical symptoms such as headaches and sore throats than others.

I

These days most economists tend to agree that the key to making people happier is to move from pure economic growth – which encourages a consumerist culture – to personal growth. According to this view, a government's priorities should be to reduce unemployment and job insecurity, improve mental healthcare and discourage the pursuit of status.

Adapted from *New Scientist*

▶ True/False/Not Given

Questions 6–11

Do the following statements agree with the information given in the text?

Write | **TRUE** | *if the statement agrees with the information*
| **FALSE** | *if the statement contradicts the information*
| **NOT GIVEN** | *if there is no information on this*

6 Not all researchers agree about how to interpret the word 'happiness'.

7 For Asian people, feeling unhappy is something to be ashamed of.

8 For North Americans, satisfaction comes from self-discipline and co-operation.

9 Japan is the only country where people have become happier in the last 30 years.

10 As people get richer they become less interested in buying things.

11 Wanting to become rich and famous can make you unwell.

▶ Multiple choice

> *Question 12*
> *Choose* **TWO** *answers A–E. Which* **TWO** *policies do economists think would help make people happier?*
>
> **A** increasing job security
> **B** working towards pure economic growth
> **C** increasing payments to the unemployed
> **D** encouraging a consumerist culture
> **E** encouraging personal growth

SKILLS PRACTICE
▶ Reference links

4 **What do the following words or phrases refer to?**

e.g. *the subject* (line 5). The answer is: *The study of happiness.*

1 *Veenhoven* (line 29)   4 *They* (46)
2 *it* (31)   5 *it* (56)
3 *it* (40)   6 *this trend* (67)

▶ Linking expressions

5 **Find and underline the following expressions in the text. Then answer the questions below.**

> *However* (line 29)   *Meanwhile* (43)   *Furthermore* (51)
> *on the other hand* (55–56)   *So* (58)

1 Which expression is a(n):
   a) **AND** expression (introducing additional similar information)?
   b) **BUT** expression (introducing different or contrasting information)?
   c) **THEREFORE** expression (introducing the logical result of earlier information)?

2 Which expression is:
   a) usually followed by a comma?
   b) used to compare two different things happening at the same time?
   c) sometimes used as the second part of a two-part expression?

Choose one of the expressions you didn't know before or don't normally use, and make a point of using it in written work in the coming week.

> ▶ **EXAM LINK**
>
> Good writers use **linking expressions** to provide logical connections between sentences and paragraphs. Using them in your own writing will improve the cohesion and coherence of your own work, which is taken into account in the exam.

Focus on grammar 2 *Articles*

KEY LANGUAGE
Articles
▶ p. 141

The double expressions *study after study* and *hand in hand* in the text are examples of fixed phrases without articles. There are a number of other fixed phrases which do <u>not</u> take articles that are worth remembering. Test yourself below then refer to the Key language bank to check your answers.

Add articles where necessary in the following sentences.

We usually have **1** .... lunch at about **2** .... midday. That's **3** .... main meal of the day for us. Then some time in **4** .... evening we might have **5** .... snack of some kind, **6** .... soup or **7** .... omelette, for example. We've been trying to lose **8** .... weight by cutting down on **9** .... sweet things and **10** .... little by **11** .... little. I think it's working.

I take **12** .... children to **13** .... school by **14** .... car but when they're older they'll be able to go on **15** .... foot because it's not far. We have to leave **16** .... home by **17** .... 7 a.m. because **18** .... traffic is so bad in **19** .... morning. When I finally get to **20** .... work I'm exhausted!

Focus on speaking 2 *Answering difficult questions*

SKILLS PRACTICE

1 If the examiner asks a difficult question in the interview, you can use an expression which gives you time to think. Study the Essential language below, then answer the following questions.

> ▶ **ESSENTIAL LANGUAGE**
>
> **Playing for time**
> That's quite a difficult question to answer. Let me think … Maybe …
> That's an interesting point.
>
> Which teacher influenced you most at school?
> *That's quite a difficult question to answer. Let me think. Maybe my Maths teacher because …*

1 What's your favourite food?
2 If you could visit any city in the world, which city would you choose?
3 What has been the best day of your life?
4 Which is the most interesting place in your country for a tourist to visit?

EXAM PRACTICE
▶ **Part 3**

2 Working in pairs, take it in turns to answer the following questions:

* Can money buy happiness? Why/Why not?
* Is it more important to enjoy your work even if you don't earn much money, or to have a successful career? Why?
* Who is your country's greatest man or woman (past or present), in your opinion? Why?
* What is the key to success in life?

IELTS VOCABULARY BUILDER

Opposites

1 Choose the correct prefix to form the opposite of the following words. Many of the answers appear in the texts in this unit.

dis-	in-	mis-	un-

1 ....satisfaction
2 ....equality
3 ....employment
4 ....security
5 ......agreement
6 ....understand

7 ....happy
8 ....flexible
9 ....interesting
10 ....interpret
11 ....appropriate
12 ....courage

Word families

2 Make nouns from the following adjectives and verbs. Check your answers by searching Focus on reading texts 1 or 2.

1 adaptable (Text 1)
2 exist (1)
3 healthy (1, 2 section C)
4 expect (1, 2F)
5 stable (1)
6 different (2B)

7 achieve (2E)
8 able (2E)
9 co-operate (2F)
10 friendly (2F)
11 observe (2G)
12 grow (2I)

Expressions with *self-*

3 Complete the sentences by choosing a suitable noun or adjective to combine with *self-*.

confident	contained	discipline	employed	esteem	expression

1 I've been self-................................ all my life and I couldn't imagine working for anyone now.
2 People who work from home need the self-................................ to get up at a set time.
3 Children do various writing and artistic activities which are designed to encourage their self-................................ .
4 It's easy to suffer from low self-................................ when you've been unemployed for a long time.
5 We need a leader who is self-................................ enough to make speeches and appear on TV.
6 After staying with an English family for three months, I moved to a self-................................ flat.

12 ▶ Buildings and structures

In this unit you will practise:
- **Listening skills:** Analysing questions; prediction
- **Writing skills:** Describing objects; discussing solutions to problems
- **Speaking skills:** Discussing buildings; giving supporting examples
- **Grammar:** Participle clauses; unreal conditionals
- **Vocabulary:** Materials and structures; pronunciation: sounds

Exam Focus

Listening: Sections 1, 4; Note completion; multiple choice; labelling a diagram

Writing: Task 1, 2

Speaking: Parts 1, 2, 3

Lead-in

A

B

1 Work in pairs to answer the questions.

a) Match the following names 1–5 to the correct pictures A–E.

b) Which is the oldest? Which is the most recent?

1 **The Great Wall of China**   ....
2 **The Taj Mahal** (India)   ....
3 **The Leaning Tower of Pisa** (Italy) ....
4 **The Great Sphinx** (Egypt)   ....
5 **The Statue of Liberty** (USA)   ....

C

D

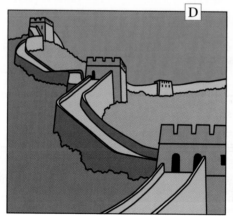

E

2 Match the pictures to the descriptions below. Write the correct letter A–E beside the text. Be prepared to say which words or phrases were important clues.

1 Built mainly of earth and stone, and varying in height between five and nine metres, this vast structure was designed as a defence against nomadic tribes. Its construction began around 214 BC.

2 It was carved out of a single block of limestone approximately 4,500 years ago. Today it is in quite a poor condition because of the effects of wind, humidity and pollution.

3   This steel-reinforced structure was designed as a gift from one nation to another. Completed in 1884, it was then transported to its final destination, where it now stands on an island.

4   It has a central dome and four minarets, at each corner. Constructed between 1632 and 1650, the entire structure is made of marble and it is considered by many people to be the most beautiful building in the world.

5   Standing 55 metres high, this structure is estimated to weigh 14,453 tonnes. However, it has foundations which are only about three metres deep. Work began on the building in 1173 but took two centuries to complete owing to serious construction problems.

3   **Which of these structures would you most like to visit, and why?**

Focus on grammar 1 *Participle clauses*

> ▶ **EXAM LINK**
>
> **Participle clauses** are common in academic writing. They are a way of combining two or more pieces of information in one sentence, and they can make a text quite dense to read. For this reason it's important to notice participle clauses in exam reading passages, and to study those sentences very carefully.

1   **Read the first sentence in description 1 (Great Wall) again. The table below shows how the sentence is constructed. Study the table and answer the questions.**

Type	Participle clause	Main clause
Past (-*ed* or irregular)	***Built*** *mainly of earth and stone, …*	*this vast structure was designed as a defence against nomadic tribes.*
Present (-*ing*)	***varying*** *in height between five and nine metres …*	

1   How many participle clauses does the sentence contain? What kind of word introduces a participle clause?
2   How many main clauses does the sentence contain?
3   Which clause contains the subject of the sentence?
4   How many types of participle clause are there? What are they called?
5   *Built* is a short way of saying: *This structure **was built**.* What grammatical structure is this?

2   **Underline the sentences with participle clauses in texts 3, 4 and 5. Circle the subject each refers to and say what type of participle clause they are.**

Focus on speaking 1 *Discussing buildings*

SKILLS PRACTICE

1 If you have to say you don't like or aren't interested in something, remember to start with a softening phrase. (See page 95)

e.g. A *Are you interested in architecture?*
   B *Not really.* **To be honest,** *I don't know anything about it.*

> ### ► ESSENTIAL LANGUAGE
>
> **Making negative comments**
>
> | I'm afraid | I'm not (very/really) interested in … |
> |---|---|
> | To be honest, | I don't know (very) much about … |
> | | I find … (quite/pretty) boring. |
> | | I (really) hate … |

In pairs, choose topics below to practise asking and answering questions. Begin: *How do you feel about …? Do you like/enjoy +-ing …?*, etc.

Give true answers and introduce negative comments with a suitable softening phrase. Give reasons if possible.

1	housework	3	politics	5	art galleries
2	cooking	4	classical music	6	exams

EXAM PRACTICE

► Part 1

2 In pairs, practise answering these questions.

- What kind of building do you live in?
- Do you enjoy visiting historical buildings?
- Do you prefer modern or more traditional architecture?

► Part 2

3 Work in pairs. Take it in turns to speak for about two minutes on this topic. Before you begin, spend a minute thinking about what you're going to say. Make notes if you wish.

> **Describe a famous building you have visited.**
>
> > **You should say:**
> >
> > > **where it is**
> > > **what it's like**
> > > **why it's famous**
> >
> > **and explain whether you would recommend other people to visit it.**

Focus on writing 1 *Describing objects*

SKILLS PRACTICE

1 Match each word below with the correct diagram A–H on the opposite page.

1	Circle ..*E*..	3	Cylinder	5	Semi-circle	7	Square
2	Cube	4	Rectangle	6	Sphere	8	Triangle

2 Make an adjective from each noun above.

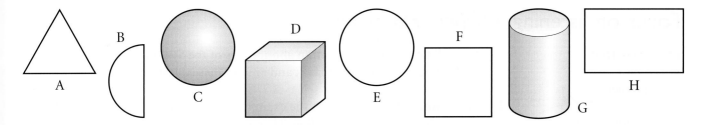

3 **Use words from the box to complete the description of the fish tank below.**

> ► **ESSENTIAL LANGUAGE**
>
> **Describing objects**
>
> **is** (approximately) … **long/tall/high/wide**.
> **has a length/height/width of** …
> **is shaped like** a sphere/rectangle/cylinder, etc.
> **is** (roughly) round/square, etc. **in shape**
>
> **consists of** … (main parts)
> **contains** … (what's inside)
> **is made of** … (materials)
> **is connected to** … (by …)

WRITING PRACTICE
There is an optional
Writing task based on
explaining how things
work on page 165.
► Practice 9, p. 165

The fish tank is **1** .... in shape and **2** .... a base
and four walls which are **3** .... glass. It is 60 cm **4** ....
by 30 cm **5** .... and has a **6** .... of 45 cm. The tank
7 .... water, fish and plants. It is **8** .... a tap by a
rubber hose.

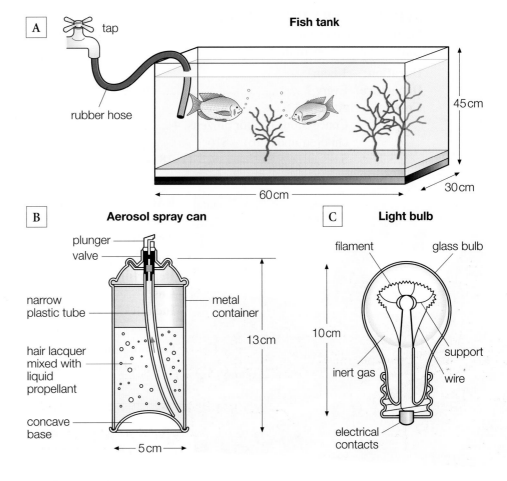

A tap

Fish tank

rubber hose

45 cm

30 cm

60 cm

B **Aerosol spray can**

plunger
valve

narrow
plastic tube

metal
container

hair lacquer
mixed with
liquid
propellant

concave
base

13 cm

5 cm

C **Light bulb**

filament

glass bulb

inert gas

support

wire

10 cm

electrical
contacts

4 **Write brief descriptions of the aerosol spray can and light bulb.**

Focus on listening 1 *Opera House Tour*

EXAM PRACTICE
▶ Section I
  Preparation

How much … ?

How long … ?

When … ?

You will hear some information about tours of the Sydney Opera House. Before you begin, study the task and answer these questions.

1 Match words 1–3 below from the exam task with the question words on the left you might hear on the recording. Then complete each question.
  1 Duration
  2 Departure
  3 Cost

2 Which answers are likely to include numbers?

3 Try to think of possible answers for questions 1, 2, 4 and 5.

Now listen and complete questions 1–10 below.

Questions 1–10
Complete the notes below.
Write **NO MORE THAN THREE WORDS AND/OR A NUMBER** *for each answer.*

SYDNEY OPERA HOUSE TOUR
Learn about the history and **1** .... of the building and visit the concert hall and opera theatre.

Duration: 1 hour
Departure: Every **2** .... (between 9 a.m. and 5 p.m.)
Cost: Adult – **3** $...............
               Concessions (senior citizens, **4** .... students and children under 16) – $16
               5 .... (1–18 people) – $432.00

BACKSTAGE TOUR
Stand on the stage, see where the orchestra plays and meet the **6** .... staff and performers.

Duration: **7** ....
Departure: 7 a.m.
Cost: **8** $............... per person
Includes: **9** light ....

For more information or to book a tour today call:
Sydney **10** ....

▶ **EXAM LINK**   Listening

Even if the instructions say you can write up to three words, some or all of the correct answers may be just one word.

Focus on listening 2 *The Itaipu Dam*

EXAM PRACTICE
▶ Section 4
   Prediction

You will hear part of a lecture on the Itaipu Dam in South America.

1 Look at the headings for questions 1 and 3. What other words could you use to talk about these points?

2 Try to think of possible answers for questions 2 (have a wild guess!), 3, 4 and 5.

3 Read through the other questions and think about the most likely answers.

▶ **EXAM LINK**

Listening
Study key words in the question like *location* or *purpose* and think about different ways of expressing this information. This will help you identify the answers more easily.

Questions 1–5
Complete the notes below.
Write **ONE WORD AND/OR A NUMBER** *for each answer.*

ITAIPU DAM: Vital statistics

Location:	Brazil and Paraguay
Completion date:	1 ....
Purpose:	Hydro-electric power
Cost:	2 $............................
Type:	Gravity
Material:	3 ....
Length:	7.8 kilometres
4 ....:	196 metres
Reservoir 5 ....:	1.02 trillion cubic feet

Questions 6 and 7
Choose **TWO** *letters A–E.*

What **TWO** problems caused by the construction of the dam are mentioned?

A People had to leave their homes.   ....
B Animals lost their habitat.   ....
C Farming has suffered.   ....
D The water from the dam can spread disease.   ....
E The land near the dam is sometimes flooded.   ....

Questions 8–10
Label the diagram.
Write **ONE WORD**
for each answer.

crest
downstream face
upstream face

8 ....
10 ....   9 ....

Focus on speaking 2 *Giving supporting examples*

SKILLS PRACTICE

When the examiner asks you about a general topic, it's a good idea to try and think of a specific example from your personal experience to support your argument. Study the Essential language and the examples below.

> ### ▶ ESSENTIAL LANGUAGE
>
> **Giving supporting examples**
> Take .... , for example.
> .... is a good example.

- Do you think children care too much about fashion these days?
  *Yes, I think some children do. **Take** my nephew, **for example**. He's only 12 but he keeps asking his mum to buy him designer jeans.*
- Are computer games a waste of time?
  *I think some games are quite educational, actually. Hangman **is a good example**. It teaches you spelling.*

EXAM PRACTICE
▶ **Part 3**

1 Think of specific examples for these topics.

- Do children get enough exercise these days?
- Should all young people aim to go to university?
- Is watching TV a waste of time?
- Are cities good places to live?
- Do people depend on their cars too much nowadays?

2 Practise asking and answering the questions. Start by agreeing or disagreeing in general, and then mention your example.

Focus on grammar 2 *Unreal conditionals*

> ### ▶ EXAM LINK
>
> **Unreal** or **Type 2 conditionals** are a useful way of discussing solutions to problems in Task 2 of the Writing paper. They allow you to imagine an unlikely or unreal situation in the present or future and talk about possible results.

1 Look at the examples and underline the *if* or conditional clause in each case.

1 If more people travelled by public transport, there would be less traffic congestion.
2 TV companies wouldn't spend money on game shows unless they were popular.
3 If the teachers went on strike, the government might take the problem more seriously.
4 A lot of these houses could collapse if there was an earthquake.

2   Say whether the following statements are True or False.

1   The *if* clause doesn't always come first in a conditional sentence.
2   You must use a comma after the first clause in a conditional sentence.
3   *If* is not the only conjunction that can introduce a conditional clause.
4   The verb in the main clause is always *would* + infinitive.

You can check your answers by referring to the Key language bank on page 143.

3   Rewrite the following as conditional sentences.

e.g.   Public transport is quite expensive so people don't use it much.
   If public transport wasn't so expensive/was cheaper, people would use it more.

1   There isn't much cheap accommodation near the college so most students live outside the area. Use: *if*
2   I'm sorry to phone you so late but I've got some important news. Use: *unless*
3   Children behave badly in school because their parents aren't strict enough with them at home.
4   The government spends so much on the army that it can't afford to fund basic services.

> KEY LANGUAGE
> Conditionals
> ▶ p. 143

4   Change the verb in brackets into a suitable form and complete each sentence.

1   If children (take) more exercise, they …
2   Drug dealers (go) out of business if people …
3   If we (invest) more money in preventative medicine, …
4   Many more people (go) to university if …
5   If air travel (be) more expensive, …

Focus on writing 2 *Presenting the solution to a problem*

SKILLS PRACTICE

1   Study the following exam task.

> You should spend 40 minutes on this task.
>
>   Write about the following topic.
>
>   ***Many cities have become less pleasant places to live in recent years.***
>   ***What do you think are the causes of this?***
>   ***What solutions can you suggest?***
>
>   Give reasons for your answer and include any relevant examples from your own knowledge or experience.
>
> Write at least 250 words.

▶ Task 2
Organising your ideas

2 Match problems 1–5 with effects a)–l) in the list below. Some problems have two effects, others three. Fill in your answers in the <u>first</u> column in the following table.

Problems	Effect(s)	e.g.	Causes	Solutions
1 air pollution				
2 traffic congestion				
3 crime				
4 shortage of housing				
5 unfriendliness				

Effects
a) Some people feel lonely.
b) It's hard to find somewhere to live.
c) It takes a long time to travel around.
d) Elderly people don't feel safe in their homes.
e) House prices and rents are high.
f) Neighbours don't speak to each other.
g) It's hard to find anywhere to park your car.
h) Buildings, furnishings and clothing quickly become dirty.
i) People are afraid to let their children go out alone.
j) You may have to accept poor quality accommodation.
k) Some people suffer from breathing or other health problems.
l) People don't help each other.

3 Work with a partner. Discuss the causes of the problems and possible solutions. Write notes about your ideas in the <u>last two</u> columns of the table.

EXAM PRACTICE

4 Now work individually to plan your writing.

1 Think – do you have any examples of problems or effects from *your own knowledge or experience*? If so, add a tick (✔) in the <u>second</u> (e.g.) column.

2 Decide which two or three main problems to include in your essay. Choose ones you think it will be easiest to talk about and which you can illustrate with personal examples and/or experience.

WRITING PRACTICE
Task 2, Guided practice
▶ Practice 10, p. 167

3 Make a paragraph plan, decide on a suitable introduction and conclusion, then write your essay.

IELTS VOCABULARY BUILDER

Materials and structures

1 Underline the four words in the following list that describe building materials. Then match them to the definitions below.

arch	dome	span	storey
brick	foundations	steel	timber
column	plumbing	stone	tower

1 a hard, strong metal containing mainly iron and used for making things like tools and parts of buildings ....
2 a hard rectangular block of baked clay used for building ....
3 natural rock often used in building ....
4 wood or trees used for building ....

2 Circle the four words in the list that describe architectural shape. Match these to the correct diagram.

1 .... 2 .... 3 .... 4 ....

3 Match the remaining words to the following definitions.

1 the distance from one side of something to the other (e.g. a bridge) ....
2 a floor or level in a building ....
3 a solid base deep in the earth on which something is built ....
4 all the pipes that water flows through in a building ....

Pronunciation: Sounds

4 Put the following words in the correct column according to how they are pronounced. There should be five words in each column.

chief	deep	design	frame	great	heat	height	key
laid	light	metre	shape	site	type	weight	

/ei/ e.g. *date*	/ai/ e.g. *wide*	/iː/ e.g. *three*

ACADEMIC WORD STUDY 6

1   The following academic words come from the text on pages 121 and 122. Match each one with an expression which means approximately the same from the box below. If necessary, go back to the passage to see how the word is used in context.

1	**random**	*at random times* (paragraph B)
2	**data**	*interpreting the data* (D)
3	**precise**	*no precise equivalent* (D)
4	**attitude**	*a fatalistic attitude* (E)
5	**distinct**	*a distinct sense of self* (F)
6	**pursue**	*to pursue … happiness* (F)
7	**significant**	*One of the most significant observations* (G)
8	**status**	*the pursuit of status* (I)

a) exact
b) without any pattern
c) follow/try to achieve
d) social position
e) important
f) facts/information
g) clearly different
h) way of thinking

Using academic vocabulary

WORD PARTNERS

2   Match each verb 1–3 with two academic words from the list below.

> *a comment   an error   a function*
> *instructions   a task   a trend*

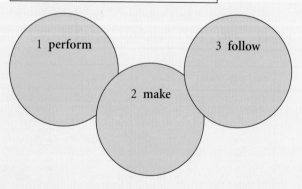

1 perform   2 make   3 follow

PREPOSITIONS

3   Complete the following sentences by adding the correct prepositions.

1   Water power can be converted .... electricity.
2   The symbols on the map correspond .... information in the Key.
3   She needs to focus more .... grammatical accuracy.
4   Conjunctions are defined .... connecting words.
5   This book must not be removed .... the library.
6   My views on the matter are similar .... yours.
7   The building was designed .... a school.
8   The study looks at different attitudes .... happiness.

SPELLING

4   The underlined words in these sentences come from earlier Academic Word Study sections but SIX of them have been wrongly spelt. Find and correct the errors.

1   It takes years for a surgeon to <u>acquire</u> the necessary skills.
2   Good <u>comunication</u> is vital in a large organisation.
3   It's a simple <u>equasion</u>: time equals money.
4   Police need to <u>estimate</u> the time of death.
5   It's difficult to <u>etablish</u> how long it will take.
6   Let me give you an <u>ilustration</u> of what I mean.
7   It's <u>obvious</u> that we need to seek expert advice.
8   I wasn't expecting a major problem to <u>ocur</u>.
9   You should only include <u>relevant</u> information.
10 I have a useful <u>tecnique</u> for learning vocabulary.

5   Choose four academic words from this page and write personal examples to help you remember them.

1   ....
2   ....
3   ....
4   ....

Check your answers on page 168 and use this page as a reference point for revision.

REVIEW 6

Grammar

SPOT THE ERROR

1 Not all the following sentences are correct. Underline the mistakes and correct them.

1 *We'll let you know as soon as we will have the results of the tests.*
2 *When I finish my degree, I'm planning to start my own business.*
3 *The hotel has a large swimming pool shaped as a circular.*
4 *The Golden Gate Bridge is made with steel and concrete. It has single span of 1,280 m.*
5 *The course consists of four modules, each lasting one month.*
6 *The museum will have to close unless more money can be found to run it.*
7 *If petrol cost more, fewer people will buy cars, and they will also use their cars less.*
8 *I do not think that people will stop to use private cars because public transport it is often is expensive and crowded also.*

MISSING WORDS

2 There are <u>ten</u> words missing from the following text. Mark the place where the word is missing and write the answers in the spaces below. The first has been done as an example.

Emperor Tenno Shomu, who ruled Japan/724 to 749, was responsible building the Hall of the Great Buddha. The temple is 45 m height and 68 m long, and it took thousands of workers more twenty years to complete. Inside the impressive building is the country's most important sculpture, colossal bronze statue of Buddha, is approximately 15 m high. The statue contains 444 tonnes of bronze as well considerable quantities of mercury and gold. According Japanese historians, the completion of the statue exhausted some of country's copper reserves and also forced the Emperor's subjects pay high taxes.

1 *from*   6 ....
2 .... 7 ....
3 .... 8 ....
4 .... 9 ....
5 .... 10 ....

Vocabulary

WORD BUILDING

3 Use the word given in capitals at the end of each line to form a word that fits the space. Make sure your answer fits grammatically as well as logically.

1 This idiomatic language is .... in such a formal letter.   APPROPRIATE
2 The government has promised to reduce the level of ....   EMPLOY
3 They had great .... in finding a suitable office.   DIFFICULT
4 The problem with the job was that the hours were ....   FLEXIBLE
5 Job .... is more important to me than money.   SATISFY
6 The country is facing an .... crisis.   ECONOMY
7 There has been a rapid .... in online banking.   GROW

Exam skills

4 Complete each piece of advice 1–8 with an expression a)–h) below.

a) question   e) topic area
b) specific information   f) word limit
c) reasons   g) skimming skills
d) mindplan   h) answers

1 To find out what a reading passage is about, use ....
2 One key reading skill is locating ....
3 When you express an opinion in the interview, don't forget to give ....
4 You can make a listening task easier by studying the questions in advance and thinking about possible ....
5 Use separate paragraphs to write about each main ....
6 A good way to prepare for Part 2 of the interview is to prepare a ....
7 Don't begin a report using the same words as the ....
8 Read the instructions for listening tasks carefully and underline any ....

137

An Introduction to the Academic Word List

Averil Coxhead, Massey University, New Zealand

What is the Academic Word List?

The Academic Word List (AWL) is a list of 570 word families that are commonly found in academic texts. This list was selected by examining a large corpus (or collection) of written academic texts and selecting the words that occurred.

The AWL includes vocabulary that occurs most often in written academic texts. These words also occur in newspapers but not as often as they do in textbooks. The AWL words appear even less in fiction.

Why is the AWL important?

The AWL is intended as a reference for students who are studying or preparing to study at a tertiary level in English. The AWL does not include 'content' vocabulary but focuses instead on the non-subject-specific vocabulary that students of any discipline will need to master in order to produce coherently-structured written assignments.

Averil Coxhead is a lecturer in English for Academic Purposes at Massey University, Palmerston North, New Zealand. She compiled the AWL in 2000. For further information on the AWL go to Averil's website at http://language.massey.ac.nz/staff/awl/index.shtml

On the right is a list of words from the AWL which are included in the Academic Word Study sections in *Focus on IELTS Foundation*. The relevant page number is shown beside the word.

Below is an extract from the *Longman Exams Dictionary* which highlights all words from the AWL in blue.

ac·a·dem·ic AC WC / ˌækəˈdemɪk / adj ◂
1 [usually before noun] relating to education, especially at college or university level OPP **non-academic:** *He possessed no academic qualifications.* | *a program to raise academic standards* | *Between 1980 and 1987 the number of academic staff in British universities declined by 12 percent.* | *a major research resource for the academic community* ▸▸**Topic Activator** HIGHER EDUCATION
2 [usually before noun] concerned with studying from books, as opposed to practical work: *the study of art as an academic discipline*
3 good at studying OPP **unacademic:** *He's not very academic.*
4 if a discussion about something is academic, it's a waste of time because the speakers cannot change the existing situation: *The question of where to go on holiday is **purely academic** since we don't have any money.* **–academically** /-kli/ adv: *academically gifted children*

AWL words featured in this book

academic *adj*	26
access *v/n*	92
(in)accurate *adj*	92
achieve *v*	70, 92
acquire (v require) *v*	114, 136
affect *v*	70
alternative (to) *n*	114
analyse *v*	92
aspect (v prospect) *n*	114
assist *v*	26, 92
attitude (towards) *n*	136
available *adj*	48
(un)aware *adj*	92
benefit (from) v	92
challenge *n*	70
comment *n*	136
comment (on) *v*	114
communication *n*	48, 136
compensate (for) *v*	114
component *n*	70
concentrate (on) *v*	114
conclusion *n*	70
consequence *n*	70
consist (of)	48, 92
(in)consistent *adj*	92
constant(ly) *adj/adv*	70
construct *v*	26
contribute *v*	92
contribution *n*	114
convert (into) *v*	136
correspond (with) *v*	136
crucial *adj*	70, 92
data *n*	92
decade *n*	70
define (as) *v*	136
definition *n*	48
demonstration	48
design (as) *v*	136
despite *prep*	48

► Key language bank

Adverbs (Unit 2, p. 19)

USE

Adverbs can be used with verbs, adjectives and also other adverbs.

ADVERBS OF TIME AND FREQUENCY

NB See table showing the positions of the most common frequency expressions on page 19.

- One-word time and frequency adverbs plus *hardly ever* normally go before the main verb, e.g. *My sister recently had a baby. It often rains in July.*
- One-word time and frequency adverbs plus *hardly ever* normally follow forms of the verb *be*, e.g. *She's hardly ever late. I'm still nervous before I give a speech.*
- Longer time and frequency expressions normally go to the end of the clause, e.g. *I go to the cinema once a week.*

ADVERBS OF PLACE AND MANNER

- Adverbs of place and manner normally go at the end of a clause. e.g. *She likes reading in bed. He explained everything clearly.*

ADVERBS OF DEGREE

- Adverbs of degree are used to say something is more or less than normal. e.g. *The situation is **extremely** serious.* The most common adverbs of degree are: *completely, extremely, fairly, highly, quite, seriously, severely, slightly, totally, very*

1 In each of the groups of words below, underline the word or expression which shows the highest frequency i.e. the one that means the most often.

 0 sometimes/never/<u>generally</u>

 1 now and then/often/seldom
 2 occasionally/hardly ever/normally
 3 frequently/rarely/sometimes
 4 every Monday/every other day/twice a week
 5 once in a while/every so often/regularly

2 Re-order the sentences below, choosing the correct position for the adverb.

 1 **hardly ever**/Ian/his vocabulary/revises
 2 who want to take/**extremely**/The number of people/has increased/the exam/**rapidly**
 3 a conventional dictionary/Ayumi/to/using/an electronic dictionary/prefers/**normally**
 4 I/**rarely**/to the radio/my listening skills/listen/I'm afraid/to improve
 5 announcement/**yet**/hasn't been/of the election/There/any/about/the date
 6 discuss/our two countries/the differences/We/between/**often**
 7 too/fast/**automatically**/lights up/The warning sign/you/approach
 8 You/**always**/carefully/in the IELTS test/must/read the questions

3 Choose adverbs from the list below to complete the following sentences. There may be more than one correct answer.

extremely fairly fully highly relatively seriously slightly strongly

 1 The situation is .... serious and we need to act immediately.
 2 They are .... opposed to the new law.
 3 There are only a few .... unimportant details to clear up.
 4 It's .... unlikely that the building will be finished on time.
 5 Sales have only been .... better than average.
 6 Fortunately nobody was .... injured in the accident.
 7 I .... understand your problem.
 8 The virus is .... dangerous to humans.

► JUST REMEMBER

Adverbs of degree are fairly common in academic texts. Using appropriate adverbs like *slightly*, *fully* or *highly* in your writing for the IELTS test will help you express yourself more precisely and will also increase your vocabulary range, which is taken into account in marking.

Articles (Unit 4, p. 44, Unit 11, p. 124)

FORM AND USE

Articles (*a/an/the/zero article*) go before nouns and noun phrases. The choice of article depends on the type of noun and also the context.

	Countable nouns		Uncountable nouns
	singular	plural	
a/an	✓	✗	✗
no article	✗	✓	✓
the	✓	✓	✓

a/an (indefinite article)

- to talk about something for the first time, e.g. *A new law has been introduced.*
- to describe something that is one of many, e.g. *London is a big city.*

the (definite article)

- to talk about something already mentioned, e.g. *The law will stop people smoking in public.*
- to describe something specific, e.g. *The pollution in the river is terrible.* (specific) **but** *Pollution is a problem.* (in general)
- when it is clear what we are talking about, either from the context or because it is the only one, e.g. *I'm going to the library.*
- for oceans, rivers, mountain ranges, plural countries and countries which have a noun in their name, e.g. *The Pacific, the Alps, the Czech Republic*
- with superlatives, e.g. *the oldest, the best*

no article (zero article)

- with plural and uncountable nouns to talk about things in general, e.g. *Pets help people relax.*
- with most names of people, places, countries, cities, streets, single mountains and lakes, e.g. *I grew up in Oman.*

Special cases
Look at the use of the zero and definite articles in the following situations:

- meals, e.g. *have lunch/dinner/breakfast*
- travel, e.g. *travel by bus/plane/on foot*
- times of day – *at night/lunchtime/midday/ten o'clock* **but** *in the morning/in the evening*
- days, months, seasons – *on Thursday/in June/in winter*

- institutions, e.g. *to go to prison* (you've done something wrong), *to go to school* (to study), *to go to hospital* (as a patient) **but** *He works at the prison. She lives opposite the hospital.*
- double expressions, e.g. *year after year, little by little, day and night, head to foot*
- other fixed phrases, e.g. *at/from home, at/to/from work, by post/email, in/to bed, in debt*

INDEFINITE OR DEFINITE?

1 **Complete the sentences with either *a/an* or *the*.**

1 .... number of students taking .... English language exam in the UK is increasing every year.
2 When I started university I met .... amazing girl called Kate who lived in .... same hall as me.
3 In Britain and Japan you have to drive on .... left-hand side of .... road.
4 .... vet is .... person who looks after sick animals.
5 We had .... accident on our way to meet .... Prime Minister.

DEFINITE OR ZERO?

2 **In the following sentences, cross out any incorrect uses of *the*.**

0 Mathieu lives in ~~the~~ Lyon.

1 I hope to study at the college, either in my country or overseas.
2 The Internet and the computers are essential for everyday life.
3 The professor who teaches us French is excellent.
4 The Everest is the biggest mountain in the world.
5 I've been working at the cinema since last Tuesday night.

3 **Add *a/an, the* or – (zero article) in the spaces below.**

1 .... 2012 Olympic Games will be held in
2 .... London, it has recently been decided.
3 .... committee of people representing different countries took several months to narrow down
4 .... choice of potential venues to Madrid, Paris and London. On 5 .... final day of the bids, famous people from each location spoke about

why their city was **6** .... best. It was **7** ....
close competition but just after **8** .... midday,
London came out on top. Among **9** .... different
projects, **10** .... huge stadium will be built in
11 .... area of South London, providing
12 .... new jobs and much needed regeneration.
Tony Blair, **13** .... Prime Minister, said he was
delighted by **14** .... decision and is confident
15 .... 2012 Olympics will be one of **16** ....
most successful ever.

Comparison (Unit 6, p. 66)

FORM AND USE

adj/adv + -er + than …

	comparative	superlative
Adjectives and adverbs of one syllable: *cheap, fast*	…*-er than*	*(the) …-est*
Adjectives and adverbs of two or more syllables: *relaxed, easily*	*more … than* *less … than*	*(the) most* *(the) least*
Irregular forms: *good, bad, little, much*	*better* *worse* *less* *more*	*(the) best* *(the) worst* *(the) least* *(the) most*

Notes
- One- and two-syllable adjectives ending in *–y* change to *-ier/-iest*, e.g. *dry: drier/driest; happy: happier/happiest*
- When a one-syllable adjective ends in a single vowel and consonant, the final consonant is doubled, e.g. *big: bigger/biggest*
- We use comparative forms to compare one noun or action with another, e.g. *The IELTS Listening module is shorter than the Writing module.*
- We use the superlative form when we are comparing one noun or action with the whole group that it belongs to, e.g. *The Nile is the longest river in the world.*
- We use *much* or *a lot* to make the comparative stronger, e.g. *The new medicine is much more effective than the old one.*

as … + adj/adv + as

- We use the *as … as …* structure to show equal comparison, e.g. *Cheetahs can run as fast as a car.*
- We use the *not so … as …* as structure to show unequal comparison, e.g. *Living in the countryside is not as expensive as living in a city.*
- We can also use the *as … as* structure to make numerical comparisons, e.g. *Nearly twice as much pollution is produced today as it was in 1970.* (See the Essential language box page 87.)

▶ JUST REMEMBER

There are two main comparative structures and it's important not to mix them up. **-er** structures are followed by **than**; **as** + **adjective** is followed by **as**. Avoid common mistakes, e.g. NOT *The bus ~~doesn't cost as much than~~ the train.*

FORMING COMPARISONS

1 Expand the notes into complete sentences using suitable comparative and superlative forms or (*not*) *as … as.*

0 Whale/large/dolphin
 e.g. *A whale is larger than a dolphin.*

1 Playing football/not dangerous/playing ice hockey.
2 Desert/much dry/rainforest.
3 River Nile/long/river/in Africa.
4 Some people learn languages/easily/others.
5 Law/popular/university course in the UK.
6 Adult dogs usually/behave well/puppies.

DESCRIBING A GRAPH

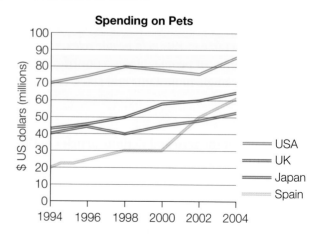

Spending on Pets

142

2 Complete the description of the graph on the opposite page using the adjective/adverb given and a suitable comparison structure.

The graph shows the amount of money spent on pets in the UK, the USA, Japan and Spain between 1994 and 2004.

In 1994 Spain spent **1** .... (little) amount of money on pets, while Japan and the UK spent about **2** .... (much) each other. However, by 2000, the gap in spending between these two countries had widened and considerably **3** .... (much) money was spent in the UK .... in Japan.

The amount spent increased in all four countries but rose **4** .... (dramatically) in Spain. In 2004 the Spanish spent **5** .... (three times/much) money .... they did in 1994.

However, during this ten-year period, the USA remained **6** .... (big) spenders on pets, with all three other countries spending **7** .... (little) on them.

Conditionals (Unit 11, p. 118, Unit 12, p. 132)

FORM AND USE

Conditional sentences consist of an *if* clause (beginning with *if/when/unless*) and a main clause.

TYPE 0

if clause	Main clause
if/when + present form	present form or imperative or *can/should*

- to describe general truths; processes, e.g. *When you add acid to blue litmus paper, it turns red.*
- to give an instruction, e.g. *If the alarm sounds, leave the building immediately.*

TYPE 1 (REAL)

if clause	Main clause
if/unless + present form	future form or *can/should/might* + infinitive

- to describe a condition that is possible in the future, e.g. *If you don't slow down, you'll have an accident. I won't call you unless I have a problem.*

TYPE 2 (UNREAL PRESENT AND FUTURE)

if clause	Main clause
if/unless + past simple or progressive	*would/could/might* + infinitive

- to describe a present or future event which is possible but is much less likely to happen than Type 1, e.g. *Crime rates could be reduced if there were more police on the streets.* (it is unlikely there will be more police)
- to talk about unreal situations or events, e.g. *Britain would be a much nicer place to live if it didn't rain so much.* (it is unlikely it will rain less)
- We sometimes use *were* instead of *was* in the *if* clause, especially in more formal speech and writing, e.g. *If the weather were better, Britain would be a nicer place to live.*
- The phrase *If I were you* is a common way of introducing advice, e.g. *If I were you, I'd write and complain.*

TYPE 3 (UNREAL PAST)

if clause	Main clause
if/unless + past perfect	*would/could/might* + have + past participle

- to imagine the result if past events had been different, e.g. *If I hadn't passed my school certificate, I couldn't have gone to college.*

Notes
- Either the *if* clause or the main clause can come first in the sentence but when the *if* clause comes first, it must be followed by a comma. Compare these examples:
  If you have a question, raise your hand.
  Raise your hand if you have a question.
- Present forms include present and present perfect tenses (simple and progressive).
- Time clauses after *when, before, after, as soon as* and *until* follow the rules for type 1 conditionals e.g. *You can't ask questions after the exam has started.*

1 Match the *if* clauses 1–6 with the correct endings a)–f). Say which type of conditional each completed sentence is, 0, 1 or 2.

1 If you miss the bus,
2 When the water level is high,
3 If the price of oil fell,
4 Unless the rains come soon,
5 If more people protested,
6 If my computer was working,

a) there is the risk of flooding.
b) the crops will die.
c) you could use it.
d) the government might pay attention.
e) there won't be another one for an hour.
f) more people would be able to afford central heating.

TYPE 2 CONDITIONALS

2 Expand the notes below to make 'unreal' (Type 2) conditional sentences. Make any changes to the verbs that are necessary.

1 government/spend more money on public transport/it/be more reliable
2 public transport/more reliable/more people/use it regularly
3 parents/give teenagers more freedom/they/fewer arguments
4 many more species of animal/become extinct/ they/not protected by law.
5 countries like the USA/stop producing high quantities of carbon dioxide/climate change/ not/be so rapid.
6 easier/give up smoking/cigarettes/not/so addictive

TYPE 3 CONDITIONALS

3 Imagine that the following past situations had been different and make Type 3 conditional sentences describing the result.

0 I couldn't take a holiday because I didn't have any money:
   e.g. *If I'd had some money, I would have taken a holiday.*

1 He didn't pass his driving test because he didn't practise enough.
2 The weather was terrible so we came home early.

3 I missed my flight because I lost my passport.
4 The traffic was so heavy that I was an hour late.
5 I lost my lottery ticket so I couldn't claim the prize.
6 I first met my husband-to-be at a party.

Countability

USE

There are two types of noun:

- **Countable nouns** describe things that can be counted. They have both a singular and plural form, which may be regular (+*s*), e.g. *job/jobs, school/schools* or irregular, e.g. *foot/feet, fish/fish*
- **Uncountable nouns** describe materials and abstract qualities, which cannot be counted. They have just one form, cannot be used with *a/an*, and usually take a singular verb, e.g. *information, water, health*

It is important to know whether a noun is countable or uncountable so you can use the correct verb form, singular or plural. But there are some nouns which can be both depending on the context or meaning. Look at these examples:

Tennis is a sport (one example) but *Sport is good for your health* .(in general)
He reads the paper every day. (= a newspaper) but *Paper is produced from wood.* (= the material)
Coffee is grown in Central America. (the substance) but *Would you like a coffee?* (an offer of a drink)

QUANTIFIERS

There are three main considerations when choosing a quantifier: grammar, meaning and formality.

Plural countable	Uncountable	Both
few, a few, not many, many, a large number of, a great many, every one of	*little, a little, not much, much, a large amount of, a great deal of*	*no, hardly any, a lack of, some, a lot of, most, all kinds of, all*
too many (i.e. more than the right amount)	*too much* (i.e. more than the right amount)	*not enough* (i.e. less than the right amount) *any* (used in negative sentences and most questions)

Notes

- *little/few* – have a negative meaning, suggesting 'not as much/many as we would like', they are also more formal, e.g. *We were given little information. Few people attended the meeting.*
- *a little/a few* – have a more positive meaning, similar to 'some', e.g. *There was a little rain in the morning. They were a few minutes late.*
- *both/neither/either* – are used to talk about two people or things, e.g. *Both Jay and Bilen live in Bristol.* (true for both) *Neither Cardiff nor Manchester has an underground railway.* (negative for both) *The shop takes either cash or credit cards.* (one or the other)
- *a little of/a few of/both of/neither of/all of* – are used with a pronoun/determiner + noun, e.g. *A few of us are going to the cinema tonight. A little of the money was spent on books, but most was used to buy new computers.*
- *all* – takes a plural/uncountable noun, e.g. *All children have to attend school*
- *every/each* – take a singular noun. *Each* is used for two or more people or things and suggests we are thinking of them separately; *every* is used for groups of three or more when our focus is the whole group, e.g. *Every child has the right to education; each member of the club has a locker.*

COUNTABLE OR UNCOUNTABLE?

1 Write the following nouns in the correct column. For each countable noun, write its plural form.

advice animal building child decade equipment facility happiness idea machine money pollution person petrol rubbish student tourism traffic tree weather

Countable	Uncountable

QUANTIFIERS

2 For each sentence below choose the most suitable quantifier.

1 Unfortunately, *a few/few* people were willing to support the project.

2 A large *amount/number* of rubbish *was/were* left after the protest.

3 *Every/All* book *was/were* destroyed in the fire.

4 Can I give you *little/a little* advice? Make time for *some/any* relaxation during your studies.

5 It would cost too *many/much* money to give *all/every* members a free ticket.

6 *Either/Both* Monday or Friday *is/are* OK for me.

7 There *was/were* a great deal of/a great many people at the meeting.

8 He has had *hardly any/a little time* off work recently and he's exhausted.

9 We haven't got *a large number of/much* choice about the matter.

10 *All/Most* people agree that global warming is a serious problem.

Expressing the future

There are several ways of expressing the future in English. The form we use may depend on how sure we feel that an event will happen, or whether we are talking about a personal intention or not. It often depends on the speaker's attitude to the event as well as how near or certain it is to the present.

FORM AND USE

The most common future forms are:

going to + **infinitive without** *to*

going to is used to talk about:

- a planned future event, e.g. *The Prime Minister is going to visit Egypt next month.*
- a personal intention, e.g. *I'm going to buy a dictionary tomorrow.*
- a prediction based on evidence, e.g. *This is going to be a difficult problem to solve.*

NB *going to* is generally less formal than *will*.

will/won't + **infinitive without** *to*

The **future simple** is used to talk about

- a future fact, e.g. *The planet will continue to get hotter unless we do something about pollution.*
- an opinion about the future, especially after verbs like *think, suppose, expect, doubt,* e.g. *I expect university fees will rise next year.*
- an unplanned event, e.g. *I'll give you an example.*

Present progressive
- for an arranged future action, e.g. *I'm leaving tomorrow.*

Present simple
- for a fixed future event, usually based on a timetable or programme, e.g. *The exam starts at 2 p.m. tomorrow.*

Notes
- See page 119 for notes on the use of present tenses with future reference in *if* and time clauses and for other useful expressions for discussing future plans.

1 Change the verbs in brackets into the correct future form and make any other necessary changes.

1   I need a good grade, so I (study) really hard.
2   The next exam (take) place on 15 September.
3   Smoking in public places (be) illegal in the near future.
4   I (see) my tutor at 5 p.m. to discuss my essay.
5   I doubt if there (be) any elephants left in a few years.
6   According to the weather forecast, it (rain) all week.
7   By 2025, the number of cars on the road (double).
8   If you don't train, you (have) any chance in the marathon.
9   The leaders of the G8 countries (meet) tomorrow in Geneva.
10   If we don't do something about deforestation, many species of animal (disappear) forever.

Modal verbs (Unit 8, p. 83)

Modal verbs are used with main verbs to express an attitude, such as: ability or prohibition. The main modal verbs are: *must, should, can, could, will, would, may, might.*

FORM
Modal verbs:
- are followed by the infinitive without *to*, e.g. *You must work hard.*
- do not take *-s* on the third person, e.g. *He should stop smoking.*
- form questions without *do*, e.g. *Can we go now?*
- have no past form
- have no infinitive. Other forms are used instead, e.g. *Will you* **be able to** *attend?* NOT ~~Will you can attend?~~

▶ JUST REMEMBER

The modal verbs *can, could, may* and *might* are a useful way of expressing a cautious opinion in academic writing, where *is* or *will* might sound too definite, e.g. *For all its problems, nuclear energy might be the only way forward.*

USE
Not all modal verbs can be used with all tenses. Look at the examples with the verb *go* in the table below.

Notes
- To express a specific past achievement, we use **was able to** ..., e.g. *My son could ski when he was six.* (general ability) *Fortunately, we were able to swim to the shore.* (specific achievement).

Modal verbs are used to show:

	Present	**Past**	**Future**
ability or permission	*can go*	*could go* (general ability)	*will be able to go*
probability (**sure → less sure**)	*can* *could* *must* *might* *may* + *go*	*could* *must* *might* *may* + *have gone*	*can* *could* *must* *might* *may* + *go*
obligation	*must/have to go*	*had to go*	*will have to go*
prohibition	*can't/mustn't go*	*couldn't go/had to stay*	*won't be able to go/will have to stay*
absence of obligation	*don't have to go*	*didn't have to go*	*won't have to stay*
advice	*should/shouldn't go*	*should/shouldn't have gone*	*should/shouldn't go*

- *have to* is modal in meaning (obligation) but not in form. It forms questions and negatives with *do* and has an infinitive and past form.

Other structures

It is possible to express the meaning of most modal verbs by using other vocabulary instead. Usually this makes the sentence more formal in style. Look at the examples below:

- *You **can** take the exam more than once./Taking the exam more than once **is allowed/permitted.***
- *You **must/have to** bring identification to the exam./It **is compulsory** to bring identification to the exam.*
- *You **can't/mustn't** use a dictionary./Using a dictionary **isn't allowed/permitted.**/Using a dictionary **is forbidden/prohibited.***

1 Each of the following sentences contains a mistake. Find the error and correct it.

0 I <u>can't</u> finish the homework yesterday.
→ *couldn't*

1 A referee of a physical sport have to be brave.
2 In the future we will must find alternative sources of energy.
3 You should to study very hard for the exam.
4 In the past only men can go to university.
5 European students haven't to have a visa to study in the UK.

2 Select the more appropriate modal verb to complete the sentences below.

1 You ***don't have to/mustn't*** use a mobile phone in a hospital.
2 In a few years time we'***ll be able to/should*** buy more powerful computers.
3 Everyone ***can/should*** clean their teeth at least twice a day.
4 I ***was able to/could*** complete all the questions in the last practice test in an hour.
5 You ***don't have to/mustn't*** have a visa to enter the country.

3 Using the words given, complete the second sentence so it has the same meaning as the first.

0 You mustn't use your mobile phone in lessons. (permitted)
It is not permitted to use mobile phones in class.

1 You can't talk in the library. (forbidden)
Talking ....

2 In some countries you must wear a cycle helmet. (compulsory)
It is ....

3 You aren't allowed to walk on the grass. (prohibited)
Walking ....

4 You are not allowed to use flash photography in the museum. (forbidden)
Flash photography ....

5 You have to have a passport to travel abroad. (permitted)
Travelling ....

Parts of speech

It is important to recognise the main parts of speech in English and understand how they work because this will help you:

- work out the meaning of unfamiliar words in reading passages of the IELTS Reading module.
- use a dictionary more effectively to increase your vocabulary knowledge.

	Definition	Examples
noun	a person, place, thing (real or abstract)	*David, Malta, pencil, happiness*
noun phrase	a group of words which can act as a subject or object in a sentence	*the motor industry, a science student*
verb	an action or state	*study, have*
adjective	describes a noun	*yellow, small*
adverb	describes when, where, or how something happens	*today, here, slowly,*
pronoun	can replace a noun	*she, it, himself, her*
article	used before nouns	*a, an, the*
preposition	used with a noun to tell us about place, direction, time, etc.	*on, at, behind*
conjunction	used to join words and clauses together	*and, so, if*

1 Say which part of speech the underlined words in the text below are.

0 <u>An</u> = *article*

<u>An</u>[0] increasing number of warm water marine fish and mammals are being spotted off the coast of <u>Britain</u>[1] according to <u>new</u>[2] research.

<u>A survey by university biologists</u>[3] suggests warmer water in the North Sea <u>is encouraging</u>[4] visits from species <u>normally</u>[5] found in more southern seas. More than 600 <u>sightings</u>[6] of dolphins and whales were recorded in a year-long study <u>by</u>[7] Newcastle University.

<u>Although</u>[8] local residents are by delighted the newcomers, scientists are concerned by the <u>potential</u>[9] long-term changes to <u>the</u>[10] ecosystem. <u>They</u>[11] warn that <u>native cold water fish</u>[12] are in danger of losing their habitat <u>if</u>[13] the temperatures <u>continue</u>[14] to rise.

Passive (Unit 7, p. 77)

FORM

be + past participle

Present simple	*is/are found*
Present progressive	*is/are being found*
Past simple	*was/were found*
Past progressive	*was/were being found*
Present perfect	*has/have been found*
Past perfect	*had been found*
Future simple	*will be found*
Modal verb (e.g. *can, would, might*)	*can be found*

The passive voice changes the object of the verb into the subject of the sentence. Look at these examples:

Active: *Scientists have found two new species of insect.*

Passive: *Two new species of insect have been found (by scientists).*

USE

The passive is more common in formal English and occurs frequently in academic texts.

The passive voice is used:

- when the agent (i.e. the person or people doing the action) is unknown or is less important than the object or action, e.g. *Diamonds have been mined in South Africa for many years.*
- when the agent is understood from the context or refers to 'people in general', e.g. *Performance in the exam is rated on a scale of 0–9.* (by the examiner – we know without being told) *Coffee is drunk all over the world.* (by people in general)
- to say who the agent is, we use *by* (e.g. *by scientists*). It is common not to include the agent in academic writing.

▶ **JUST REMEMBER**

The following passive stuctures can help give your written English a more academic style. They are a good way at avoiding sentences beginning *I think …* or *People …*

It is often said that …
It is generally agreed that …
It is sometimes argued that …

ACTIVE OR PASSIVE?

1 Decide whether the verb forms in the sentences below are active (A) or passive (P). Underline the verb form in each case and write A or P next to it.

1 The National Gallery has recently bought a large oil painting by Van Gogh.
2 The painting has been hung in the large entrance hall.
3 Visits to the museum are expected to double in the coming weeks as people flock to see the new piece.
4 Van Gogh was not successful during his lifetime.
5 It was only after his death that his talent was recognised.
6 His painting 'Sunflowers' was sold for a record-breaking sum by the London auction house, Sotheby's.

2 Complete each of the following facts about ice cream using a passive construction. Choose from the verbs below.

allow employ make produce say sell sell call

1 More than 500 ice cream flavours .... commercially by the food industry. They include garlic and oriental spiced curry. However, 90% of all ice creams which .... in the shops are vanilla-flavoured.
2 The average British ice cream .... of 50% air, 33% water and no milk.
3 There are more than 1,000 ice cream companies in Britain and the business .... to be worth more than £1 billion a year.
4 A team of workers .... at Ben and Jerry's ice cream factory in the USA to go round telling jokes and making the other staff laugh. They .... the Joy Gang.
5 The dancers of the Bolshoi Ballet .... to eat ice cream because it's too fattening.
6 Special ice creams for dogs .... in US supermarkets.

3 Complete the text below by changing the verbs in brackets into the passive. Make sure that you use the most appropriate tense.

In the past very little **0** *was known* (know) about the problems of waste disposal. It **1** .... (assume) that we could carry on making waste and burning it or burying it in the ground. However, the damage that **2** .... (do) to our environment in recent years by such behaviour **3** .... (now know).

New laws mean that rubbish cannot simply **4** .... (throw away). The quantities of waste sent to landfill sites have to **5** .... (reduce) or councils **6** .... (fine) by the Government. Many local councils now provide recycling schemes so that materials such as waste paper and plastic **7** .... (take away) and **8** .... (use) again.

Every year 3% more waste **9** .... (create) by the UK, so as well as recycling, it is important that we try to reduce our waste too.

Past perfect

FORM

	Simple *had* + past participle	Progressive *had* + *been* + present participle
+	*I had finished …*	*She had been talking …*
−	*They hadn't begun …*	*We hadn't been working …*
?	*Had you seen …?*	*Had it been raining …?*

USE

We use the **past perfect simple**:

- to make it clear that an action was completed before another past action started, e.g. *I had just finished high school when I met my friend Iva.*
- to explain a past situation, e.g. *I felt confident at the interview because I had prepared thoroughly.*
- in reported speech, where the past simple and the present perfect in the original words are changed to past perfect, e.g. *'We've had useful talks'. The president said they had had useful talks.*

We use the **past perfect progressive**:

- when the first action continued for a period of time or was not finished, e.g. *They had been studying for hours when the phone rang.*

We just use the past simple for both actions when:

- The order of events is clear from the context, e.g. *Women were not able to vote until 1918, when the law changed.*
- The second action happens very quickly after the first or is a result of the first, e.g. *We stopped work when the fire bell rang.*

> ▶ **JUST REMEMBER**
>
> One use of the past perfect that is important to remember for Writing Task 1 is **by** + past time, e.g. *By 2000, sales had risen to 1 million.*

1 Four of these sentences contain errors in verb forms. Find the mistakes and correct them.

1 I didn't visit the university before I applied to study there.
2 The reduction in student fees hadn't happen when I started university.
3 The lecture already started by the time we arrived.

4   The price of oil had been fallen steadily until 2004.
5   Many people hadn't been flying before the low-cost airlines started offering cheap flights.

2   Complete the following sentences by putting the verb given into the past perfect simple/progressive or past simple tense.

0   When she _died_ (die), Mrs Liu _had been_ (be) married for 86 years.

1   Fatima .... (be) worried because she .... (not remember) to do her homework.
2   I .... (realise) I .... (lost) my key when I .... (get) home.
3   The driver .... (drive) for eight hours when the accident .... (happen).
4   .... Clemence .... (learn) English before she .... (come) to the UK?
5   The class .... (not begin) when they .... (arrive).
6   The average number of people per family .... (fall) to under five by 1890.
7   House prices .... (rise) steadily for 18 months so the bank .... (decide) to raise interest rates.
8   Tatiana .... (not meet) Tetsuya before they .... (start) college together.

Past simple (Unit 3, p. 32)

FORM

	Regular e.g. *work*	**Irregular** e.g. *begin*
+	*I worked …*	*She began …*
−	*They didn't work …*	*We didn't begin …*
?	*Did you work?* *When did you work?*	*Did it begin?* *When did it begin?*

	to be
+	*I was there.* *They were there.*
−	*I wasn't there.* *They weren't there*
?	*Were you there?* *When were you there?*

Many <u>common</u> English verbs, including some useful ones for Writing Task 1, are irregular, so it's important to try and learn them.

USE

• to talk about an action that was completed before now, e.g. *I finished high school in 2000.*
• to show the order of past events, e.g. *I stayed in London for a few weeks before I came to Bristol.*

Spelling Tip!
Some regular verbs ending in *-y* have a spelling change in the present and past simple endings. The rules are:
• e.g. *enjoy* → *enjoys, enjoyed*
  If the letter before the *-y* is a vowel (*a,e,i,o,u*), we keep the *-y*.
• e.g. *study* → *studies, studied*
  If the letter before the *-y* is not a vowel, we change *-y* to *-i*.

Watch out! *say* is irregular! *say* → *said* → *said*

TIME EXPRESSIONS

Time expressions often need a preposition before them. The most common are *at*, *in* and *on*.

at +		*on* +
time (*7.30*) festivals (*Ramadan*) *night, the weekend, midday, midnight, the beginning/end of the year/ month*		day (*Saturday*) date (*24th June*)
in +		**no preposition**
month (*April*) year (*2001*) season (*winter*) time of day (*the morning*)		*last/next*, this/that, every/all (day, week, year, etc.)

1   Complete the sentences by changing the verb in brackets into the past simple. Be careful, some verbs are irregular.

1   Sickness rates .... (go up) last month.
2   .... the cost of childcare .... (fall) at the start of the year?
3   I .... (not/leave) school until I .... (be) 18.
4   When .... you .... (start) learning Hindi?
5   The mechanic .... (fix) my car very quickly.

6 The flu .... (not/spread) as fast as they .... (believe) it would.

7 What .... her job at the restaurant .... (involve)?

8 He .... (can/not) find a job for many months.

SPELLING

2 Change the following verbs into their 3rd person present simple form and their past simple form.

enjoy	enjoys	enjoyed	study		
carry			stay		
marry			try		
say			worry		

TIME EXPRESSIONS

3 Put the following time expressions into the preposition table below.

Monday   midday   all year   next week   26th May every day   New Year   2006   the summer the weekend   January   last weekend   the evening my birthday

at	on	in	no preposition

4 Each of the sentences below contains an error. Find it and correct the sentence.

1 The number of dentists rised last year.
2 Stress caused 10% of sickness at 1997.
3 I studied English and French last year.
4 When he worked in a factory, he didn't got paid very much.
5 Why didn't the employees be happy?

Present perfect (Unit 5, p. 54)

FORM

	Simple *have/has* + past participle	Progressive *have/has* + been + present participle
+	*They have walked.*	*He has been walking.*
–	*She hasn't walked.*	*We haven't been walking.*
Yes/No ?	*Have you ever run a marathon? (Yes, I have./No, I haven't.)*	*Has he been studying at college? (Yes, he has./No, he hasn't.)*
Wh- ?	*Which countries have you visited?*	*How long has he been playing tennis?*

USE

The **present perfect** is used when there is a strong link between the past and the present. We use it to talk about:

- an action or state that began in the past and still continues, e.g. *I've been doing karate since I was five.*
- a recent past action with a present result or effect, e.g. *The price of petrol has gone up 5%.*
- a past action or event, when the time is not given or is not important, e.g. *Ahmed has won many trophies for swimming.* If we want to say when exactly, we need to use the past simple, e.g. *Ahmed won many trophies for swimming between 1990 and 2000.*

Notes

- The **present perfect progressive** is used to talk about an action which is incomplete or temporary, or when the results can be seen, e.g. *I've been jogging (that's why I'm so hot).*
- Stative verbs are not normally used in the present perfect progressive. For a list of common stative verbs see page 153.

▶ **JUST REMEMBER**

DON'T use the present perfect to talk about past events when the time is mentioned or when it is understood, e.g. *I had an interview last week* (NOT *I've had an interview last week*); *We exchanged phone numbers when we met* (NOT *... when we've met*).

BEEN V GONE

- *gone* refers to an incomplete trip, e.g. *They've gone to France.* (they're not here)
- *been* refers to a complete round trip, e.g. *They've been to France.* (and are back again)

FOR AND SINCE

The present perfect is often used to show how long a situation has continued, e.g. *I've known her for ten years. I've lived here since 2000.*

- *for* is used with a period of time e.g. *six months, two years, a long time,* etc.
- *since* is used with a point in time e.g. *1997, 5 o'clock, I was a child,* etc.

EVER/NEVER/ALREADY/YET

- The adverbs *already* and *never* normally go before the main verb, e.g. *He's already received his results. We've never met before.*
- *ever* is mainly used in questions. It comes before the main verb, e.g. *Have you ever been to Shanghai?*
- *yet* is used in questions and negatives at the end of a clause, e.g. *I haven't decided what course to do yet.*

1 Put the verbs in brackets into the present perfect simple tense.

Since its invention, the mobile phone **1** .... (go) from a luxury possession for the rich to an essential everyday item for many people. In Britain, mobiles **2** .... (almost completely/remove) the need for public telephone boxes.

As technology **3** .... (develop) over the years, mobile phones **4** .... (grow) smaller and more versatile and their capabilities **5** .... (greatly/increase). As a result, they **6** .... (become) as much fashion accessories as communication tools. One company **7** .... (even/make) a mobile phone for dogs – although this **8** .... (not achieve) much popularity yet. As the demand for phones **9** .... (rise), this **10** .... (mean) an increase in profits for mobile phone companies. There is no denying that modern communication is big business.

FOR OR SINCE?

2 Write the following expressions in the correct column to show which are used with *for* and which are used with *since*.

a few years   I started high school   a couple of days 2001   March   months   this morning   ten minutes last summer   a decade   several weeks

for	since

PRESENT PERFECT OR PAST SIMPLE?

3 For the sentences below choose the more appropriate verb form, present perfect or past simple.

0 I *worked*/*'ve worked* for a bank until I was 26.

1 The number of households with seven people *decreased*/*has decreased* from 35.8% in 1790 to 1.14% in 1990.

2 The Government *increased*/*has increased* its spending on sport in the last ten years.

3 I*'ve known*/*'ve been knowing* my friend Luca since we *were*/*'ve been* at school together.

4 My father *started*/*has started* the company 20 years ago.

5 My family *lived*/*has lived* in Hong Kong for over 10 years now.

6 I *took*/*have taken* the test a week ago but I *didn't have*/*haven't had* the results yet.

Present progressive

FORM

be + **verb** + *-ing*

+	I *am*/you *are*/she *is* preparing to take IELTS.
–	I'm not/they aren't/he isn't living alone.
?	Are you learning English? Where is she studying?

USE

The **present progressive** is used to talk about:

- actions which are happening at or around the moment of speaking, e.g. *My family is visiting me this week.*
- a temporary, changing or developing situation e.g. *More people are keeping pets each year.*
- a future arrangement, e.g. *I'm taking the IELTS exam next month.* (it's planned and paid for)

Stative verbs are not normally used with progressive forms. They describe passive states rather than actions, and the most common ones are:

> **Mental and emotional states:** *believe, hate, know, like, prefer, remember, think* (= have an opinion), *understand, want, wish*
> **Use of the senses:** *appear, feel, hear, look* (= seem), *see, seem, smell, taste*
> **Other:** *belong, consist, contain, depend, mean, measure, need, own, possess, weigh*

1 Not all the following sentences are correct. Identify any errors and correct them.

1 Why does Kira learning Italian?
2 What is *migratory* meaning?
3 In my country, the number of unemployed people is steadily rising.
4 The book is belonging to me.
5 I'm thinking of buying a new computer.
6 I'm spend a lot of time studying for this exam.

2 Underline the more appropriate present form, simple or progressive, in the sentences below.

1 What *is/does* this word *mean/meaning*?
2 The sun *sets/is setting* in the west.
3 Numbers of bald eagles *increase/are increasing*.
4 Samir *works/is working* very hard to learn more vocabulary before the next exam.
5 I *enjoy/am enjoying* reading newspapers regularly.
6 An increasing number of people *become/are becoming* interested in conservation.
7 *Do/Are* you usually *speak/speaking* English with your friends?
8 Today they *practise/are practising* English pronunciation in class.
9 Some people *believe/are believing* that elephants *never forget/are forgetting*!
10 He *moves/is moving* to Russia in two years' time.

Present simple (Unit 1, p. 7)

FORM

	I /you/we/they	he/she/it
+	*read …*	*reads …*
−	*don't read …* BUT: *be → am not/aren't*	*doesn't read …* *be → isn't*
Yes/No ?	*Do you read everyday?* (*Yes, I do./No, I don't.*)	*Does she read books?* (*Yes, she does./No, she doesn't.*)
Wh- ?	*When do you read?*	*When does he read?*
	If the question word *who, what* or *which* is the subject of the question, we do not need to use auxiliary *do*, e.g. *Who likes reading newspapers?*	
'be'?	If the main verb of the question is *be*, again we do not need to use the auxiliary *do*, e.g. *Where <u>is</u> your town? <u>Are</u> you a student?*	

USE

We use the **present simple** to talk about:

- regular habits and routines, e.g. *I always read at bedtime.*
- a general truth, e.g. *It rains a lot in the UK.*
- a scientific fact, e.g. *Water boils at 100°C.*
- a mental or emotional state, e.g. *I think I understand the present simple.*
- 'timetable' future, e.g. *The train to London leaves at 8.30 p.m.*

Note

Verbs can be active or stative. **Active** verbs like *read* or *rain* tell us about events or actions. **Stative** verbs like *think* or *belong* tell us about a passive state. We generally use simple tenses with stative verbs. See box opposite for a list of some common stative verbs.

Spelling

+-s or +-es?

For most verbs we just add -s. However, if the verb ends with -ch, -x, -o, -ss, or -sh, we need to add -es. e.g. watch ➜ watches

For -y ➜ -i + -es rules see page 150.

1 Change the following infinitive verbs into their 3rd person singular form.

assess	*assesses*	say	
catch		spend	
fix		visit	
go		wash	
miss		write	

2 Complete the sentences using the most appropriate verb below. Each verb is only used once and there is one extra.

0 Hye-Shin *studies* English at a college in Brighton.

agree   arrive   be   enjoy   go   practise   read rise   spend   ~~study~~   watch

1 It .... (not) always important to understand every word when you read.
2 My friends and I .... playing computer games.
3 Marco .... jogging every morning and .... television in the evening.
4 How long .... (you) studying every day?
5 The sun .... (not) in the west, but in the east.
6 I .... (not) with you, I think Spanish food is great!
7 The plane from Milan .... at 16.25.
8 .... (he/often) a newspaper?

3 Put the words in each group in the correct order to make a sentence, and change the verb in brackets to the correct form.

1 He/to/Brussels/the/in/once a week/company's head office (fly)
2 the Internet/regularly/to/Many people/buy plane tickets (use)
3 in/some of/the/the/world/tallest buildings/Taipei (have)

4 hardly ever/UK/serious/The/earthquakes (experience)
5 week/The/a/average junior doctor/60 hours/(work)

4 Expand these notes into complete questions and then give answers. You may need to change the verb in brackets to the correct form or add extra grammatical words such as prepositions or articles.

1 What/thermometer/(measure)?
2 What/we (call)/person/(repair) cars?
3 How many/states/USA (consist of)?
4 Which country (produce) most crude oil/year?
5 you (know)/where/find/the Eiffel Tower?

Relative clauses

FORM AND USE

Relative clauses provide information about the people, things and places we are talking about, using relative pronouns.

Relative pronouns
- **People** (*who, that*), e.g. *The person* who *discovered penicillin was Fleming.*
- **Things** (*which, that*), e.g. *It's a problem* that *we need to solve.*
- **Places** (*where*), e.g. *I still live in the house* where *I grew up.*
- **Time** (*when*), e.g. *We met at a time* when *we were both students.*
- **Reason** (*why*), e.g. *I can't think of a reason* why *anybody should object.*
- **Possessive** (*whose*), e.g. *This course is for students* whose *first language is not English.*

There are two types of relative clause:

A **defining relative clause** provides information which is essential to the meaning of the sentence, e.g. *The shop where I bought my computer has closed down.* Without *where I bought my computer* we wouldn't know which shop we were talking about.

Notes

- *that* is often used instead of *who* and *which*, especially in speech, after superlatives and quantity expressions such as *anything, nothing, all, many*, e.g. *The biggest problem that we face is ignorance. Everyone that took part received a certificate.*
- The relative pronoun can be left out when it refers to the object of the sentence, e.g. *The biggest problem * we face is ignorance.* (* which/that)
- Commas are not used before the relative pronoun.

A **non-defining relative clause** gives us extra information about the people, things and places we are describing. The sentence would still be understandable without the relative clause, e.g. *My professor, who is Japanese, told me that my essay was excellent.*

- *That* cannot be used.
- The relative pronoun cannot be left out.
- Commas are used to separate the relative clause from the rest of the sentence.

► **JUST REMEMBER**

Relative clauses are a good way of increasing the grammatical range of your writing by avoiding too many short simple sentences with the same subject.
If you're unsure about which relative pronoun to use, it's safest to use **who** for people and **which** for things, as these are the most common.

DEFINING RELATIVE CLAUSES

1 **In these sentences the relative pronoun has been left out. For each one, decide what the missing pronoun is. If the sentence is grammatically correct without it, put the relative pronoun(s) in brackets.**

0 *Here is the book (which/that) I borrowed from you.* **Not essential**

00 *The doctor ..who.. treated him at the hospital was from Senegal.* **Essential**

1 The number of people .... were affected by the factory closure was close to 500,000.
2 The dolphins .... have been seen off the coast of Wales are believed to be breeding there.
3 The photos .... the paparazzi took of the pop star were never published.

4 Everyone .... uses a mobile phone for more than one hour a day may be risking their health.
5 The researcher, ... results appeared in last week's *Global Report*, has admitted they were false.
6 The university .... I studied has obtained a large grant from the Government to modernise the facilities.

NON-DEFINING RELATIVE CLAUSES

2 **Rewrite the following sentences including the information in brackets as a relative clause.**

0 Ben Nevis is climbed by nearly 20,000 people each year. (It is the tallest mountain in the UK.), e.g. *Ben Nevis, which is the tallest mountain in the UK, is climbed by nearly 20,000 people each year.*

1 William Shakespeare wrote 37 plays during his lifetime. (He was born in Stratford-upon-Avon.)
2 My college has recently bought ten plasma screen televisions. (They cost £2,000 each.)
3 Microsoft is probably the most successful computer software company in the world. (It is owned by Bill Gates.)
4 They bought the house 20 years ago. (Property prices were much cheaper then.)
5 The University of St Andrews is one of Scotland's top universities. (Prince William studied there.)
6 Dubai has an increasingly international population. (It has a very high standard of living.)

Writing practice bank

This section contains model answers to exam topics in the units and other guided practice tasks.

Words printed in blue in this section are from the Academic Word List (see page 138).

► **Task 2**
Paragraphs

Practice 1 (Unit 2, p. 24)

1 Study the following model answer to the task on page 24.

> In years gone by, before the age of the telegraph or telephone, letter writing was the main means of communication for most people. Since then we have developed faster and more direct ways of contacting people, and personal mail has become relatively rare.
>
> It is true that in many cases where our parents would have written a letter, we prefer to pick up the
> 5 phone, to email or even to text instead. These are perfectly suitable ways of inviting friends to call round or exchanging news with a family member, for example, and they have the advantage that the communication is immediate and we can receive a reply very quickly. In business, too, fax and email are extremely useful.
>
> However, in my opinion there are times when there is no alternative to a letter. Letters are generally
> 10 more formal and carefully composed than emails. This makes them more suitable for occasions when they are likely to be kept and re-read, perhaps several times, by the recipient, as with formal letters of thanks or sympathy. In addition, letters provide a written record, unlike telephone calls, so they are also a better way of setting out an important or complex argument, as in official complaints or legal matters.
>
> In conclusion, I would definitely agree that there are fewer times when we need to write letters than in
> 15 the past. On the other hand, I feel there are still some important occasions when a letter is the most appropriate form of communication.
>
> (248 words)

2 Now answer these questions.

Organisation
  1 How many paragraphs are there?
  2 What is the main topic of each paragraph?

Linking expressions
  3 Which expression is used to link the ideas in paragraphs 2 and 3?
  4 Which phrase is used to introduce a second argument in paragraph 3?
  5 Which phrase is used to link the two contrasting ideas in the last paragraph?

Reference links
  6 What does *These* refer to? (line 5)
  7 What does *This* refer to? (10)
  8 What does *they* refer to? (11)

Vocabulary and grammar structures
  9 Find at least three different tenses or other verb forms.
  10 Find at least ten adjectives.

▶ Task I

Practice 2 (Unit 4, p. 41)

1 **Study table A below and answer the questions.**

Reading the data

1 What do the numbers 26, 25, etc. represent?
2 How many countries were surveyed?
3 What was the time period?

Identifying significant
trends

4 Did the age of marriage rise, fall, or remain the same in most of the countries? (The **general trend**)
5 There was **no change** in one country. Which one?
6 In which country was the age of first marriage highest in all these years?

A **Age of marriage**
Average age of women at first marriage 1980, 1990, 1998

	1980	1990	1998
Sweden	26	28	30
Denmark	25	28	30
Ireland	24	28	28
Germany	23	26	28
Spain	24	25	27
Canada	23	26	27
USA	23	25	26
Russia	23	23	23

B

Marriage and divorce statistics

Country	Marriages per year		Divorces per year	
	1981	1994	1981	1994
USA	10.6	9.1	5.3	4.6
UK	7.1	5.9	2.8	3.5
Japan	6.6	6.4	1.3	1.5
Finland	6.3	4.9	2.0	2.7
Germany	6.2	5.4	2.0	2.0
France	5.8	4.4	1.6	1.9
Italy	5.6	5.0	0.2	0.5
Denmark	5.0	6.8	2.8	2.6
(figures given per thousand people)				

2 **Now study table B above and answer the questions.**

Reading the data

1 What do the figures 10.6, 9.1, etc. represent?
2 How many countries were surveyed?
3 What was the time period?

Identifying significant
trends

4 How many countries had more marriages in 1994 than 1981?
5 What can you say about **the general trend** in marriage in the ten countries?
6 How many countries had more divorces in 1994 than in 1981?
7 What can you say about **the general trend** in divorce in these countries?
8 Which countries were **exceptions** to this general trend?
9 Which country had the lowest number of divorces in both 1981 and 1994?

TASK APPROACH

- Always begin Task 1 with a brief **introduction**, saying what the diagram is about and giving any necessary information such as the time period and country the data relates to.
- When you describe the information, it's best to move from general to specific.

3   **Read this short description of table A and then answer the questions below.**

> As we can see from the information, there was a **general** trend for women to get married later in most countries. In 1980, the average age of marriage for women was about 24, but by 1998, this **had risen** to about 28. The biggest increase **over the** period was in Iceland where the marriage age **rose** seven years from 23 to 30. **By comparison**, the increase in Germany and Denmark was five years, and in Sweden, Norway, Ireland and Canada it was four years. The only **exception to** this trend was Russia where there was no change in the marriage age.

Write down:

1   a phrase which describes an overall change
2   two past tense forms of a verb which means *go up*
3   a phrase which introduces a different example
4   a phrase which means the same as *between 1980 and 1998*
5   an expression which means *something which does not follow a general rule*
6   a phrase which introduces a detailed description

4   **Fill in the gaps in this description of table B with one or two words, or a number.**

> As we can see from the information, there was a **1** .... for the number of marriages to decrease over **2** .... in most of the countries. In 1981, the USA had the most marriages (10.6 per thousand) but by **3** .... this had fallen to **4** .... The number of marriages also fell substantially in Finland and **5** .... The only country where there was an increase in the number of marriages was Denmark.
>
> By **6** ...., the rate of divorce increased in most countries over the same period. The only **7** .... to this trend were Germany, where there was no change, and the USA and Denmark, where the figure fell. The country with the fewest divorces in both 1981 and 1994 was **8** ....

5   **Write down:**

1   a verb which means *go down* or *get less*. The noun has the same form.
2   two irregular past tense forms of another verb meaning *go down*
3   a noun which means *going up* or *getting more*. The verb has the same form.
4   two superlative forms
5   a very useful word for describing data which means *number*

▶ Task 1
Describing data

KEY LANGUAGE
Comparison
▶ p. 142

Practice 3 (Unit 6, p. 65)

1 Use the information in the table on page 65 to complete this description. Write one or two words in each space.

> The table gives information about four animals, polar bears, lions, grizzly bears and snow leopards. It shows the 1 .... of the animals' natural territories and also their infant mortality rate when they are kept in captivity.
>
> As we can see from the data, polar bears have an average territory of approximately 79,000 sq km, which is by far 2 .... of the four animals. Polar bears also have a 3 .... minimum territory than the other animals (1,200 sq km). On the other hand, the grizzly bear has 4 .... minimum territory of the four (0.5 sq km). According to other information in the table, lions travel about 11 km a day, which is 5 .... distance of the four, while the animal with 6 .... infant mortality rate when kept in captivity is the polar bear (65%). By contrast, grizzly bears have a zero infant mortality rate.
>
> These figures provide useful data about which animals are 7 .... suited and which are 8 .... suited to a life in captivity.

2 Now answer these questions about the language used in the description.

1 How many main sections does this description have? What are they?
2 Does the writer express his/her opinion about keeping animals in captivity?
3 What phrase is used to introduce the description (and could be used to introduce many other descriptions)?
4 What phrase is used to introduce a detailed description of the table?
5 Find two phrases which are used to introduce a very different example.

▶ Task 2
Presenting and justifying
an opinion

Practice 4 (Unit 6, p. 68)

Study the following model answer to the exam topic on page 67 and answer the questions below.

> Most people who have seen a lion or tiger in a cage have felt concerned that such a magnificent beast is unable to move about freely or hunt. Those who feel strongly about animal rights go further and argue that there is no justification for keeping animals in zoos. **However**, it is
> 5 important to look at both sides of the argument.
>
> Supporters of zoos would argue that there are many benefits to keeping animals in captivity. One of the most important is that people learn more about animals first-hand than they do from books. **For example**, when

children see a gorilla close-up, they are often interested in finding out
10 about its life and about threats to its survival. **For this reason**, zoo
animals have been called 'ambassadors for the wild'. **In addition**, zoos can
play an important role in conservation by establishing breeding
programmes for endangered species.

On the other hand, those who oppose zoos would argue that it is cruel to
15 keep wild animals in captivity. **This applies particularly** to large species
like polar bears or lions, which have large territories in their natural
habitat. Keeping such animals in unnatural conditions causes stress,
which can lead to high infant mortality rates. **A further argument against**
zoos is that most people who visit zoos want entertainment rather than
20 education. **While** they are happy to take a few photos, they are not
necessarily interested in learning about the animals.

On balance, I feel that zoos do have a role to play in the 21st century.
However, they need to consider the animals' welfare above everything
else, and also to concentrate on education and conservation rather
25 than simply entertaining the public.   (278 words)

1 How many times is the pronoun *I* used in the essay?
2 Is the writer for or against zoos? How do you know?
3 Find one way of describing people who are <u>for</u> zoos.
4 Find one way of describing people who are <u>against</u> zoos.
5 How many arguments <u>for</u> zoos are mentioned?
6 How many arguments <u>against</u> zoos are mentioned?
7 Find two phrases which introduce extra arguments (for or against).
8 Find a phrase which introduces a different point of view.
9 Find a phrase which introduces a specific example (para 3).
10 Which expression is used to introduce the last paragraph?

▶ Task I
Describing data

Practice 5 (Unit 7, p. 80)

1 **Match descriptions 1–3 of rainfall with the graphs A–C.**

1 There is little or no rain **during** the dry season which **lasts from** December
to February. **During** the summer months, rainfall **increases** steadily,
averaging around 35 cm **in** July and August. *Graph …*

2 This country has one of the wettest climates in the world, with rainfall
reaching a peak of 45 cm **in** July **during** the rainy season. *Graph …*

3 There are two rainy seasons, the main one **during** April and May when
rainfall **reaches** around 20 cm, and another **during** October and November,
when rainfall is lighter. *Graph …*

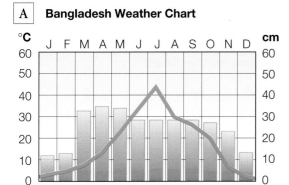

A | Bangladesh Weather Chart

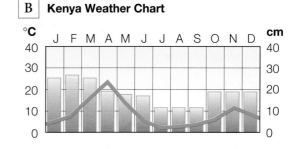

B | Kenya Weather Chart

Key

Average daily temperature — Rainfall

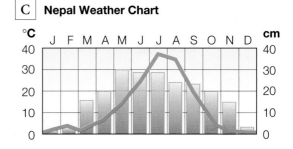

C | Nepal Weather Chart

2 Complete these sentences describing the temperature ranges shown in the graphs. Write one to four words or a number in each space.

A Temperatures in Bangladesh **average around 1** .... **during** the dry season which **2** .... from December to February. They rise rapidly in March and then **3** .... for the rest of the year, varying **4** .... 22°C .... 25°C.

B **5** .... months in Kenya are **from** January **to** March when temperatures **6** .... 25°C. **7** .... the dry season from July to September, temperatures **8** .... around 10°C.

C Nepal has a wide temperature range with **9** .... of about 3°C **during** the winter months and **10** .... of about 30°C **in** May.

► **ESSENTIAL LANGUAGE**

Describing graphs

increase/rise (steadily/gradually/sharply/rapidly) **to**
drop/fall

reach a peak/a minimum/a maximum of (around)
average (around)
vary between ... **and** ...
remain (fairly) **constant.**

in/during (a period of time)   *In 1900; during the winter*
throughout (a period of time)   *throughout the year*
from ... **to** ... (two points of time)   *from May to December.*

3 Use the information in graphs D and E to write short descriptions of the climates in Cambodia and Canada.

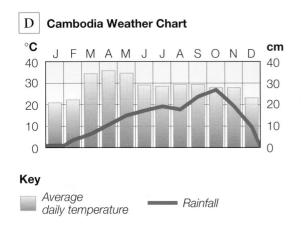

D **Cambodia Weather Chart**

Key

Average daily temperature   ━━━ Rainfall

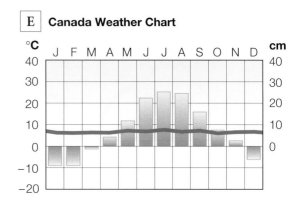

E **Canada Weather Chart**

▶ Task 2
Selecting information

Practice 6 (Unit 8, p. 89)

1 Read the following writing topic and underline the key words.

> Write about the following topic:
>
> *Recent research suggests that children are spending increasing amounts of time on the Internet. Should we be worried about this or not?*
>
> Give reasons for your answer and include any relevant examples from your own knowledge or experience.
>
> Write at least 250 words.

2 Decide whether the following ideas are: definitely relevant ✓, possibly relevant ✓? or irrelevant ✗ and complete the table below. Discuss your ideas with another student if possible.

	✓	✓?	✗
a) The Internet began with four computers in 1969.			
b) Children don't learn social skills from computers.			
c) Computer crime is a serious problem.			
d) Long hours at a computer keyboard can cause physical problems.			
e) The Internet is a convenient way of buying many items.			
f) Computer games can be educational.			
g) Even elderly people can use the web, e.g. to play chess.			
h) Using the Internet develops useful computer skills.			

3 Think of at least one more argument in favour of Internet use by children, and one against. Try to find at least one example from your own experience.

4 Make a plan, following the model on page 89, and then write your answer.

▶ Task 2
Presenting the solution
to a problem

Practice 7 (Unit 10, p. 108)

Study the following model answer to the exam topic on page 108 and answer questions 1–10 below. The questions focus on the criteria which are used to assess your work in the exam.

Smoking is an expensive habit which pollutes the environment and carries serious health risks, yet a third of the men in the world smoke. It is also a sad fact that one in five teenagers take up the habit when they are as young as 11. Of course, there is one interest group, the tobacco industry, which is more than happy with this situation, since its profits depend on our addiction to cigarettes.

5 These statistics are particularly depressing because the link between smoking and cancer, heart disease and other serious illnesses has been known for many years. We must also remember that apart from harming the individual, smoking represents a huge cost to society. The money we spend on treating smoking-related diseases could be used for much better purposes, such as helping to feed the world's poor or paying for medical research.

10 So why, despite all the evidence, do people still smoke? The obvious answer is that cigarettes are highly addictive, so that it can be extremely difficult to give up. Another answer is the power of peer pressure, especially amongst young people. In my view, the most important thing is to discourage people from starting to smoke, and we could do this by increasing the tax on tobacco and banning cigarette advertising. I also feel that people who want to quit should be given as much advice and support as possible.

15 In conclusion, I believe that we should do everything we can to reduce the number of smokers in society. However, it is not enough to provide information about health risks, we also need to use a variety of strategies to tackle the problem.

(276 words)

Task response: *Have you discussed all parts of the task?*
1 Why should we be concerned about smoking, according to the writer?
2 How many solutions are proposed? What are they?
3 Find examples from the writer's own knowledge or experience.

Coherence and cohesion: *Is your writting well-organised? Are ideas linked logically?*
4 What main topic area does each paragraph cover?
5 Underline all the linking expressions you can find.

Lexical resource: *Is there a good range of vocabulary?*
6 How many words or phrases to do with smoking can you find?
7 Find three ways of introducing a personal opinion.

Grammatical range and accuracy: *Is there a variety of sentence structures? Is the writing reasonably accurate?*
8 Underline three examples of the passive voice.
9 How many modal verbs can you find?
10 Find a question in the text. Why do you think this is used?

► Task I
Describing data

Practice 8 (Unit 10, p. 112)

1   Study *Figures 1* and *2* below and answer the questions.

Figure 1

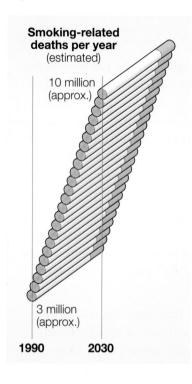

Figure 2 The smoking habit

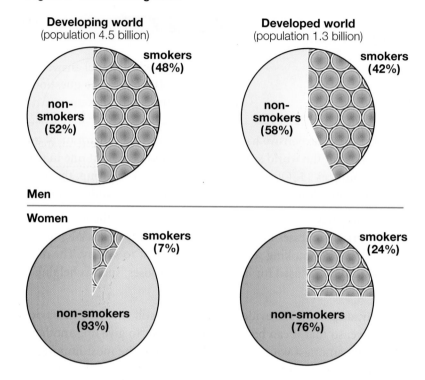

► Reading the data

1   What is the subject of *Figure 1*?
2   What period of time is covered in *Figure 1*?
3   In *Figure 2*, what do the two circles above the line represent? And the two below?
4   What do the two circles on the left represent? And the two on the right?

► Identifying significant trends

2   Now answers questions 1–6 below.

1   Describe the change which is shown in *Figure 1*.
2   According to *Figure 2*, generally speaking, who smokes more – men or women?
3   Which group represents the largest percentage of smokers? What is the figure?
4   Which group represents the smallest percentage of smokers? What is the figure?
5   Compare male smokers in the developed and developing world.
    Use: *There are … more …*
6   Compare female smokers in the developed and developing world.
    Use: *There are … x times more …*

DESCRIBING THE DATA

3 **Complete the following brief descriptions by writing one or two words or a number in the spaces.**

Figure 1 shows the estimated number of smoking-related deaths per year over a **1** ....-year period. We can see from the diagram that smoking was **2** .... approximately 3 million deaths in **3** .... The number of deaths has continued to **4** .... since then and this trend is expected to continue **5** .... 2030.

Figure 2 **6** .... the percentages of smokers and non-smokers in both the developing and the developed world. We can see **7** .... the diagrams that, in general, male smokers outnumber female smokers in the world. The **8** .... percentage of male smokers is in the developing world, where almost **9** ....% of men smoke. This is slightly **10** .... than the **11** .... for male smokers in the developed world (42%). By **12** .... , only 24% of women in the developed world are smokers, **13** .... the figure for female smokers in the developing world is even **14** .... (7%).

▶ Task 1
Explaining how things work

Practice 9 (Unit 1, p. 129)

1 **Study the diagram and then complete the description below. Choose answers from the box.**

How a water tower works

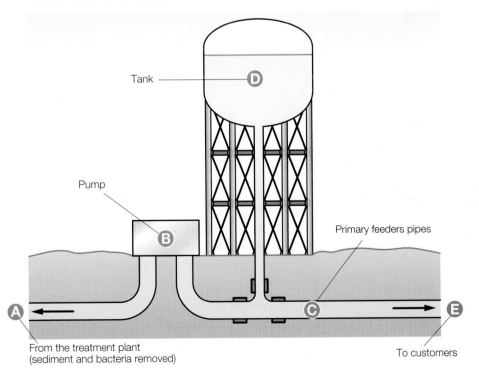

Tank — Ⓓ

Pump

Ⓑ

Primary feeders pipes

Ⓐ

Ⓒ

Ⓔ

From the treatment plant
(sediment and bacteria removed)

To customers

165

A water tower **1** .... a large tank (**D**), which **2** ....
water and which **3** .... high enough above ground to provide
the necessary level of water pressure for a community. The tank
4 .... to the water system's primary feeder pipes (**C**) by a
5 .... pipe. Drinking water for a town is first treated in a water
treatment plant (**A**) to **6** .... sediment and bacteria. A pump
(**B**) then **7** .... it *via* the primary feeder pipes to the customers
(**E**). If the community demands more water than the pump can
8 ...., the water flows out of the tank to meet the need.

is connected to   sends   consists of   vertical
is raised   contains   remove   supply

2   **Write a short description of the tower windmill below and how it works.**

A tower windmill

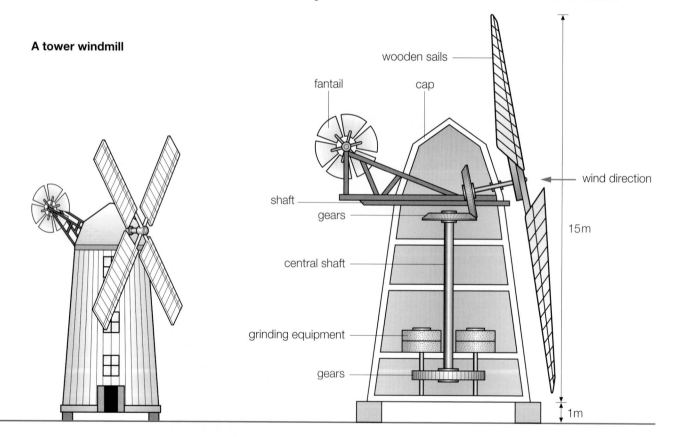

Begin: *A tower windmill is specially
designed to use wind power to
drive machinery for grinding corn
into flour.*

It consists of …
The sails are connected to … by …
The windmill also contains …
As the sails turn they …

Useful language

vertical/horizontal
at the top; at the bottom/base
on one side; on the other/opposite side
on the upper/lower floors/levels

► Task 2
Presenting and justifying
an opinion

Practice 10 (Unit 12, p. 134)

1   a) **Study the following exam task and underline key words.**

> You should spend 40 minutes on this task.
>
> Write about the following topic.
>
> > *Most governments use public funds to try to protect their*
> > *architectural heritage in some way.*
> >
> > *Is this a good use of public money in your view?*
> >
> > *Which kind of old buildings should be preserved and how should*
> > *they be used?*
>
> Give reasons for your answer and include any relevant examples from your
> own knowledge or experience.
>
> Write at least 250 words.

b) **Answer the questions below.**

► Analyse the question

General

1   Are all old buildings 'architectural heritage'? If not, which kind of buildings
deserve to be preserved?

2   Can you think of any examples in your country/internationally to mention?

For

3   What can we learn from old buildings?

4   What is lost if an important old building is destroyed?

5   How can old buildings be used?

Against

6   What are the problems of preserving old buildings?

7   Can you suggest more important things to spend money on?

8   What other sources of money can you think of, apart from public funding?

► Plan your answer

2   Make a plan, following the model on page 89. If necessary look back at the
language for giving reasons and arguments on page 68, and also the
impersonal expressions on page 107.

► Write your answer

3   When writing your answer, rember to divide your essay into clear paragraphs
and to link your ideas logically. If you are planning to take the IELTS exam
soon, try to complete the task in 40 minutes.

► Check your answer

4   When you check your work, first look for your 'favourite' mistakes, then check
for any other mistakes with spelling, punctuation, articles, subject/verb
agreement, and tenses.

Answer keys

Unit 5
Lead-in (p.50)
Athletes with the Largest Hearts
1 *Tour de France* cyclists
2 Marathon runners 4 Boxers
7 Weightlifters 8 Swimmers
10 Decathletes

Unit 7
Lead-in (p.72)
1st Bicycle (63%)
2nd Electricity (20%)
3rd Vaccination (9%)
4th Computer with World Wide Web (8%)

Unit 8
Focus on speaking 1 (p.85)
Percentage of people who said they could not bear to be without:
1 mobile phone (77%)
2 access to the Internet (51%)
3 satellite/cable TV (40%)
4 email (32%)
NB 9% of young people said they could live without all of these items.

Focus on speaking 2 (p.88)
(1 = most popular; 8 = least popular)
1 Send/receive email
2 Get news
3 Check the weather
4 Research a product before buying it
5 Do research for school or training
6 Get travel information
7 Look for health/medical information
8 Buy a product
9 Participate in an online auction

Unit 9
Focus on speaking 1 (p.94)
1 d) 2 b) 3 c) 4 b) 5 c)
6 c) 7 a) 8 a) 9 c) 10 a)

Unit 10
Lead-in (p.104)
1 70% 2 10 million
3 100,000 4 4 5 40%
6 230 7 5 8 300,000 9 20
10 37

Focus on speaking 1 (p.105)
1 B 2 B 3 C 4 C 5 C
6 A 7 A 8 B 9 C 10 C

Focus on grammar 2 (p.111)
A: An estimated number of annual deaths caused by crocodiles is 600–800.
B: Sharks cause about 10 deaths per year.
C: It is estimated that around 22 people die annually as a direct result of a wasp or bee sting.
D: Mosquitoes transmit malaria which kills 1–3 million people every year.
E: 50,000–100,000 people die from snake bites every year.
F: Tigers are responsible for approximately 70–80 human deaths a year.
G: There are very few reports of death caused by spiders – an estimation is 2–4 per year

Academic Word Study 1 (p.26)
1 1 help 2 build 3 show
   4 get 5 buy 6 need
   7 answer 8 choose
2 1 Adj 2 Adj 3 Vb 4 N
   5 Vb 6 N 7 N 8 N
3 a) 1 b) 7 c) 5 d) 3 e) 6
   f) 4 g) 8 h) 2
4 1 substitute 2 item
   3 obtained 4 require
   5 extract 6 techniques
   7 construct 8 relevant

Academic Word Study 2 (p.48)
1 1 demonstration
   2 equation 3 illustration
   4 immigration
   5 investigation 6 legislation
   7 location 8 participation
2 Incorrect words: 1 big
   2 clearly 3 big 4 lasts
   5 make 6 do
3 Possible answers
   1 Most families **consist of** only two or three people.
   2 The company introduced pay cuts **despite** angry protests/**Despite** angry protests, the company …
   3 The police still haven't **established** who carried out the crime (yet).
   4 The government has various **options**.
   5 There is an error in the **data**/The **data** contains an error.
   6 In recent years there has been a **trend**/the **trend** has been for people to marry later.
   7 You should start with/by giving a **definition** of 'success'.
   8 There isn't much/There's very little … accommodation **available**.

Academic Word Study 3 (p.70)
1 1 N, plural, c) 2 Vb, e)
   3 N, b) 4 Adj, g)
   5 Adv, h) 6 Vb, f)
   7 N, a) 8 Vb, d)
2 1 components 2 monitor
   3 affect 4 consequence
   5 constantly 6 crucial
   7 achieve 8 decade
3 1 facing 2 reached 3 gave
   4 have 5 doing
   6 play/have
4 Suggested answers:
   1 a serious/major **challenge**
   2 a final/clear **conclusion**
   3 a clear **indication**
   4 major/significant/serious **consequences**
   5 fascinating/in-depth/important **research**
   6 a crucial/important/significant **role**

Academic Word Study 4 (p.92)
1 NB These words normally end with *-ize* in American spelling
   1 analyse 2 summarise
   3 emphasise 4 minimise
   5 maximise 6 symbolise
2 Suggested answers
   1 The temperature varies between 10°C and 40°C.
   2 Using calculators/The use of calculators in the exam is prohibited./It is prohibited to use calculators in the exam.
   3 I can't access/I haven't got access to/I have no access to the Internet on my present computer.
   4 Low cost flights have contributed to the growth of tourism.
   5 The whole community will benefit from the sports facilities/The sports facilities will benefit/be of benefit to the whole community.
   6 The majority of people/the population live by the coast.
3 1 *in*accurate 2 *un*aware
   3 *in*consistent 4 *in*flexible
   5 *il*legal 6 *un*predictable
   7 *ir*relevant 8 *un*reliable
   9 *in*secure 10 *in*significant
4 1 data (p.26) 2 crucial (70)
   3 period (48), obtained/achieved (26) 4 consist of (48) 5 assist (you) (26)
   6 monitor (70), options (48)

Academic Word Study 5 (p.114)
1 1 economical 2 logical
   3 medical 4 physical
   5 psychological 6 technical
   7 mechanical 8 identical
2 1 economic 2 resource
   3 estimated 4 acquired
   5 factor 6 transferred
   7 visible 8 aspect
3 1 to 2 on 3 for 4 on
   5 of 6 from 7 as 8 in
4 1 contribution/contributor
   2 disposal 3 erosion
   4 exclusion 5 identification
   6 reaction/reactor
   7 removal 8 substitution/substitite

Academic Word Study 6 (p.136)
1 1 b) 2 f) 3 a) 4 h)
   5 g) 6 c) 7 e) 8 d)
2 1 **perform** a function, a task
   1 **make** a comment, an error
   1 **follow** instructions, a trend
3 1 into 2 with/to 3 on
   4 as 5 from 6 to 7 as
   8 to/towards
4 1 ✓ 2 communication
   3 equation 4 ✓
   5 establish 6 illustration
   7 ✓ 8 occur 9 ✓
   10 technique

Review 1 (p.27)
1 1 He doesn't spend enough time (on) <u>studying</u> for his exam.
   2 I enjoy listening <u>to</u> folk music <u>very much.</u>
   3 She goes to college <u>once a week</u> <u>to</u> study computing. OR <u>Once a week</u> she goes …
   4 <u>Slightly more than</u> or <u>Just over a</u> quarter of university students have part-time jobs.
   5 The job requires someone who can speak Russian <u>fluently.</u>
   6 Electricity <u>costs</u> exactly the same (amount of money) <u>as</u> gas.
   7 Climbing has <u>fewer</u> participants than skiing/There are fewer participants in climbing than skiing.
   8 <u>In</u> my opinion, the government should encourage people <u>to</u> save money.

2 1 to; on   2 into
   3 At; at; by   4 in; in
   5 On; with   6 At; as; on
   7 for; on/about   8 for
3 2 carefully
   3 communication
   4 grammar   6 interesting
   7 language   8 pronunciation
   11 successful
4 1 B   2 C   3 A   4 C   5 A
5 1 The present and past
     simple. They make up 80%
     of all communication in
     English.
   2 60 minutes/one hour
   3 Three   4 60 minutes/one
     hour   5 Two

Review 2 (p.49)

1 1 became   2 brought up
   3 could   4 caught   5 cost
   6 fell   7 froze   8 went
   9 knew   10 made   11 paid
   for   12 rose   13 set up
   14 spread   15 took
   16 thought
2 *the*: A (something unique),
   D (something specific and/or
   clearly defined), F (rivers,
   oceans, countries with a word
   like *state* or *republic* in their
   name), H (superlatives)
   a: C (something unspecific)
   no article: B (uncountable
   nouns in general), E (most
   names of people and places),
   G (plural nouns in general)
   1 (*no article*) children; (*no
   article*) games; *the* Internet
   2 (*no article*) Tiredness; *a*
   break; *the* M4 motorway
   3 *an* increase; *the* number;
   (*no article*) traffic accidents;
   the last ten years
   4 (*no article*) women; *an*
   increasingly important role;
   the labour market; *the* 20th
   century
   5 (*no article*) Spain; *the* most
   popular; (*no article*) UK
   residents; *the* USA
3 1 qualification
   2 agricultural   3 tolerant
   4 trainee   5 Inexperienced
   6 responsibility
   7 explanation   8 height
4 1 prepare; notes
   2 underline/highlight
   3 discussion; four; five
   4 understand; choose/select
   5 spelling

Review 3 (p.71)

1 1 began   begun
   2 bought   bought
   3 chose   chosen
   4 did   done
   5 ate   eaten
   6 found   found
   7 gave   given
   8 lost   lost
   9 made   made
   10 put   put
   11 saw   seen
   12 spoke   spoken
   13 stood   stood
   14 told   told
   15 understood understood
   16 won   won
2 1 I arrived   2 ✓   3 ✓
   4 The lorry contains
   5 lives in; it has a length of
   6 is declining; being shot
   7 a happier child   8 ✓
   9 the tallest   10 ✓
   11 better than
   12 The government said
3 2 approximately
   3 argument   6 disappear
   9 height   10 immoral
   11 responsible
   12 spectator
4 1 On   2 By/In   3 By   4 In
   5 On   6 As   7 in   8 on
   9 in   10 on   11 to   12 on
5 1 C   2 B   3 A   4 B   5 C
   6 A   7 A   8 C   9 B
   10 C

Review 4 (p.93)

1 1 The graph shows the
     difference between male
     and female wages.
   2 … but less than 20% of
     women enjoy watching
     football.
   3 … twice as high as
     electricity use in summer.
   4 … a small/slight increase in
     the number of visitors
   5 … twice as many Korean
     speakers as Dutch speakers
   6 Overall we can see that
     most electricity is used for
     heating rooms.
   7 … compared with men.
   8 if the price of tickets
     increases any more, people
     might not be able to buy
     them.
2 *At*: A, F, J, L
   In: C, D, E, G, I
   On: B, H, K
4 1 majority   2 day
   3 amount   4 area
   5 climate

5

Ooo
benefit
bicycle
countryside
diagram
estimate
industry
Internet
medical
mountainous

oOoo
analysis
appropriate
community
development
humidity
geography
industrial
majority
technology

6 1 T (*p.73*)   2 F (*75*)
   3 T (*77*)   4 F (*87*)   5 F (*89*)

Review 5 (p.115)

1 1 is generally agreed (that)
   2 too dirty (for people) to
     swim in
   3 despite the fact that it is
   4 clear enough (for you) to
     see
   5 a (very) good chance of
     surviving
   6 in/by comparison with
   7 was responsible for
   8 to raise money by selling
2 1 C   2 B   3 A   4 C   5 B
   6 A
3 1 harmful   2 solution
   3 Industrial   4 investigation
   5 presence   6 scientific
   7 depth   8 threatened

Review 6 (p.137)

1 1 … as soon as we have the
     results …
   2 ✓
   3 shaped like a circle/which is
     circular in shape
   4 … is made of … It has a
     single span …
   5 ✓   6 ✓
   7 … fewer people would buy
     cars/a car, and they would
     also use …
   8 … will stop using private
     cars because public
     transport is often expensive
     and also crowded/both
     expensive and crowded.
2 Missing words
   1 from (*Example*)
   2 responsible for
   3 in height   4 more than
   5 a colossal   6 Buddha,
   which   7 as well as
   8 According to
   9 the country's   10 to pay
3 1 inappropriate
   2 unemployment
   3 difficulty   4 inflexible
   5 satisfaction   6 economic
   7 growth
4 1 g) (*p.3*)   2 b) (*13*)
   3 c) (*18*)   4 h) (*43*)
   5 e) (*45*)   6 d) (*58*)
   7 a) (*87*)   8 f) (*106*)

Key Language Bank
Adverbs (p.140)

1 1 often   2 normally
   3 frequently   4 every other
   day   5 regularly
2 1 Ian hardly ever revises his
     vocabulary.
   2 The number of people who
     want to take the exam has
     increased rapidly.
   3 Ayumi normally prefers
     using an electronic
     dictionary to a conventional
     one.
   4 I'm afraid I rarely listen to
     the radio to improve my
     listening skills.
   5 There hasn't been any
     announcement about the
     date of the election yet.
   6 We often discuss the
     differences between our two
     countries.
   7 The warning sign lights up
     automatically when you
     approach too fast.
   8 In the IELTS test you must
     always read the questions
     carefully.
3 1 extremely
   2 strongly/seriously
   3 fairly/relatively
   4 highly/extremely
   5 slightly   6 seriously
   7 fully   8 highly/extremely

Articles (p.141)

1 1 The; an   2 the; the
   3 the; the   4 A; a   5 an; the
2 1 I hope to study at ~~the~~
     college …
   2 The Internet and ~~the~~
     computers are …
   3 ✓
   4 ~~The~~ Everest is the biggest
     mountain in the world.
   5 ✓
3 1 The   2 –   3 A   4 the
   5 the   6 the   7 a   8 –
   9 the   10 a   11 the   12 –
   13 the   14 the   15 the
   16 the

Comparison (p.142)

1 1 Playing football is not as
     dangerous as playing ice
     hockey.
   2 A desert is much drier than
     a rainforest.
   3 The River Nile is the
     longest river in Africa.
   4 Some people learn
     languages more easily than
     others.
   5 Law is the most popular
     university course in the UK.
   6 Adult dogs usually behave
     better than puppies.
2 1 the least   2 as much as
   3 more; than

4 (the) most dramatically
5 three times as much; as
6 the biggest
7 (much) less

Conditionals (p.143)

1 1 e),1 2 a),0 3 f) ,2
  4 b),1 5 d),2 6 c), 2
2 1 If the government spent more money on public transport, it would/might be more reliable.
  2 If public transport were more reliable, more people would/might use it regularly.
  3 If parents gave their teenagers more freedom, they would/might have fewer arguments.
  4 Many more species of animals would become extinct if they were not protected by law.
  5 If countries like the USA stopped producing high quantities of carbon dioxide, the climate change wouldn't/mightn't be so rapid.
  6 It would be easier to give up smoking if cigarettes weren't so addictive.
3 Suggested answers:
  1 He would have passed his driving test if he had practised more./He wouldn't have failed his driving test if he had practised more.
  2 If the weather hadn't been so terrible, we wouldn't have come home early.
  3 I wouldn't have missed my flight if I hadn't lost my passport.
  4 If the traffic hadn't been so heavy, I wouldn't have been an hour late.
  5 If I hadn't lost my lottery ticket, I would have been able to claim the prize.
  6 If I hadn't gone to the party, I wouldn't have met my husband-to-be.

Countability (p.144)

1 **Countable**
animal–animals
building–buildings
child–children facility–facilities
idea–ideas machine–machines
person–people
student–students tree–trees
Uncountable
advice equipment happiness
money petrol pollution
rubbish traffic tourism
waste weather
2 1 few 2 amount was
  3 Every; was 4 a little; some

5 much; all 6 Either; is
7 was; a great deal of
8 hardly any 9 much
10 Most

Expressing the future (p.145)

1 1 'm going to study
  2 takes place/will take place
  3 will be illegal
  4 'm seeing/am going to see
  5 'll be 6 is going to rain
  7 will have doubled 8 won't have 9 are meeting
  10 will disappear

Modal verbs (p.146)

1 1 A referee of a physical sport **has to/must** be brave.
  2 In the future we **will have to find** …
  3 You **should** study very hard …
  4 In the past only men **could go** …
  5 European students **don't have to have** …
2 1 mustn't 2 'll be able to
  3 should 4 was able to
  5 don't have to
3 1 Talking in the library is forbidden.
  2 It is compulsory to wear a cycling helmet in some countries.
  3 Walking on the grass is prohibited.
  4 Flash photography is forbidden in the museum.
  5 Travelling abroad without a passport is not permitted.

Parts of speech (p.147)

1 1 noun 2 adjective
  3 noun phrase 4 verb
  5 adverb 6 noun
  7 preposition
  8 conjunction 9 adjective
  10 article 11 pronoun
  12 noun phrase
  13 conjunction 14 verb

Passive (p.148)

1 1 has (recently) bought – A
  2 has been hung – P
  3 are expected – P; flock – A
  4 was not – A
  5 was recognised – P
  6 was sold – P
2 1 are produced; are sold
  2 is made of 3 is said
  4 are employed; are called
  5 aren't allowed 6 are sold
3 1 was assumed 2 has been done 3 is now known
  4 be thrown away 5 have to be reduced 6 will be fined
  7 are/can be taken away
  8 (are) used 9 is created

Past perfect (p.149)

1 1 ✓

2 … hadn't happened …
3 **had already started** …
4 **had fallen** …
5 **hadn't flown** …
2 1 was; hadn't remembered
  2 realised; had lost
  3 had been driving; happened
  4 Did; learn; came
  5 hadn't begun; arrived
  6 had fallen
  7 had been rising; decided
  8 hadn't met; started

Past simple (p.150)

1 1 went up 2 Did; fall
  3 didn't leave; was
  4 did; start 5 fixed
  6 didn't spread; believed
  7 did; involve
  8 wasn't able to
2 1 carries; carried
  2 marries; married
  3 says; said
  4 studies; studied
  5 stays; stayed 6 tries; tried
  7 worries; worried
3 **at**: midday.; New Year; the weekend
  on: Monday; 26th May; my birthday
  in: 1999; the summer; January; the evening
  no preposition: last week; last weekend; all year; every day
4 … **rose** last year. 2 … **in** 1997. 3 I studied …
  4 … **get paid** … 5 Why **weren't** the employees ~~be~~ happy?

Present perfect (p.151)

1 1 has gone 2 have almost completely removed 3 has developed 4 have grown
  5 have greatly increased
  6 have become 7 has even made 8 has not achieved
  9 has risen 10 has meant
2 **for**: a few years; a couple of days; months; ten minutes; a decade; several weeks
  since: I started high school; 2001; March; this morning; last summer
3 1 decreased 2 has increased
  3 've known 4 has started
  5 has live 6 took; haven't had

Present progressive (p.152)

1 1 Why **is** Kira learning …
  2 What **does** *migratory* **mean**?
  3 …is **rising** steadily.
  4 **belongs** … 5 ✓
  6 I'm **spending** …
2 1 does; mean 2 sets 3 are increasing 4 is working
  5 enjoy 6 are becoming
  7 Do; speak 8 are practising 9 believe; never forget 10 is moving

Present simple (p.153)

1 1 catches 2 fixes 3 goes
  4 misses 5 says 6 spends
  7 visits 8 washes 9 writes
2 1 isn't 2 enjoy 3 goes; watches 4 do you spend
  5 doesn't set 6 don't agree
  7 arrives 8 Does he often read
3 1 He flies to the company's head office in Brussels once a week .
  2 Many people regularly use the Internet to buy plane tickets.
  3 Taipei has some of the tallest buildings in the world.
  4 The UK hardly ever experiences serious earthquakes.
  5 The average junior doctor works 60 hours a week.
4 1 What does a thermometer measure? (Temperature)
  2 What do we call a person who repairs cars? /(A mechanic)
  3 How many states does the USA consist of? (50)
  4 Which country produces the most crude oil a year? (Saudi Arabia)
  5 Do you know where to find the Eiffel Tower? (Paris)

Relative clauses (p.154)

1 1 who (Essential)
  2 which/that (Essential)
  3 which/that (Not essential)
  4 who (Essential)
  5 whose (Essential)
  6 where (Essential)
2 1 William Shakespeare, who was born in Stratford-upon-Avon, wrote 37 plays during his lifetime.
  2 The 10 plasma screens which/that my college has recently bought cost £2,000 each.
  3 Microsoft, which is owned by Bill Gates, is probably the most successful computer software company in the world.
  4 They bought the house 20 years ago, when property prices were much cheaper.
  5 The University of St Andrews, where Prince William studied, is one of Scotland's top universities.
  6 Dubai, which has a very high standard of living, has an increasingly international population

▶ Audio script

Unit 2, Focus on listening 1

Letters and sounds 1 (p.17)

EXERCISE 2
1 B-A-C-K-E-R
2 G-A-D-G-E-T
3 C-H-E-R-V-I-L
4 H-E-N-B-A-N-E

EXERCISE 3
1 T-O-A-D H-A-L-L
2 S-A-N-D-R-I-N-G-H-A-M
3 M-A-N-S-F-I-E-L-D P-A-R-K

Unit 2, Focus on listening 2

Introducing listening skills (p.18)

EXERCISE 1
1 For passengers on Platform 4 awaiting the arrival of the 10.24 to Exeter, we regret to inform you that this train is currently running fifteen, that's one-five, minutes late. The delay is due to signalling problems in the Reading area. We apologise for any inconvenience this may cause.

2 Police are continuing to hunt for prisoners who escaped from Longmead Gaol last night. One man has given himself up and police say they are confident of recapturing the rest in the next couple of days. There has been an earthquake measuring 5.5 on the Richter Scale in Japan …

3 Things are fairly quiet at the moment in the city. But for those of you heading onto the motorway the news is not so good, I'm afraid. We're getting reports of a lorry shedding its load on the southbound carriageway near Junction 8. So be prepared for delays.

4 (*SM = Sally Meakin; I = Interviewer; BT = Bill Turnbull*)
   SM Right, well, first of all, thanks for coming in. My name's Sally Meakin and this is my colleague, Bill Turnbull …
   I Hello.
   BT Hi, how's it going?
   SM … And what we'd like to do today is find out a bit about you, discover what makes you tick. OK?
   I OK.
   SM So let's begin. Now you say on your application form that you enjoy a challenge, and I wonder …

5 OK, now the first thing we have to do is to make sure you all know how to get on correctly. So watch me first. You face the back of the horse, take the reins in your left hand like this, right? Put your left foot in the stirrup, grasp the back of the saddle with your right hand like this, and up you go!

EXERCISE 2
1 Short city breaks are very popular these days. And there are some great package deals available this autumn. For example, you can have three nights for the price of two in <u>Paris</u>, staying in a three-star hotel, but only if you're free to travel this weekend …

2 (*TA = Travel agent; C = customer*)
   TA Flight Savers, Can I help you?
   C Hello, yes, I'm looking for a cheap flight to <u>Sydney</u>.
   TA Single or return?

3 **A** I'm doing a project on <u>Japan</u> as a tourist destination.
   B Sounds interesting. Do you get to go there?
   A I wish!

4 Hi, Andy. Could you do me a favour? I'm up to my eyes at the moment. Yes. But we need to get those samples to our agent in <u>Washington</u>. Could you give the couriers a ring and arrange a pick-up ASAP? You will? Many thanks.

5 OK everyone! Now on Saturday, there's a trip to see an exhibition of photographs by Julia Margaret Cameron, if you're interested. Cameron was born in 1815, in <u>India</u>, if I remember rightly, and she was one of the first women to become a professional photographer. Anyway, it's a fantastic exhibition …

EXERCISE 3
1 We'll start off in the south east. Here there's quite a bit of cloud around and I think we'll see some bands of rain during the afternoon. As a result, temperatures are unlikely to rise above <u>15 degrees</u>. Next I'll take the whole of the north and west …

2 Now here's something that might interest you. It's a studio apartment, so OK it's tiny, but it's right in the central business district. And that's <u>800 dollars</u> a month. It's a pretty good price for the location – what do you think?

3 And now for the financial news. According to a report published in *Home Buyer* magazine, property prices in certain areas have risen <u>12 per cent</u> in the last year. This means that it's becoming even harder for young people to get a foot on the property ladder.

4 A major power failure left almost all of Italy without electricity yesterday. The blackout extended from the Alps in the north to Sicily in the south, cutting power supplies to around <u>57 million</u> people. Transport was disrupted as traffic lights broke down and trains and trams stopped running.

5 In my lecture today, I want to look at the work of the Irish writer, Frank O'Connor, who is best known for his short stories. O'Connor was born in Cork, Ireland in <u>1903</u>. He was an only child and most of his childhood was spent in considerable poverty …

Unit 4, Focus on listening 1

Letters and sounds 2 (p.42)

EXERCISE 1

1	child	6	eye
2	height	7	quite
3	great	8	break
4	weight	9	buyer
5	flight	10	neighbour

EXERCISE 2

1	said, paid	The answer is *said*.
2	many, lazy	The answer is *many*.
3	reason, measure	The answer is *measure*.
4	chief, friend	The answer is *friend*.
5	guess, queue	The answer is *guess*.
6	leisure, seize	The answer is *leisure*.
7	breathe, breath	The answer is *breath*.
8	pretty, plenty	The answer is *plenty*.

EXERCISE 3

1 Albany A-L-B-A-N-Y
2 Carlisle C-A-R-L-I-S-L-E
3 Mainstay M-A-I-N-S-T-A-Y
4 Channing C-H-A-N-N-I-N-G

Unit 4, Focus on listening 2

International Friendship Club (p.42)

S = Simon; M = Maria

S   2466. Simon speaking.

M   Hello. Is that the right number for the International Friendship Club?

S   Yes, that's right. How can I help?

M   I picked up a copy of your newsletter in the Students' Union, and I was wondering if you could tell me a bit more about the club?

S   Yes, of course. We set up the club three years ago as a way of promoting international understanding. So we've been established for a while now. And, there are meetings every Thursday evening, during term time that is.

M   Thursday, right.

S   Yes, we usually show a film or maybe run a competition of some kind. But mostly it's an opportunity for people to get together, relax, make friends. And we also produce a regular newsletter – I think you said you'd seen a copy of that … ?

M   The newsletter? Yes, it looked interesting.

S   So you know it's got loads of information about what's on in the area and about living in Britain in general. We also have quite a busy social programme with outings to places of interest like London or Oxford.

M   Sounds great.

S   And one other thing to mention. We like to encourage people to attend regularly and play a real part in the club. So we give special certificates as a reward for active participation. It's something you can put on your CV, for example.

M   I see. And, I meant to ask does it cost anything to join? Is there a fee?

S   Yes, membership costs £5 for a term but you can save a bit of money if you pay for the whole academic year. Then it's only £12, instead of £15. That doesn't include special trips. But they're subsidised by the university, so they're not too expensive. The Oxford trip only costs £10, for example.

M   So, how do I go about joining?

S   Right, well I'll take a few details now if I may, so I can send you a welcome pack. That's got all the information you need. Then if you're happy to go ahead, perhaps you could send us a cheque for your membership fee?

M   Fine.

S   OK. So could I have your name please?

M   Maria Lanzerac.

S   Sorry, could you spell that for me?

M   Yes, Lanzerac, L-A-N-Z-E-R-A-C.

S   Right. And where are you from, Maria? I should be able to tell from your accent but …

M   Don't worry. Most people think I'm from Australia but I'm actually South African.

S   That's somewhere I've always wanted to go! Now your address. Do you live in the city?

M   Yes, I'm staying at 47 March Street, Southville.

S   47 … Sorry, what was the street name again?'

M   March Street. Like the month.

S   OK. So you haven't got far to come, have you? And how old are you, if you don't mind my asking?

M   I'm 22. 23 next month, actually.

S   Right. And last but not least, I just need to know what course you're doing?

M   Art History. I'm on the MA course.

S   Fantastic. Well, I think that's all I need for now. You should get the pack in the post tomorrow. Just give me a call if you've got any questions.

M   Thanks. Bye.

Unit 6, Focus on listening 1

Wildlife Film Festival (p.63)

EXERCISE 1

1 2.365%
2 1,100
3 5.45
4 577204
5 01628 351940

Unit 6, Focus on listening 1

Exam Practice (p.63)

Right, well we come to the part of the programme where we look at what's on in our area. And this week we've got something really rather special to look forward to. It's a Festival of Wildlife Films at the Regent Arts Centre. The festival runs for Saturday and Sunday and it's got something for everyone, whether you're 8 or 80! I've only got time to tell you about a few of the films on offer, but at least it'll give you a flavour of the programme.

OK. So first off on Saturday morning is a film called *My Life as an Ant* which starts at 10.30 a.m, have I got that right? … Yes, 10.30. This is definitely one for the children. The leading character is a tiny ant, just one centimetre long. And he introduces us to his world as he travels around, looking for food to take back to his family. *My Life as an Ant* was made using the latest digital technology, and it comes from Japan. From what I've heard, the close-up images of the insect world are pretty amazing,

OK, well if you're not into creepy-crawlies, and I know some people aren't, we can move from one of the smallest creatures to one of the largest, because there's another great film on Saturday evening. This one's called *Ocean Oasis*. It's an American production and it was filmed in the oceans around the coast of Mexico. It's a film that takes you into the fantastic life and colours of the coral reefs. And there's also some amazing film of scientists swimming side by side with huge sea creatures like giant manta rays and even whales. This is a real adventure for the mind and senses.

Moving on to Sunday, we've got two more great offerings. First at 11 in the morning there's a film from China called *The Mystery of Yunnan Snub-nosed Monkey*. This is very special. It took ten years to make and it's the first real in-depth study of these monkeys which live deep in the forests of south west China. Apparently there's under <u>fifteen hundred</u> of them left now, so they're obviously in real danger of extinction. Anyway it's a wonderful film and it won a TVE Award last year. Not sure what that stands for, exactly … Anybody know? No, no one in the studio knows. I expect one of our listeners will have the answer.

The last film I'm going to tell you about is on Sunday afternoon. It's called *Riverhorse* and it was made by a team of film-makers from the <u>UK</u>. It's the story of a family of hippos living by an African river, and the film follows the family over a two-year period. In that time the film-makers managed to get incredibly close to the hippos as well as to crocodiles and other river animals. *Riverhorse* also won a film award last year – it won the 'Animal <u>Behaviour</u>' category of the Panda film awards.

So that's just four of the fabulous films on offer at the festival but there's plenty more to choose from, as well as competitions and activities for children. For more details, just give the Box Office a ring. The telephone number, if I can just find it … Yes, the number to ring is <u>973 4617</u>. I'll repeat that 973 4617.

On now to the sporting fixtures for the weekend, and here's Amy to give us the details …

Unit 6, Focus on listening 2

The right to roam (p.65)

T = Tutor; L = Lisa; J = Jamie

T Is everyone here now? Lisa? Jamie? Maria? Good. Well, we're continuing the module on 'Animal Rights' and I think Lisa, you're going to talk to us about your assignment, right?

L Yes.

T And what topic have you chosen?

L The problems of keeping large animals in zoos.

T Fine. And where did you get your information?

L Partly from an article I read, about some research they've done, and also from the Web.

T OK. And do you know who carried out the research?

L Yes, the research was done by <u>Oxford University</u>. I've got the researchers' actual names here somewhere …

T Don't worry about names now, but you'll need to mention them when you write up your assignment. And the other thing you should mention if possible is where the results of this research were published. Do you know that?

L Yes, it was in a scientific journal … called *Nature*, I think. Let me just check … Yes, that's right, *Nature*.

T Fine, carry on.

L OK, well we all know that there are problems with keeping large animals in zoos. When you put lions or tigers, for example, into tiny cages, they often don't breed successfully. That's because of <u>stress</u>, because they're used to having large areas to wander around in. But different animals need different amounts of territory and that's what this research looked at.

J You say different animals need different amounts of territory. Could you give us some specific examples, Lisa?

L Yes, I've got information about four animals; that's the polar bear, <u>lion</u>, grizzly bear and snow leopard. The scientists looked at the average territory these animals had in the wild. And the results were pretty amazing. For example, it turned out that a polar bear has an average territory of around <u>79,000</u> square kilometres!

J Did you say 79,000?

L Yes. That's what the report says,

J Wow!

L And the second thing the study looked at was the <u>minimum</u> territory that could support these animals. The minimum territory for a polar bear is still enormous, it's 1,200 square kilometres. On the other hand, grizzly bears only need a minimum territory of <u>0.5</u> of a square kilometre, which means they're more likely to do well in a zoo.

J Could you repeat that figure, Lisa?

L Yes. '0.5 of a square kilometre'. OK?

J Thanks.

L The third thing the scientists looked at was the average distance an animal travels <u>in a day</u>. And here it's the lion that comes top. A lion travels 11 kilometers a day, and a polar bear, 8.8. By contrast, grizzly bears only cover about <u>1.5</u> kilometres and snow leopards slightly less.

The final thing in the study was the infant mortality rate, that is how many young animals die before they're 30 days old, I think it is. Anyway, the polar bear, has a really high infant mortality rate. It's 65 per cent, which is highest of all. Snow leopards do better, with a rate of <u>14.3</u> per cent, but grizzly bears do best of all with 0 per cent infant mortality.

T Is that it?

L Yes, that's as far as I've got.

T Fine, very interesting. But can you draw any conclusions yet?

L Yes, well, basically I think zoos need to decide what kind of animals they should keep. If they're a small city zoo, for example, they should forget about lions, because they need plenty of space, and I'm not sure anyone should keep polar bears at all.

Unit 8, Focus on listening 1

Mobile phone safety (p.84)

T = Tutor; D = David Myers

T So now, just to finish off this morning's session, I've asked the college Health and Safety Officer, David Myers, to say a few words about mobile phone safety. David …

D Thanks, Miranda. Yes, mobiles are an essential part of everyone's life these days, aren't they? And it's hard to believe that hasn't always been the case. Actually, did you know that the first mobile network was only opened in 1979? It's no time at all, really. That was in <u>Japan</u>, by the way. Since then, of course, mobile phone ownership has gone through the roof. In 1990 only about 1 per cent of people in the EU had a mobile, for example, but by 2003 the figure had gone up to <u>about 80 per cent</u>. That's a fantastic increase over such a short space of time.

So why all the fuss about safety? Well, this is quite a hot topic right now, as you probably know. Basically, the concern is that mobile phones work by sending out <u>radio waves</u> and people think that these could damage body tissue and even cause cancer. However, I should say that there's still quite a bit of disagreement among experts about this.

D So, I'd like to pass on to you the latest advice about using mobiles safely. A lot of it's common sense really, I suppose. For example, you should only use the phone when necessary, and you should <u>try to keep your calls short</u>. Don't stay on the phone for hours! Incidentally, you may think the phone is safe when it's on standby, but actually it's still giving off radio-waves. So <u>when you're carrying the phone around, try to keep it away from your body</u> if you can. Put it in your bag or in a backpack, not in your pocket. But then you'll need to be more careful about security, obviously.

Now there are a few things to remember when you're buying a phone. First, look for a model with a long 'talk time'. That means <u>the radio wave emissions it gives out will be less powerful</u>. And less powerful means less risk to health, remember.

You also need to check the 'SAR' value of the phone. That's the amount of radiation that the handset transmits. <u>It's best to avoid phones that have a high 'SAR' value</u>. The higher the 'SAR' value, the more radiation they transmit, which is bad news. Also, <u>don't buy a phone with an internal aerial</u> if you can possibly help it. Many experts think an internal aerial is more dangerous because it's closer to your head. And they think we should keep the aerial as far away from our head as possible.

Something I think I forgot to mention was <u>try not to use your phone when reception is weak</u>. A weak reception means the phone needs more power to communicate to the base station and so the radio wave emissions will be higher.

Finally, there are lots of gadgets around that promise to protect you from harmful radiation – you've probably seen the adverts – but <u>only buy ones that have been independently tested</u>. Otherwise, there's no guarantee at all that they'll work and you'll probably be wasting money.

Well, that's all the advice I have for you now. I hope you'll think about it. Many thanks.

Unit 8, Focus on listening 2

Txt don't talk (p.90)

A = Andy; M =Mary

A Hi, Mary. How are you?

M Fine, thanks. Come in and have a seat. So, how are things going? With the presentation, I mean?

A Not too bad, actually. I found that survey you sent me really useful.

M The one about young people and mobile phones?

A Yes. It's got some interesting facts and figures in it that I think we could use.

M Great.

A They show how incredibly important mobile phones are to young people. For example, did you know <u>that 75 per cent of teenagers use their phones at least once a day.</u>

M Three quarters! That's a lot.

A But actually texting is an even bigger thing with young people nowadays. About 90 per cent of them send at least one text message a day, believe it or not. And if you look at the UK as a whole, people are sending over 2 billion text messages a month. What's so amazing is that <u>it's gone from zero to 2 billion</u> in such a short time

M That's an amazing increase. You know, we could design a graph to show that.

A Great idea! It would be good to have some graphics. By the way, what do you think the peak time for sending text messages is?

M I don't know. Seven thirty? Eight o'clock at night?

A Well, it is at night but apparently <u>it's between ten thirty and eleven</u>.

M That's quite late. I'm surprised!

A What you have to remember about mobiles is that they're part of young people's self-expression. Part of their identity. For example, the way you carry your phone is very important. The most popular place is in your pocket, apparently. And <u>the last place you should keep your phone is on your belt.</u> That's a really big fashion mistake. For most of the teenagers in the survey anyway.

A Now you were going to talk about the different functions of mobile phones, Mary, weren't you? Which functions did you decide to cover?

M Well, the most popular, obviously, is text messaging. But you seem to have a lot of information on that already. So I'll leave that to you, if that's OK.

A Fine, so you won't cover text messaging but … ?

M Well, I'm going to look at <u>using a mobile to take photos</u>. I know not all phones have cameras at the moment, but the number's going up all the time.

A And are you going to deal with sending pictures as well as taking them?

M No. I think it might take too long. But I'm definitely going to look at <u>the kind of games you can play on a mobile</u> because that's the next most popular activity after texting.

A Right. And how about video?

M I think video is still a pretty specialised thing at the moment. Not that many phones have it yet. So I'm not covering that, no. But <u>the other thing I'm going to look at is voicemail</u>. It's not quite as popular with teenagers as the other functions but about two thirds still use it.

M OK, are we nearly done?

A Pretty much so, I think. It's an interesting subject though, isn't it? I mean, you know my younger brother?

M Michael?

A Yes. Well, Michael's 17 now and he's exactly like the teenagers in the survey. <u>He always has the very latest model</u>, and he's always flashing it around. <u>He even uses it as an alarm clock to remind him about appointments and things.</u>

M That's very organised of him! Yeah, my cousin Cindy's like that as well. She told me she has to have the phone with her 24 hours a day. <u>She even keeps it under her pillow when she goes to bed at night!</u> Can you believe it? But the problem is it's easy to run up huge bills. I know someone who got into trouble like that. Linda Hall, do you know her?

A No.

M Well, Linda was sending 20 or 30 texts a day and it was costing over £100 a month.

A What happened?

M Eventually <u>her mother put a limit of £30 on her phone bill</u>. That's all she can spend a month, and she hates it. Anyway, enough of that. I think we've done quite well, don't you? We've sorted out who's doing what. Shall we meet again next week?

Unit 10, Focus on listening 1

Countdown to a healthier life (p.106)

P = Presenter; R = Roger Armstrong

P As you probably know, this is National Stop Smoking Week. And today in the studio we have Roger Armstrong to tell us about some of the benefits of giving up smoking. Roger …

R Thanks, Sally. Yes, I think we've all heard enough bad news. We know about the harmful effects that smoking can have on our bodies and our health. But now for the good news. Let's look at what happens when you finally decide to stop.

Well, the amazing thing is that your body starts to recover almost immediately. For example, both your blood pressure and your pulse will return to normal levels just <u>20 minutes</u> after your last cigarette. And you'll probably also notice an improvement in your circulation, particularly in your <u>hands and feet</u>. So, if you're the kind of person whose hands and feet go blue at the least sign of cold, this could be the answer!

OK. Then eight hours after you stop, the <u>oxygen level</u> in your blood will return to normal, that is to the normal oxygen level of a non-smoker.

After 24 hours – that's just one day, remember – all the carbon monoxide will have left your body. And this is the point when your <u>lungs</u> begin to clear, to clear out all the debris that's collected in them. So don't be surprised if you develop a cough for a few days. That's a sign that your lungs are recovering.

Now, all the nicotine will leave your body in 48 hours – or two days after you stop. Incredible. And you'll also begin to notice an improvement in your sense of <u>taste and smell</u>. That means you'll be able to enjoy food a lot more. Just one more benefit!

Then after 72 hours, you'll find your <u>breathing</u> has become much easier. And you'll also experience an increase in your energy levels.

As time goes on, your circulation will continue to improve. And then some time between 2 and 12 weeks after you first stopped smoking, you'll notice that walking and <u>exercising</u> have become a lot easier. In fact, exercising can be fun again. You'll soon be cycling or playing tennis without having to keep stopping for a rest.

After 3–9 months, any remaining breathing problems you've had, like coughing or shortness of breath, will get better. In fact, your lungs will increase in efficiency by <u>up to 10 per cent</u>. That means you'll be able to exercise more intensively and also go on for longer.

Looking further ahead, <u>five years</u> after you give up smoking, your risk of having a heart attack will fall to about half that of a smoker.

And finally, ten years after you first gave up, your risk of getting cancer will also fall to about half that of a smoker. Meanwhile, your risk of having a heart attack will now be the same as someone who <u>has never smoked</u> at all.

So, don't delay, give up today! That's the health message I want you all to go away with. It's worth it, believe me! You'll feel some of the benefits almost immediately, but in the long term, you could be saving your life.

Unit 10, Focus on listening 2

Milestones of medicine (p.109)

(*T = Tutor; S = Sara*)

T OK, I think we're all here now. And today Sara, you're doing a presentation on a medical topic, I believe.

S That's right, I wanted to look at some of the key discoveries in medicine over the years. And I thought it would be easy, to be honest, because there's so much information on the Internet, and in the library. But I actually found I had a real problem, because there are just so many amazing developments that <u>it was really difficult to make up my mind which ones to talk about</u>.

I mean where do you start? You can go right back to prehistory if you want. Because people were actually performing operations ten thousand years ago, you know. It's incredible. Anyway, I've picked out some developments that I think are important and I've put them on a time line, which you can see on this chart I've made. The dates are at the bottom, going from left to right. OK?

And we start in 1615 with the clinical thermometer. This was invented in <u>Italy</u> by a physician called Sanctorius. The thermometer made it possible to take human temperature for the first time, which is such an important step in so much medical diagnosis.

Also in the seventeenth century, an Englishman called William Harvey discovered the circulation of the blood. That was in the year <u>1628</u>. It was a really important breakthrough even though most doctors at the time thought the idea was ridiculous.

Moving on to the next century, 1733 was the year when Stephen Hales, another Englishman, measured blood <u>pressure</u> for the first time. He actually measured the blood pressure of both animals and humans, in fact.

There were lots of medical discoveries during the nineteenth century and one of the most important, in my opinion, was <u>general</u> anaesthetic. Can you imagine having a major operation without anaesthetic? Well, that's how it was for most patients in previous centuries, unfortunately. Then in 1846 general anaesthetic was first used in America.

My last important discovery was in 1895. That's when X-rays were developed in <u>Germany</u>. X-rays have transformed medicine since then but they were actually discovered completely by accident.

S Now I'd like to finish by mentioning a few important medical treatments which have been developed in the last hundred years or so.

The first is **penicillin,** which was discovered in 1928. At first nobody realised how it could be used. Then a few years later, scientists decided to try <u>using penicillin on laboratory mice</u>. That's how they found that penicillin can successfully kill many serious infections.

Next is probably the most common drug of all – something we all reach for when we have a headache – **aspirin.** This was originally <u>extracted from meadowsweet, which is a member of the rose family, and which grows wild in many parts of the country</u>. It had been used for years as a traditional painkiller, in fact.

Beta blockers are an important group of drugs which are used to treat high blood pressure. Drug companies were very excited about them when they were first developed in the 1960s, but a few years later it was found that some patients were suffering heart failure and other <u>damaging conditions</u>. Since then, further research has produced a new generation of beta blockers.

Insulin was discovered by two Canadian scientists who <u>first tried it on a dog</u> which was seriously ill with diabetes. A few hours later the dog sat up and barked. After that success, they treated a young boy whose health improved almost immediately, and nowadays insulin allows diabetics to live almost normal lives.

Cortisone is often used to treat arthritis. The scientists who originally discovered the hormone in the 1940s won a Nobel Prize for their work. Nowadays a synthetic version is used, but doctors have to control the dosage carefully because they've found that patients who take it over a long period run the risk of <u>developing conditions like diabetes or high blood pressure</u>.

T Thanks, Sara, that was really good. Thank you. I think we'll all take a short break now …

Unit 12, Focus on listening 1

The Opera House Tour (p.130)

T = Tim; E = Erica

E Hello

T Erica? Tim here.

E Oh hi, Tim. Sally said you might ring. You're going to Australia, right? And you wanted some information about tours of the Sydney Opera House?

T That's right. I haven't got an Internet connection at the moment.

E No problem. I got a printout from the Opera House website. Let me just get it … right. Opera House Tour. OK. It says: 'This is our most popular tour …', blah blah. 'Visitors are given a fascinating account of the history and <u>architecture</u> of the building.' You see the concert hall, the opera theatre, you hear about the current programme, et cetera. What else do you need to know?

T Does it say how often the tour goes?

E Let me see … it's a one-hour tour and, yes, 'it leaves every <u>half hour</u> between 9 a.m. and 5 p.m.'.

T Right, every half hour. So they're pretty frequent. And does it say how much the tour costs?

E I think so, yes at the bottom here – adults … <u>23 dollars</u>. But there are some concessionary rates for, um, senior citizens, and also <u>full-time</u> students, plus kids under 16. So remember to take your student card and you'll only have to pay 16 dollars. Which is pretty cheap, actually. But they can also arrange a <u>private tour</u> if you wanted. That's for a group of up to 18 people and it costs, … wait for it! 432 dollars!

E OK. The other option is the Backstage Tour. Let me read you what it says about that. 'An opportunity to explore behind the scenes at the Opera House. Appear on the stage and see where the orchestra plays.' You also get the chance to chat to some of the <u>technical</u> staff and maybe even some performers, if you're lucky …

T Sounds really great but how long does that one take?

E Um, that's <u>two hours</u>, so twice as long as the first one. But there's an early start – it goes at 7 a.m.

T And how much is that?

E Let me see … <u>a hundred and forty dollars</u>.

T That's per person, right?

E Yes, per person. I think it's something pretty special. And apparently, included in the ticket price, you also get a light <u>breakfast</u>. Which would be very welcome, I should think, after that early start!

T Right. I'll have to give it some thought.

E Well, anyway, if you are interested, I'd try and book well in advance if you can. I think the tours get quite booked up.

T OK.

E There's a number you can call for bookings or if you want more information. Have you got a pen handy?

T Yup. Fire away.

E OK. It's <u>9250 7250</u>. That's Sydney, obviously. Did you get that? 9250 7250.

T Got it. That's brilliant, Erica. Thanks a lot.

Unit 12, Focus on listening 2

The Itaipu Dam (p.131)

Hello and welcome to this, the fourth in our series of public lectures on Big Buildings. Today we're going to take a look at the Itaipu Dam in South America. You may not know too much about Itaipu but it's been named one of the 'Seven Wonders of the Modern World' by the American Society of Civil Engineers. And in this lecture, I hope to explain some of the reasons why.

OK, let's begin with a few facts. First of all, where exactly is the Itaipu Dam? Well, it's on the Parana River, close to the border between Brazil and Paraguay. Construction began in 1975 and the dam was only finished in <u>1982</u>. Two years later it started generating electricity and it's now one of the largest hydro-electric power plants in the world. The total cost of building was <u>20 billion</u> dollars. That's right, 20 billion!

In design, it's what is called a gravity dam, which means it relies on its immense weight for stability. The main section is made of <u>concrete</u>, actually 15 times the amount of concrete that was used in creating the Channel Tunnel between England and France.

To give you an idea of size, the dam is 7.8 kilometres long, with a <u>height</u> of 196 metres. The reservoir behind the dam is huge – almost fifteen hundred square kilometres and the reservoir <u>capacity</u> is 1.02 trillion cubic feet. With such a massive capacity, no wonder it took fourteen days to fill!

This dam really is an amazing feat of engineering. Engineers actually had to change the course of the Parana, which is the seventh largest river in the world, and move 50 million tons of earth and rock in the process.

With any success story, I suppose there are bound to be a few problems. One is that the Itaipu Dam sometimes gets blocked with mud and silt, which is expensive to clear. But more seriously, <u>this mud and silt carries bacteria, which can be transmitted in the water and cause illness in the people who use it</u>. So it's essential the water's kept clean. The other main problem was that when the land was originally flooded to create the reservoir, they destroyed <u>a large area of rainforest, which was home to many birds and other forest creatures and sadly they died</u>. Since then, however, seven new protected areas have been created for wildlife.

OK, now before I go on, has anyone got any questions? … No? Well, I'd like to look at the construction of the dam in a bit more detail. So, if you could all look at the cross-section of a dam on the sheet I gave out … OK? Look at the left side, which is the side facing the reservoir. Can you see the point at the very bottom of the dam on the upstream face? That's called the 'heel', H double E, L, just like part of your foot. And the same point at the bottom of the downstream face of the dam is called, anyone care to guess? That's it, the 'toe' also like the toe on your foot. What else should I mention? Yes, the top of a dam, that's the part you can see above water, the 'crest', and then the base or ground on which the dam is built is the 'foundation'. I think that's all you need for now.

Now, I've got a few more diagrams … if you'll just bear with me while I find out how to work this projector …